Childhood Memories of East Anglian Life

C

A CASTELL PUBLICATION

Presented & Edited by Mel Birch

e

ISBN 0 948134 47 X

Published in Great Britain by
Castell Publishing, Mendlesham, Suffolk, England IP14 5RY

Printed in Great Britain by
Barnwell's Print Limited, Aylsham, Norfolk NR11 6ET

The publishers acknowledge the use of articles and illustrations selected from those previously contributed to, and published in editions of the East Anglian Magazines from the 1940s and 1950s

Childhood Memories of
EAST ANGLIAN LIFE

Recollections of life in Town & Country around 100 years ago

And what is our life but a day ?
A short one that soon will be o'er;
It presently passes away,
And will not return any more !
Tomorrow may never arise,
And yesterday's over and gone:
Then catch at today as it flies,
'Tis all we can reckon upon.

Acknowledgements

We would like to acknowledge the use of articles and illustrations taken from The East Anglian Magazine editions between 1947 and 1959 in compiling this publication. The year that the articles were first published is shown in brackets against the name of the author.

We further acknowledge the following authors who provided the original articles for the EAM:

Margaret Storer; Gwenyth Dyke; S. P. Goddard; Edith Southwell; Mary H. Vennard; Jessie Mallows; Emily E. Gray; R. H. Futter; Miriam Sykes; E. A. H. Ward; Barbara Smitherman; Godfrey Windham; Evelyn Barrett; Arthur H. Pye; Keith Irvine; W. F. Turner; Rev. C. E. Woode; Phyllis Pearce; Kate Elizabeth Chapman; Walter Tye; J. A. E. Kitchen; George W. Giffen; Rev. J. R. M. Wright; F. C. Oakley; Fred D. Cross; Mrs Scarfe Webb; Cedric W. Mays; Gladys V. Nunn; Hugh Barrett; C. E. Woodrow; M. Janet Becker; A. W. Osborne; Mary Durham; D. A. Chillingworth; H. W. Turney; Florence E. Burroughes; G. A. Dunn; D. Murrell Simmons; Alick Reeve; D. E. Hurr; Alice Sterry; George J. M. Baker; Michael Cornell; Sylvia Hayman; E. L. Barrett; Marguerita S. S. Bird; R. Hemstedt; Gladys O. Howard; Ernest De Caux Tillett; Guy P. J. L'Estrange; Alice Mary Bond; Cecile Arburn Spring; Phyllis Mills; L. J. Tibbenham; L. R. Garrard.

the following Illustrators:

Jennifer Kent; Nancy Blyth; Joan Pickford; Mary Jarvis; Andrew Dodds; Beryl Irving; Mary Tye; Bernard Reynolds; Slader Hoare; Paul Hogarth; Marjorie Budd; R. Sell.

and the following Photographers:

L. Sewell; John Tarlton, A.I.B.P., A.R.P.S.; J. Limmer; F. Jenkins; C. R. Temple; E. S. Singleton Ltd.; Ramsey & Muspratt; Tudor Photos, Ipswich.

Above : 'Red Polls, motionless as bronze statues'. A Leslie Moore drawing from "Call me at Dawn" by Percy Edwards. 'What is our life but a day?' a poem by Ann Taylor (1782-1866).

Contents

An Introduction

THE NEW MILLENNIUM would seem an appropriate time to reflect on the last hundred years or so, and to mark the many changes that have taken place in people's lives, particularly here in East Anglia. Reproducing articles written in the mid twentieth century about their childhood, by East Anglians - most of whom are regretfully no longer with us, having themselves joined the lost past of which they wrote - provides not only a unique insight into life at the turn of the last century, but a reminder of the 'modern' life they themselves were experiencing in the 1940s and '50s.

Although the book has been divided into sections highlighting the various aspects of town and country living, by the very fact that these are reminiscences many subjects are touched upon within each article.

We see life through a child's eyes at school and at play; what they wore; what they ate; what games they played; how they travelled; first tentative steps in employment; relation-ship with their parents and teachers, and fleeting glimpses of how those parents lived, earned their living and made ends meet.

But the book not only seeks to save for posterity the written images of a bygone age, but also to commemorate the much lamented East Anglian Magazine. For about forty years this worthy publication encapsulated the thoughts and mood of the period as it affected East Anglians, in notes, letters, poems, articles, stories, photographs and illustrations. These items were, in the main, provided by local readers and ex-patriots around the world where the magazine was distributed and had a regular following. This was an age when people contributed, not for any financial gain, but for the joy of playing their part in promoting the region and enlightening its inhabitants; an age when people expressed a pride in their environment and its history.

In post-war Britain when this attitude began to change, so did the fortunes of the magazine. The old generation made way for the young who, for the most part, possessed a 'live for today' attitude, with scant regard or tolerance for how things used to be. There was also an increasing influx of newcomers to the area, bringing with them an ignorance of country ways and customs, and little inclination to learn. People were no longer prepared to take the time to contribute articles and debate local issues - the life-blood of the magazine, and with increasing costs and growing competition for the not-unlimited pool of vital advertising revenue, it became commercially uneconomic to continue. Its ultimate demise was not only a great disappointment for its loyal readership but for those who worked on the magazine and strove tirelessly in its support. Their obvious enthusiasm was clearly evident in each monthly issue, produced from the heart with a real love for the subject.

You may yet discover an old copy of the magazine tucked away on the shelves of some secondhand bookshop to remind you of all that was best in regional publishing, but in the main it has gone, receding into the mists of time along with the majority of its readers and contributors. We hope this book will go some way to reviving those memories and providing a memorial to a fondly remembered magazine and a less frantic and in many ways more fulfilling age.

Mel Birch

Childhood Village Life

Fast Falls the Eventide

Margaret Storer (c1956), Illustrated by Jennifer Kent

OLD Mrs Hazell, in her 90th year, lived with her unmarried son, Joe. They had a young teenage girl to 'live-in' and do the housework.

Joe, who worked for my father, came to me one day in great haste. 'Miss, will you goo and see what's the matter a' mother. The gal she've just come fer me and she saay: "Joe, that there owd hin's a-gitten out o' the pot. Oi doon't know what tew dew."'

I went along to the cottage and found Mrs Hazell and Phoebe in a state of great excitement. They had a fowl boiling on the stove and one leg had 'kicked' up the lid of the saucepan. I pushed it in and placed a flat iron on top for a weight.

All the time Mrs Hazell was recounting the tale for my benefit:

'Oi were a-setting boy the winder, thinking about when Oi were a gal and Phoebe she come a-running in. "Ma," she saay - she allus call me Ma. "Ma," she saay, "that there owd hin's a-gittin' out the pot. Wot'll Oi dew?" she say. "Tha's a-gittin' out the pot?" Oi saay? "Yis," she saay, "Wot'll Oi dew?" "Yow'd better goo and tell Joe," Oi saay.'

She paused. Then with a beaming smile: 'Thank yer kindly, miss, fer comin'.'

'You're kindly welcome,' I replied.

Mrs Hazell was a dear old soul without a tooth in her head. As she talked, her chin went up and down, almost meeting her nose at times. When she laughed, which was quite often, one could see the back of her throat.

Many a tale she has told me of her young days. Her father was gamekeeper on an estate not far from Sudbury. 'Oi moind the day when th'owd squoire wot now is were born. Noin year owd Oi were at the toime and Oi hed moi pinny full o' iggs. Summat startled me - Oi fergit wot it were now - and Oi dropped the lot! Tha's how Oi remimber the daay.'

At an early age she went into service and was unhappy living in the town. There were little children for her to mind and if one of them refused to finish a boiled egg the maid was expected to finish it herself. 'Ugh!' she would say expressively.

Once she went to London by the old horse coach. 'That took us tew daays and a noight to git there. At noight there were an owd lantern hung up insoide an' that kep' on a-swingin' an' a-swingin'. Fair made me sick that did.'

The old mind wandered somewhat and I never succeeded in finding out how many stops were made on the way to rest or change horses nor yet to which part of London they journeyed. The lantern was the thing she remembered most clearly.

NOW, in her widowhood, she lived in a pretty little cottage with thatched roof and a porch. Honeysuckle climbed round the porch and in the garden grew old apple trees, roses, cabbages and all sorts of lovely things including, of course, the Suffolk primroses and violets in season.

In the summer she would sit at the open window of the kitchen, her 'summer room' as she called it. Over the fireplace hung the old shepherd's crook. I think it had belonged to her husband, memory of whom was hallowed by silence.

The little parlour was the 'winter room' and there she would sit by the fire, cosy and stuffy, with walls covered thick with photographs and pictures, thick curtains at door and window, thick heavy table-cloth and mantel border with a row of little wool balls hanging from it. There were cases of stuffed birds and rabbits which stared at me with glassy eyes.

Sometimes on winter evenings my father would come with me, bringing his fiddle, and we would sing hymns and songs which the old lady knew. She would join in with her high-pitched, quavering old voice, sweet as a robin's when it did not crack. Like a robin's, also, were her bright, sparkling brown eyes.

Joe seldom joined in the singing but would sit with his hands on his knees, a smile on his good-tempered, contented face, in silent appreciation.

'Swift to its close ebbs out life's little day
'Earth's joys grow dim, its glories pass away.'

How true those words, sung by that aged voice. But the joys were dimmed only by a mellow, kindly shade. They were by no means lost.

'Where is death's sting?
'Where, grave, thy victory?'

As we sang, a memory would sometimes send a flash of merriment into the old lady's eyes and her face would crease all over with laughter wrinkles.

'Did Oi iver tell yer . . . ?' she would say and off she would go on some tale of long ago, taking us with her, back through the years.

'Did Oi iver tell yer about them owd Miss Eglantine's? Tew sisters they was, owd maids yer know. Good women they was, used to take soup and the loike to the sick folk and dew all sorts o' kind actions. They'd be in the family pew of a Sunday mornin' as reg'lar as reg'lar. They allus kep' a bottle o' wine and a cake riddy, dew anyone 'ud feel faint loike. That were kep' in a little builden' in the chu'chyard. We called it the fainten' house. It were used a lot!'

ONE day in May - it was one of those lovely days that sometimes happen along when the hawthorn is in bloom - I sat with Mrs Hazell at the open window. The heavy perfume floated in and the old woman sniffed the air thoughtfully. 'That dew stink roight noice but that allus moind me o' moi Polly.' The old face clouded and the bright eyes were dimmed with tears as she continued: 'She doid in Maay. She were a lovely gal, only nointeen when the good Lord saw fit to take her home. Hair loike an angel, she had, and her eyes they was as bleew as they little owd bleew flowers what grow b' the soide o' the rood. Yew know what Oi mean, the flowers drop off if yer pluck 'em

- brids' eyes we used to call 'em. Her skin, that were just loike the Maay blossom, white as snow, wi' little bits o' pink. She had lovely rosy cheeks - you'd niver a' thought she were so ill. Oi didn't think she were quoite so bad till the doctor he saay she hid to hive new milk ivery daay. Then I knew that were serious, cos yer see we niver had only skim milk in them daays, ordinary toimes.

'Oi moind the the daay afore she died she saay: "Mother," she saay, "dew yew git me some o' that there Maay. That dew stink suffin bewtiful." She did want it so bad. Oi had a rare owd job not ter give in. But o' coorse Oi had t'refuse her. "Oi dussent bring that into the house gal," Oi saay. "Don't yew know tha's unlucky?"

'She doid that night and Oi did wish Oi'd let har hev har way. That couldn't ha' bin wus luck than losin' har loike that, could it?'

She were moi fust baby, lovely she were. Oi never hed another loike what she wus. Oi got another gal, yer know, married she is and livin' in furrin' parts, out Che'msford way somewhere. Married an undertaker and now thinks she's too grand to visit her owd mother."

Mrs Hazell sighed. Then, as she saw her son returning from his work, her face brightened.

'There's Joe,' she cried cheerily. 'He's good to his mother, moi booy is. You wouldn't think to see him now that when he were born yew could hev put him in a point pot, sich a little owd moite he were.'

'Now then mother, yew jawin' 'bout that there point pot agin. How dew yew know Oi would ha' fitted in that, dew yew niver troid ter shove me in?' Joe, beaming all over his honest, open face, came in and took his mother's fragile hand in his big paw.

At that moment Phoebe appeared, carrying a kettle, which she had just filled at the pump in the yard. As she crossed the kitchen to the stove a few drops of water splashed over the side of the kettle.

'Look what yew're a-doing of, Maw,' cried the old lady sharply. 'Dew yew goo and git the dwile, gal, doon't that'll make a mark on the floor.'

'Mother,' said Joe soothingly, 'what about that butter?'

Phoebe flashed him a grateful smile as with haste she wiped the little splashes from the floor. Mrs Hazell gave a chuckle and, quickly back in the past, continued her tale.

'When the nuss picked him up - not one o' them young lidies loike what does it now but a woman gettin' on loike. She'd hed foive herself and buried four o 'em so she'd hed some experience yew see. Well when she picked him up she saay: "He's not long f'r this world, m' dear. Yew'll niver rare that little owd booy."

'Oi started to croy and she saay: "Howd yer row, woman, that on't help nuthen'." Then she took and she rubbed him all over with fresh butter, face an' all over his little owd hands and fit. Then she wrapped him up toight with his arms str'ight down b' his soides. He were quoiet fer a time but later on, a'ter she'd gone home, he begun to shreik and Oi couldn't make 'm stop nohow. At last Oi

onwrapped the shawl a bit, so's he could git his little owd hands out. One o' they was full o' butter and he shoved that in his mouth and sucked the butter off. After that Oi allus put just a little bit o' butter on his fist to keep him quoiet. Some saay that's whoy he grew s' big. Oi niver had no more trouble along o' he, only when he hed the whoopin' corf now, and thin he wouldn't ate his mouse. They don't give 'em meece f'r th' whoopin' corf now, dew they? They did uster saay that were the best thing f'r that, cooked, yer know, not just a raw one. His father, he caught a noice fat owd mouse and skint it for him. Oi froid that but owd Joe here wouldn't ate it. He were six year owd at the toime and he hollered and made himself corf so Oi hed to give in to him an' let him goo without. he got better all roight, soo that din't really matters, did that?'

AS time went on the old lady grew gradually more feeble and took to rising later in the morning and going to bed at dusk. Later she would stay in bed for a whole day now and again and then for two or three days at a stretch.

One day she sent for me. She had been in bed for nearly a week and seemed quite content to stay there but was rather agitated.

'Do yew goo downstairs, Phoebe,' she said. Then: 'hev the gal gone?'

I nodded.

'Now Oi must tell yer. Oi told a loi.'

She paused, embarrassed, and I began to feel rather uncomfortable myself and tried unsuccessfully to think of a suitable remark. At last she reached for my hand and pulled me near enough to wisper: 'Oi towd yew Oi was nointythree an' Oi'm on'y nointytew.' Then, more brightly: 'But Oi'll be nointythree come Michaelmas. Tha's three months' toime, ain't it? If Oi'm spared.' I stayed chatting with her for a while and left her sleeping peacefully. That night she died, still sleeping.

That Dear, Dear Lady and her Tales of Long Ago

Gwenyth Dyke (c1951)

THE village where I spent my childhood lies on the border of that deserted region along the Suffolk coast. I remember with fascination the stories the old people used to tell. I remember particularly one old lady, well over 80, whom I was fortunate to visit regularly over a period of years and as I grew older it was my delight to see through her eyes the vision of the past take shape and grow and populate.

Her very appearance was conducive to traditional tales, for she more closely resembled the 'White Witch' of legend than anyone else I ever saw. She was tiny and bent double, active and strong, and she dug her garden and cleaned her house with a surpassing vigour which seemed to grow with the years. Her face was deeply lined and pitted and from above her withered rosy cheeks peered two shrewd, intelligent, beady eyes set in deep hollows of massed and entwined wrinkles. Her mouth was small and shrunken and her hooked nose and chin almost met. It was a lively, gallant, interesting face under the wide, black hat, natural gaiety struggling with inculcated piety, a face which suffered no delusions about the world but still challenged it with enjoyment and strength.

Often since then, examining the brasses of her 17th century counterparts with wide hats and shrewd, puritan, independent faces, surrounded by bands of linen about the neck, bodies decorously aproned and girdled, I have been struck with the exactitude of the likeness: and almost seen, as I once saw, the worn hands plucking and smoothing the apron, as the old voice told tales of the old Suffolk, always in the background of her mind.

Those stories! With the condiment of a rich dialect to add to their savour, they combined the joy of legend with the certainty of truth. For no imagination could have reproduced so faithfully the oddities and touches of human nature. Through her parents she could feel back to the first years of the 19th century, when the Martello towers were building and the talk was all of Bonaparte - and smuggled 'runs.' My old lady's mother had lived in a lonely cottage on the wild heaths outside Butley, near the famed Hatchley Barn, now surrounded by acres of sombre fir and pine but then free and open as the sky. She - child about 1810, I should imagine - had been able to recall the jingling of harness and the tramp of feet, muffled commands and dragging sounds in the dead of the winter night, 150 years ago. And her parents, in their turn, had known the infamous Luff and Will Laud and poor Margaret (Catchpole) and were related to the horse thief, John Cook, who betrayed Margaret. Once this little girl, the mother of my old lady, had wakened and cried at the sounds below, and the smugglers, to quieten her, had brought her a tiny wooden barrel, polished and shiny, with which they had bribed her not to tell of her nightly alarms. This barrel had an honoured place on the chiffonier and as the inheritor of all these stories talked I could watch the flames leap and die in its brilliant surface.

HER father's family, at that same period, kept the Greyhound at Pettistree - the old timbered inn looking over the churchyard yews and the level fields. He, as a young boy, could remember being dragged, sleepy and protesting, from the bed he shared with his brothers and sisters, at the dead hour of a summer night, to run fast to Wickham across the fields and rouse the grocer for beer and cheese to feed a cavalry troop on its way from Yarmouth to London after the battle of Waterloo. The officers slept in his bed and the troops and horses were bedded on thick straw in the deep lane between the inn and the turnpike road. Over a hundred years later his younger daughter could still evoke the stamp and clink of the harness in the silent dawn through which they vanished on the London road.

The London road was a fascination to the big, gay, handsome boy in his teens, and once he ran away from the farm to ride the leading horse of the stage coach and six all the way to London. Three weeks was he gone, his then widowed mother weeping for his loss and the younger children wide eyed and sad at his disappearance. Then with the next Yarmouth coach he rode back, to tell of London and its marvels 'never more to stir foot out of East Anglia until his dying day'.

At one of the farms where he worked as semi-skilled labourer, training gradually to become horseman, he met and fell in love with the smuggler's black-eyed grandchild from Butley and after their marriage they were promoted to keep the lodge at Loundham Hall. All my old lady's early memories centred on the low-storeyed, gloomy cottage at the edge of a plantation, surrounded by rhododendrons - wet and dank in winter, deeply shaded in the hot summers of eighty years ago. As the youngest child, at home long after the others were out to service or farmwork, she would run to open the gates and curtsey as the carriages passed; and once a lady visitor, taking a fancy to the little girl, gave her a bottle of wonderful scent. Tragedy ended the tale, or rather tragi-comedy, for one washing day, when steam hung heavy in the kitchen, she tried to reach it from the shelf over the sink, and it overbalanced, the contents falling into the water, turning it deep rosy pink - 'like magic' - and so liberally scenting the shirts and smocks that for the next fortnight 'father got a rare leg pulling in the stock yards, him going round pale pink and smelly.'

THEN came service, in one of the tall houses by Melton Hill and later on in one of the big mansions surrounded by a well-kept park. But she soon left to marry and rear her own family in the tiny cottage where I knew her. Hers was a busy, active life - chapel and its weekday meetings and services, treats and burials . . . the children . . . the mending . . . the washing . . . the brewing . . . the baking . . . the garden . . . and later still the nephews and grandchildren coming home from the Boer War or the Great War . . . picture postcards of queerly-named places . . . the folding cup of a gentleman in khaki . . . the framed velvet, embossed views of Cape Town and the Veldt, Brussels and Cologne . . .

Now, in my time, all were scattered and gone. None was left to be spanked or chivvied but the big Timmy who, true to tradition, sat upon the three-legged stool waving his striped tail and washing his striped ears. As I used to sit and watch the sun sink below the geraniums in the window and the bees grow less busy in the lavender, the visions grew and grew, to be shattered by her vehement change of tone as the delinquencies

of the village boys or a turbulent disagreement over right-of-way with the aggressive next-door-neighbour came into her thoughts and the Victorian peace faded.

That peace was to suffer more than from those depredations, for during the Second Great War there came two small, scared boys, evacuees, who were quite convinced that she was a witch! Curranty cake and Sunday school, a Saturday walk to 'my daughter's' and a daily ruthless cleansing, combing and scrubbing, soon dispelled their fears. And at night, all unknowing, they were put into the same bed from which, once, a boy was turned to make room for the veterans of Waterloo. The next door neighbour's iniquities were lost in those of Hitler, whose 'old aerioplanes dropped their bumbs' and shook the plaster off the ceilings.

It was with regret that later, away from the village, in the rush and roll of approaching 'D-Day,' I heard of the death of my old lady - a regret deepened by the consideration that I had never heard more of her unique stories, or recorded them sooner; and mingled with gratitude to the friend who opened my eyes to the bygone Suffolk I never knew.

Portrait of Two Grandmothers

S. P. Goddard (c1957), Illustrated by Nancy Blyth

THE garden gate of the little cottage was still the same shade of red. The box hedge was still clipped to the same height. Nothing seemed to have changed very much since those memorable school holidays, except that there were now television masts on certain houses along the road.

In those school days the cottage was the home of my paternal grandmother. I remember it so well. On the small table that one encountered upon entering was a large white horse fashioned by some unknown craftsman in plaster. Grandmother assured everyone that this was very valuable, that she had once been offered a handsome sum for it by a stranger. This table also supported every conceivable kind of ornament so closely placed that not the smallest space was left vacant.

˙ The whole room was furnished in the same fashion. The walls were lined with photographs of my ancestors and these Sunday-suited and feather-hatted personages never failed to fill me with apprehension. It was, no doubt, one of those bearded gentlemen who provided my first impressions of the Deity. Among the vast collection of articles, useful and useless, that stood on the bureau was a water weather-glass, in which Grandfather had great faith, and one wall supported a large picture in remarkably bright colours of General Gordon in the act of departing from this world.

Under the window there stood a horse-hair sofa on which Grandmother used to climb in haste in order to examine the rare passers-by. I can still hear her urgent request: 'Pass me my glasses.' She would then consider the direction and pace of the passer-by and debate for some time his destination and purpose, giving special attention to anyone who passed at regular weekly intervals.

On Sundays two young ladies who lived in a nearby house would be collected by their swains and 'taken off'. Grandmother would demand that everyone come to the horse-hair sofa and witness this. She would point out their short dresses, bright colours and excited laughter and solemnly declare they were 'going to the bad'.

Grandmother was very patient and understanding despite the narrow ideas that were the fashion of the country folk of her day. Only once did I see her slightly impatient and put out. The cause of this was the escapade at the bottom of the garden by my cousin and myself.

The small wooden building that went with the property was at a great distance from the house. To reach it one had to pass one other cottage and two back gardens (even in those days I remember pondering the terrible possibilities of a weak stomach combined with a bad winter). Attached to this building and part of it was a cesspool and we conceived the idea of collecting tin cans and floating them upon its surface. Soon we decided they were ships that had to be sunk and we proceeded to sink them with the aid of bricks from a nearby pile. After a short time, of course, we were

smothered from head to foot in splashes and all the 'ships' that could be found were sunk. It was Grandfather who discovered us and I shall always remember his pained expression as he commenced to raise the sunken fleet with the aid of some garden implement, contriving at the same time to keep his distance from the stirred up contents of the pool. I cannot remember any punishment we may have received but it was punishment enough to note Grandmother's displeasure as we were cleaned up.

IT was during these holiday excursions that I was initiated by Grandfather into the art of catching eels. The process consisted of first making a 'bab'. To accomplish this one had first to dig up a quantity of worms and then thread them on to a length of worsted (a gruesome process). The result was then folded into a ball, the idea being that the eel would bite on the juicy bundle of worms and get its teeth stuck in the worsted, and then before having time to reach for a toothpick it would be thrown on to the bank. Skinning the catch was another gruesome process (eels always seem to be alive even when chopped up in small pieces and put in the frying pan). The head was speared with a fork and pinned down to a board, the skin being then cut below the head and peeled off. My first taste of eels, however, compensated for all this. I thoroughly enjoyed them.

Eight o'clock was bed-time for the entire household. Townspeople stayed up much later, Grandmother was prepared to admit. She would imply, however, that what went on after that hour was better not enquired into. Persuading Grandmother to read or tell stories of her young days was one method of prolonging the retiring hour. She would read to Grandfather from the local newspaper (Grandfather being unable to read). I remember she was particularly fond of the column by 'XYZ' which she would pronounce 'X wyer Z'. I also remember her pronunciation of chemist as 'kimister'. This interlude would, however, be short-lived and off we had to go to bed.

The mornings were perhaps the most exciting part of the day, with prospects of long days in the sun with our homemade pop-guns and bows and arrows. The king harry in his cage by the window would begin the day by singing his hymn to the first slanting rays of the sun. It is now, quite rightly, accepted that wild birds should not be caged. But I shall never believe that this bird was unhappy. He was Grandfather's bird and he became unhappy only when the old man died. After a few weeks he died also.

The smell of cooking pervading the whole house heralded breakfast and it is perhaps the smell of cooking which is strongest in my memory. Grandmother used a dutch oven and on the days when it was in use the smells that issued from that black cavern were something never to be forgotten. It is curious to note those products which are now advertised and guaranteed to dispel the smell of cooking. But perhaps in these days, they really are an asset.

At this point, while on the subject of food, my memory begins to digress to my maternal grandmother. She also 'kept a good house'. She was, however, in her habits entirely different from my paternal grandmother. Being a town dweller, she kept to the tradition by beginning to retire at midnight. This process occupied some time, since her clothes had always to be neatly folded or put on hangers and the whole house put in order.

A servant girl once employed by Grandmother was well aware of her passion for having everything done in the correct manner. On being asked if she had put any salt in the potatoes, the poor girl, no doubt thinking that any excuse was better than none, answered that there was no room left in the saucepan.

Grandmother's 'front room' was reserved for Christmas parties only. During the rest of the year it was forbidden even to open the door for fear of incurring the most awful penalties. I used to play guessing games with myself as to what Grandmother had to keep secret in this room all through the year. At Christmas, however, there was no restriction of any kind. The entire family was allowed to spread itself. Grandmother would insist on all her children and grandchildren being present, no excuse being accepted.

The room could only be described as a Victorian museum. Everything that could be associated with the period was crammed into it. Wax flowers, clocks and snowstorms under inverted glass bowls; plates with raised patterns hung on the walls; warming pans; fans and ostrich feathers; a three-

cornered cupboard containing the special crockery to be used only on occasions such as this; a musical box; and so great a collection of photographs and pictures that after filling all the wall space they had overflowed on to the many small tables; an aspidistra; a harmonium and the inevitable horsehair sofa as the crowning piece.

This room was an ideal setting for Grandmother's old-fashioned Christmas parties, which used to continue into the early hours of the morning. Should anyone consider retiring before 3 a.m. Grandmother would enquire after their health and suggest a little something to 'buck them up'.

She was a great letter writer, always keeping in touch with her huge family. She was always suspicious of the postal authorities' care in handling her letters and after sealing and stamping them she would press them under a heavy layer of books overnight, to make sure they were well stuck down.

I have often wondered why education seemed to be confined to the female sex in those days (neither of my grandfathers could read). Whatever the reason it was certainly not because grandmothers had more time to spare.

These, then, are the memories I have of my grandmothers, each so very likable, each so very different in habits. Perhaps the only point on which they were in complete agreement was the correct method of commencing a letter . . . Dear Eliza (they would begin), I now set down to write a few lines to you . . .

As I Look Back

Edith Southwell (c1956), Illustrated by Joan Pickford

I WAS born on 5 April 1876 in a large, old-fashioned house in a small village between Dereham and Cromer. It was a house with a lovely garden, an orchard and greenhouses in which grew peaches, tomatoes and cucumbers. It also had a vine with hundreds of large bunches of grapes. They were so fine that when, in adult life, I saw the much-talked-of Hampton Court vine in full fruit, I said: 'Why, my father's were much better than that!'

I was the youngest of sixteen children. Yes, I said sixteen. I had ten brothers and five sisters. All the boys but one followed the gardening and fruit-growing trade. The one became a baker and confectioner but knowing his private garden, and seeing his ability and taste, I have always felt he was the most likely one to have made a big success as a gardener.

I, too, loved garden work, hard though it was, and spent all my 'out of school' hours in the greenhouses or garden, tying up hundreds of tomato plants, watering and weeding.

All sorts of jobs fell to my lot - even bird scaring. I had a platform erected, with a bell and clappers to frighten the birds from a field of turnip seed. Perhaps it was my voice which had the most effect, however, for out in the fields by myself I annoyed none but the birds, and I used to recite my parts in readiness for the Sunday school anniversary - good practice it was too! I must have had a good memory, for I took part in ten or twelve pieces, as they were called. It was always my lot to give the 'begging piece'. Why, I don't know, for I don't think I am an expert at cadging now - I hope not.

The Sunday school was connected with the small chapel which was then called the United Methodist Free Church. The superintendent minister lived at Holt, four miles away. He came about once a quarter only. On the other Sundays we had local preachers. They were volunteers, of course, and not very local, for they came from Cley, Salthouse, Briningham and other places and as they were not provided with (or allowed expenses for) any means of transport but had to walk many miles in all weathers, very often they would be half an hour late and, fairly often, did not turn up at all.

Then it was that we had a 'few words' from my father or someone else in the congregation. I well remember that on many Sundays the congregation consisted only of about twelve of my own family and three or four others, as people had become so tired of being without the appointed preacher. Although it was a small village then, it had churches for the Congregational, Wesleyan, Primitive Methodist, Salvation Army and Church of England worshippers, to say nothing of a large mission hall a mile out. So there was a wide choice. I often wished I could take advantage of it but I had to stick to the sinking ship, so long as my family was at the helm.

MY Sunday began at 9 a.m., when I went ahead to light the chapel fire ready for 9.30 a.m. school. It was an iron stove with pipe to the roof. I delighted in seeing it get red hot. We had only one and a half hours of school, then my sister and I would go to the Congregational service at 11, home to dinner and back to Sunday school at 1.30, followed by a service in our chapel 2.30-4. Then home we went to tea, to which the preacher of the day generally came, and back to chapel for 6.30-7.45 p.m., after which there was a prayer meeting.

Oh dear, how often I have knelt on the floor and gone to sleep with the murmur of people's prayers in my ears. I knew every word that was coming, as it was the same each time and from the same people. My chapel life didn't end on Sundays, either, as my family took on the job of filling and cleaning lots of oil lamps and cleaning the chapel (no pay of course). I became so weary of it all, I said openly one day: 'I wish the old chapel would blow down.' It had a slate roof which used to rattle when it was windy. Well, many years after I had left home, I had a post-card telling me it *had* blown down. It was no longer being used as a Methodist church but by the Salvation Army and luckily no one was in it.

My parents have long since gone to rest at the age of 86 and 87. They had a hard life with such a large family to bring up and very little money to do it with. There were no family grants then and no free education. Although we had to take twopence a week each, even that meant a lot in those days. Yet I honestly think one heard less grumbling about ways and means than now. Doctors, too, had to be paid and, speaking of them, I remember very vividly having had tooth-ache for some days and as there was no dentist near I walked four miles to Holt to let our doctor draw it. He said: 'Sit down and wait.' Well, I waited while he vaccinated about thirty babies. After that he took out my tooth and said: 'You're a Briton.' I told him I needed to be, to watch that performance. And then came a four mile walk home again.

That was only one example of the 'good old days'.

I attended what was then called a national school. It was built on a common quite a mile from where I lived but many had to go there from three or four miles off - there were no buses then. In bad weather we took our dinner and were able to sit by the fire and have it. It was a good school in every way and its lovely big rooms and windows would put some present-day schools to shame.

We had an excellent master who took a real interest in his scholars and if anyone showed an inclination for more learning he would have classes at his house three evenings a week and coach us in special subjects. A great number of fully-qualified teachers have him to thank for getting them through the queen's scholars examination (that was Queen Victoria) which entitled them to become teachers without a college course. He was vexed with me because I did not choose teaching but preferred domestic work. (Well I've had my share of that!)

At sixteen I thought, as many girls do, that I would like to go away from home into a domestic job, so I answered an advertisement and got the post first go. Many said: 'Oh, you'll be home in a week.' 'No,' said I, 'I'll stay a year even if I don't like it,' and I did stay a year and I didn't like it. But then I was asked to go into a doctor's house near London and there I stayed four and a half years and was very happy. Then I had an accident to my knee and had an operation at home and decided not to go back.

For one year after that I went to a blind lady with whom I lived as companion house-keeper. It was a family we had been friendly with for years. The father was a dear old gentleman of 89 and loved me to spend hours reading to him.

After that time my brother lost his second wife, leaving a tiny baby girl, so asked please would I go and keep house and bring up baby. I said yes I would and I was with him for four years. He was a baker and confectioner at East Dereham. We did a lot of out-door catering - school treats, cricket luncheons, flower shows, freemasons' dinners, and soon I gained much experience in cooking and planning and I loved the work. Then - and a big then - along came the man who looked at me and looked again, why, I know not, but he is the man I married and he is now sitting near me having a game of draughts with a boy from over the road.

I did not leave my brother without help, for he married just before I did, so that I could look after the business while he went on his honeymoon.

IT was on Easter Monday 13 April 1903 I was married. It snowed heavily. We went to Croydon from Norfolk that day and by the time we arrived a black fog had descended and the cabman had to lead his horse and use a lamp to find the house we wanted.

We have had many foggy patches since then but also much sunshine.

You will smile at this experience of the bridegroom. I had nursed my small niece for three weeks previous to my wedding. She had had a very bad turn of whooping cough - and in the house where we spent our wedding night there were three children all whooping for all they were worth. I was already very hoarse and coughing but I thought it was the foggy journey. However, soon after the household had gone to rest, as I was then coughing badly, my husband went exploring to find mustard to make a plaster for my chest. However, it did not cure me and I was very ill after we returned to our own home - a narrow escape, it was said, but care and a good doctor pulled me through.

I don't advise mustard plaster, neither does my husband now. I think he would say: 'If you have chest trouble or bronchial coughs, give up smoking, as I did thirty yars ago.' He has been marvellously well since then.

MY parents (both born in 1834) lived to celebrate their 65th wedding anniversary, so I don't think hard work or large families shorten one's life. My brothers all reached 80 and over, one 89. I now have three sisters living - 81, 89 and 90 - and carrying on fairly normally.

My husband and I celebrated our golden wedding on 13 April 1953. We have had much happiness in spite of (or perhaps because of) many trying periods of struggle in business and more than one serious illness, through which we nursed each other.

Our tastes are simple - books, walks and in my husband's case, his church choir and choral society are his only recreations. Alas! I am very deaf, so music is denied me. He is a non-smoker, very seldom (about once a year) goes to the cinema or any other expensive entertainment.

There are many who tell you that when poverty comes in at the door love flies out the window. Personally, I say this is not true, for I quite think that the troubles we have shared have cemented us closer together.

The Simple Joys of Edwardian Childhood

Mary H. Vennard (c1956), Illustrated by Jennifer Kent

IN 1902 my father, a retired sea-captain, rented an old Suffolk farmhouse. It had four bedrooms not counting the attics, a huge drawing-room, a sitting-room, a kitchen, a dairy and the sort of pantry that one can walk round - the only kind for me!

It was a typical East Anglian farmhouse, yellow-washed and gabled, flanked by orchards that were thick with primroses and violets in the spring, overlooking the village green and with a giant horse-chestnut whose pink and flame-coloured candle-like blossoms brushed the bedroom windows.

If I remember rightly the rent was £18 a year and here it was, a year later, that I was born, thus joining the proud company of those entitled to be known as 'Silly Suffolks'.

In his childhood days my son, brought up in an age of austerity, had most of his pleas (particularly regarding ponies and large dogs) answered with the stock remark: 'We cann't afford it, dear,' or 'There simply isn't room.' In spite of the modern advantages he enjoyed, when I told him about my childhood days he used to gaze at me with awe and say: 'But, Mummy, you must have been *rich*.'

Looking back, I could almost agree with him. But in those days of cheap food and labour we did not consider ourselves anything but an ordinary middle-class family and not so well-off at that. Now, as I do my housework and reluctantly wash and iron for the family, I think how easy life must have been . . . and so, perhaps it was for families like ourselves, with a modest but adequate income.

It was not so good, however, for the farm labourer and his wife with the many children, to whose cottage my father used to drive me in the pony-trap to distribute old toys after Father Christmas had showered me with new ones.

Not so good, either, for old Martha who daily fetched our milk from the farm and water from the pump for a pittance. She looked like a witch without her broomstick, wore about five petticoats in various stages of disrepair and loved to receive a pair of father's old boots which she wore until they fell to pieces and then begged for more.

TALKING of Christmas and looking back on the Christmases I spent in that little Suffolk village . . they seem to me to be quite Dickensian. Father bought coal by the wagon-load and whisky by the crate, while the slaughter that went on in the farmer's poultry yard hardly bears thinking about. It all sounds so affluent - until you remember that whisky was 3s. 6d. a bottle and coal less than £1 a ton.

During the war, when I scraped and scrounged to give my little son a party, I used to think of Christmas at Weylands. The pathetic little branches in the shops, that called themselves Christmas trees and cost the earth, brought to mind the stately fir which used to brush the low ceiling of our drawing room and was loaded with glittering tinsel, coloured glass balls and crowned with a pink or white fairy.

Our Christmas party was quite an event and all the children in the village used to come. The modern idea of fun seems to be to tear round the house playing cowboys and indians with complete disregard for hostesses' beds or furniture and the only way to make the little dears behave is to let them watch the television. Even then the programme does not always suit their sophisticated taste. I am afraid our party games and charades would bore them stiff. However, we enjoyed them!

And at the finish the oil lamps would be put out and we would walk down the passage to the 'back-us' by the light of flowing Chinese lanterns in different colours and shapes which my father had brought from abroad. On the kitchen table there would be a huge dish of raisins over which my father would pour a libation of brandy and then set the whole thing alight. Then we all snatched in the dancing blue flames for the raisins!

Another Dickensian touch was the visit of the carol singers. They always finished their tour at our house where Mother and Helen awaited them with hot mince-pies and coffee and father welcomed the men with a little something to keep out the cold. Perhaps it was just as well that ours was the last visit of the evening or the harmony might have suffered!

They needed no police permit in those carefree days and were to my mind infinitely preferable, with their untrained, but sweet voices, to the highly proficient but impersonal choirs provided for us nowadays by the radio.

Among the girls was my friend and mentor Katie. Her sister Helen came to work for my mother straight from school and subsequently became a marvellous cook. Katie was still at the little village school but she spent all her spare time with me and we found a thousand things to amuse us. Every child, in the past or of today, has loved picking flowers. But in those days, it seems to me, the flowers were so much more profuse. The borders of the roads, the banks and ditches, were thick with primroses and dog-violets. In the meadows we gathered bunches of slender grasses with little quivering buds which we called 'ladies hair'. They were much prized by the cottagers for putting in vases on their mantelpieces.

No one ever seemed to growl at us for playing in the meadows, whereas nowadays everywhere is jealously fenced off and children chased away or told to play in the playground provided by a thoughtful council. Those iron swings and other contraptions could never make up to me for the joys of the open fields where we gathered moon daisies in the summer, went gleaning in the autumn and tobogganing in the winter. In addition to wild flowers we picked the brightest blooms from the garden and sandwiched them between squares of glass which we called 'peep-shows'.

If it rained, there was always the shed next to the stable, where the pony's hay was kept, and here we would retire with a pile of Beatrix Potter books and read the adventures of Mrs Tiggy Winkle or Squirrel Nutkin. Next door lived Sanger, our white pony, so-called because of his habit of racing round the village green in circles like a circus pony. Besides Sanger, we had an old English sheepdog, a large and very spoilt tabby cat and a wonderful parrot called Peter who swore at the cat, barked at the dog and adored Helen who fed him with pieces of fried egg at breakfast time. He would pace frantically up and down his cage imploring her to 'save a little bit for the poor old bird'. There were also pigeons and ferrets but the former avoided me and I avoided the latter who had once nipped me on the ankle.

When the children of the village had their annual school treat they would drive in beautifully decorated farm wagons, festooned with flowers, to a selected field where they (and I) would scramble for nuts, run races and consume large quantities of buns. Father used to drive behind the wagons in our trap. This was an affair with two large wheels at the back and two small wheels, mounted on a separate axle and easily turned, at the front. Sprouting from the well of the trap was a solid mast bearing a square sunshade with scalloped edges or, in bad weather, a large black umbrella. I would imagine this conveyance to have been a close relation to Genevieve.

Another excitement, for the children at least, was the arrival on the village green of a travelling mission, in a horse-drawn caravan from which services were conducted. All the children, whether Church or Chapel, attended the service especially arranged for them and we sang lustily: 'Let us gather at the fountain, the be-yewtiful, be-YEWtiful fountain.' I still possess a photograph of us ranged round the caravan, all the girls in white pinafores, except Katie, resplendent in her new sailor-suit, and me, with lace unmentionables showing well below the plimsole line.

THE death of King Edward VII symbolizes for me the end of a carefree childhood, for, soon after, my father (who, incidentally, greatly resembled the late king in appearance) also died and our home was broken up.

My mother moved to a tiny house in Felixstowe where arrangements had been made for me to go to school and where my ripe Suffolk dialect was severely frowned upon.

Helen, my dearest companion and mentor, found another post to which she tearfully departed.

My sister took Peter to her home where a careless maid left him in the summerhouse one chilly night and he 'took sick and died'.

Bobs, the cat, was too old to be moved and a neighbour, who loved him dearly, gave him a home where he spent the rest of his life in luxury.

Joe, the sheepdog, also old and feeble, had to be destroyed and there was left only Sanger. My mother gave him to a friend on the condition that he should never be re-sold. The day before we moved, the man came to take him away. My eyes still smart as, through the years, I hear Sanger's hoofs trotting into the distance, beating the retreat to my Edwardian childhood.

Old Mary

Jessie Mallows (c1957)

O NE of my earliest recollections is of Old Mary, bandana handkerchief on head, clay pipe in mouth, seated on the doorstep of her thatched cottage, watching the world go by.

It was a different world she looked upon from that of today. Although her cottage stood at the junction of the London-coast roads it meant nothing, for motor cars had not come into being. Within her range of vision was the fine old coaching inn but its importance had declined with the advent of the railroad and was used only by those who called for a drink. Except on market days at the nearby town, when every form of wheeled vehicle passed through the village, movement was mainly confined to the residents of the district going about their various callings.

Mary must have been a handsome young woman, for her appearance was impressive even with grey hair and lined cheek. When young she had linked her life with that of Percy, ignoring the legal bond, and they had raised a family. The old rector, during whose long tenure of office every parishioner had become a friend, had appreciated the fidelity of the union and had not thought fit to censure its irregularity.

His successor was a young man and the parish was his first charge. A scholar, he had a boyish charm of manner which soon made him popular in the parish. His views on Christian living were sharply defined and at times thundered forth from the pulpit. That two of his parishioners should be living in a manner contrary to Christian principles was grievous to him and in friendly visits to Mary he tried to persuade her to conform to the law of the land and of the Church. But the niceties of the law, and the tenets of religion, were not matters of interest to Mary. She was a law unto herself and the young rector was soon made aware of it.

Yet a Sunday came when an astonished congregation listened to the banns of marriage being published of Percy and Mary and heard themselves asked if they knew cause or just impediment why these persons should not be joined together in holy matrimony.

'Parish relief' were the murmurs from various members of the congregation as they left the church. It is possible that the need for the dole - eightpence in cash and a half stone of flour per person per week, considered sufficient in that day to provide sustenance for the body and for the grant of which a respectable status must be proved - had caused Mary to take a step which no admonitions of the Church could bring about.

A day came when Mary, bent with age, and Percy, still upright but spindly, took a walk and by a circuitous route entered the church and made their vows to keep each other until death did them part.

WAGES were poor in those days and older people had difficulty in finding the means to live.

Percy's work was that of a bricklayer but I cannot recall his working in that capacity. To make a few shillings Mary would, in the summer months, compound a drink from horehound, a plant which grows wild in the country lanes. On coming home from school on warm days we children would be allowed to take a jug to Mary's and, on payment of one half-penny, have it filled with what to us was a delectable drink.

Osiers grown on land bordering the rivers were cut in the winter months and peeled in the warm weather. The peeling of the rods, which gave employment to many, was mainly carried out on the osier grounds but Mary, who earned a few shillings this way, worked outside her back door and I was interested to watch her as with strong movement she pulled the rods through the stripping frame.

After Percy's death Mary took her blind brother Barney to live with her. Another brother, handsome old Tom, the embodiment of a successful dealer, lived a few miles away. He was what is known in country parlance as 'well breeched' and his hand was often in his breeches pocket for Mary.

At the office where I was employed, word was brought to me that I was wanted at the public counter. On reaching it I found Tom waiting to speak to me. Without prelude he said: 'I've jest sin yer father in the town. I've bin asking him yer mother's age. Why, she's gitting to the afternoon ain't she?'

We had some conversation about other things and I asked if he had been to see Mary lately. He was somewhat uncomfortable at the question and murmued 'No no', then burst forth with: 'It's like this here. Barney and I don't talk alike. Barney want me to help him put a tombstone to his wife's grave. I say: "No, Barney," I say, "I niver thought anything of yer wife when she was liven' and I think no more of her now she's dead." '

Mary died as yeomanry entered the village on the outbreak of war and Tom's heart was broken when a much-loved grandson lost his life in that war. Mary's cottage has been demolished and where it stood the road has been widened to allow the surge of traffic. Where Percy tilled his vegetable patch, grass and flowers flank a filling station into which cars are passing all day. The inn is as important to the motorist as it was to the traveller by stage coach. But at times the busy scene changes and in retrospect I see the quiet street, the sunlight glancing on the mellow bricks of the inn and casting the shadow of the eaves on the plaster walls of the cottage and, seated on the doorstep, Old Mary smoking her pipe.

Getting Married at the End of the 19th century

Emily E. Gray (c1954)

IN those days every young man and girl used to attend church or chapel and that was where they started looking for a sweetheart. That was generally how things began, on winter evenings, mostly, after the service. A shy young man would step up to two girls as they went home. He'd begin talking to one of them but he wouldn't have the courage to go right home with her the first time. But after about three Sundays he would become a little more sure of himself and the other girl would then leave the field to her friend. Thus things progressed a bit and the couple would be 'walking out.'

There was no fuss about engagements and engagement rings for the working people of those days but when the young man bought the wedding ring he generally bought what was called a 'keeper' with it and then he would start in earnest to save for a little home. No young man at that time thought of marrying a girl unless he had a home for her and had paid for it.

I remember in my own case my young man started to save for his home by keeping fowls and pigs. Wages were very low but during harvest a single man could earn as much as a married man and that meant he could save a clear £5. He used to pay six shillings a week to his mother for board and washing and everything included.

About the only holiday farm workers had was the Monday and Tuesday of Whitsun week and then some of them would have a 'day out' at the nearest town. But I have heard the old people say that those who went to the village inns at Whitsun had a high old time. There would be dancing all night and in the morning about five

o'clock they fried sausages for breakfast. Then they went back to work, thinking they'd had a wonderful time.

ABOUT two years after courting had started in earnest thoughts would turn to marriage. The girl would try to contribute things to the home. Her trousseau, which often consisted of half-a-dozen of everything, was often made of brown calico by the girl herself - and many a happy thought went into the work.

Then the great day arrived. The wedding party always walked to church. There would be about six of them. Behind the bride and her father walked the bridegroom and a bridesmaid, then the best man and perhaps another bridesmaid or the girl's mother. Sometimes they would walk two miles like that. Of course, coming back, the bride and bridegroom would walk in front and the people would call out 'good luck' to them as they passed.

The wedding celebrations started only after their friends had finished work for the day, as so many of them could not afford to have money deducted from their wages for lost time. The party was held at the bride's home and the guests took their presents with them . . . a set of jugs, some cups and saucers, a mirror, a saucepan.

Then they settled down to a good meal and the celebrations continued until about two o'clock in the morning. Then everyone went home for they had all (excluding the bridegroom) to be at work next day and in the summertime work started at six.

The bride had probably been in service in a gentleman's house and she found that there was much for her to learn when she had to start house-keeping on her husband's income of fourteen shillings a week. I well remember the first time I went shopping. I saw a tin of fruit on the grocer's shelf and thought how nice it would be to take it home for Sunday dinner. But I soon learned that our money wouldn't cover such luxuries, although the cost was only 7d or 8d for a 2 lb tin.

The first day, when my man went off to work, he said to me: 'I have mixed the food. Will you feed the pigs at mid-day?'

That was work very new to me. I took the pail, opened the pigsty door and as I turned round to pick up the pail out bolted the pigs. They ran all over the fields, with me after them. Of course, I couldn't catch them.

When my husband came home and asked if I'd fed the pigs I had to confess that I'd lost them. But he found them again.

Then in the harvest time the women had to help with the barley. It was called gavelling. If the wives didn't do it the men had to pay other women and it cost them two shillings a day. Taking the harvest, as it was called, was usually worked out at so much per acre per man. A man could generally earn about £10 altogether. He worked early and late and if the weather was kind perhaps he could finish in a month. One never sees nowadays a man setting out about five o'clock in the morning, with a big frail of food and a half-stone bottle of home-brewed beer strapped together and slung over his shoulder, the bottle hanging in front.

But harvest was a lovely time. The women would take their children with them into the fields about four o'clock in the afternoon and deliver tea to their men - 'beaver' we used to call it.

I could write a book about all the ways we had of making our money last out. We never dreamed of getting into debt by more than two shillings even if a really bad week occurred.

My first baby came along at the end of the first year. It was necessary to save up fifteen shillings to pay the doctor and that was all. There were no district nurses or midwives but generally a woman, a really kind person, would come in and neighbours always helped each other at a time like that, for you did the same for them when their own turn came.

I remember how I stormed because my husband bought a pram for five shillings from his brother who was in the second-hand trade. He thought it was the best he could do. I expected an awful old thing, something I should be ashamed to go out with. But it happened to be a very smart, stylish pram with big bicycle wheels and tyres. It was boat-shaped and had springs and was brass where today it would be chromium. How we polished that brass and shone it up! I was, after all, very proud of that pram when we took it down to the village.

At Christmas, when we had the children, we used to buy ginger-beer and a few biscuits and pretend that we had wine and cake after dinner. Simple pleasures . . . but how happy was our home. With all the things the children have now, are they really any happier than mine were?

The Simple Life

R. H. Futter (c1951)

Far from the madding crowd's ignoble strife
Their sober wishes never learned to stray.

THE rural population which has replaced the descendants of Gray's 'rude forefathers of the hamlet' are so changed in habit and outlook that no poet of the future will be able to sing of their 'sober wishes' or their non-straying habits. After an absence of nearly sixty years I returned to find the countryside - save for a rash of council houses - little changed, but I look in vain for anyone resembling 'Hodge, the poor honest country wight' of the old doggerel rhyme.

This village of which I write was a real village, a self-contained rural community dominated by one of the many fine churches of East Anglia. A fair cross-section of the population would show the parson, the squire, doctor, schoolmaster, a few private residents, a number of small, independent tradesmen long since, alas, driven out by mass production, and the aforesaid Hodge and his numerous progeny.

My earliest recollections are of the time when Joseph Arch (or 'Arch Joe' as some of his opponents dubbed him) thought he could improve the labourer's lot and incidentally do himself a bit of good by organising a labourers' union.

This was a time when the rectory was the real centre of parish life. Everybody, barring perhaps the village poacher and bad man, which few villages lacked, went to service at least once on Sundays and explanations were due from absentees. In our enthusiasm for the present, I think, if we are honest, we must admit that we have lost something in the abandonment of this and other disciplinary habits, which at least exacted a certain sacrifice of inclination and broadcast what one of our old-time statesmen called 'the salutary influence of example.'

Our rector was an evangelical of the old school who always preached in a black gown with little Geneva bands and all the responses were recited, the public's contribution being led, or followed as it too frequently was, by old George X, the parish clerk, who was very deaf and soon got a lap or two behind, a circumstance that did not worry him in the least as he had no idea he was holding up the traffic. He occupied the ground stall of the old three-decker pulpit which has these many years passed into the limbo of forgotten things, like the church-going habit and a number of other ancient customs which I miss.

The standard wage for the labourer was 12s. 6d. for a horseman and 10s. a week for the ordinary labourer. Holidays, except a day at Christmas and Easter, were non-existent and amusements, except what the people contrived for themselves, few and far between. Not many could read or write and quite an appreciable number never went - or wanted to go - beyond the parish they were born in.

Yet, in his way, Hodge got as much out of life as he wanted and was indeed rather surprised when Joe Arch opened up a view of a rural Utopia to be attained by organisation. He worked hard indeed for a mere pittance. But for all that, he brought up a large family of decent, God-fearing men and women who I think would compare very favourably with the products of the present generation. How it was done must be a complete mystery to modern parents.

TWO characters stand out in my memory of those days. One was old John X, the village pig butcher, rat and mole catcher and week-end barber. Today I suppose he would be called a rodent operator. He used to wear what was called a Newgate fringe, very popular at the time - a clean-shaven chin with a short surrounding whisker. He was bounded to the north by an ancient bowler hat and clad, over-all, in an old frock coat.

He always shouldered on a short spud his ferret-box, while he carried at the trail an old gaspipe muzzle-loader. What he did not know about the virtues and vices of the country for miles around did not matter. He was a skilful butcher and my father used to say it was almost a pleasure for a pig to be killed so scientifically.

He used to shave the old gaffers on a Saturday night. None of them had any teeth and old John used to shove a couple of fingers in their mouths to stretch their cheeks to give the razor a chance. For tuppeny clients he had a wooden spoon.

The other character was a well-to-do farmer who was something of an innocent. One of the bugbears of those days was chaff-cutting because of the difficulty of getting horses to tread the monotonous round and some joker sold him the idea of putting up a windmill as a power unit.

The mill was duly erected but, because of the variable nature of the wind and the load, proved an utter failure. Nevertheless, his nephews, with a little assistance from my brothers and myself, found it extremely diverting to set the thing going. When the wind was right, we used to shove the belt on and let her rip. The old chaff-cutter stood in the root house and with a plentiful supply of turnips we would bombard the knives, creating an amazing display of vegetable pyrotechnics which delighted us almost as much as it annoyed the farmer.

I knew well the agricultural labourer of Joe Arch's day and I know that he worked hard and long and was underpaid. But I deny that he was any less happy than his modern fag-smoking, football fan, picture fan and dog racing counterpart.

He found his pleasures in the simple things of life. He ran the whole gamut of human emotions and neither millionaire nor trade union organiser can do more.

The enduring satisfactions do not come from football pools, cinema or similar diversions but from the simple things which Burns had in mind when he wrote:

To make a happy fireside clime
For weans and wife -
That's the true purpose and sublime
Of human life.

If it be true, as the scriptures have it, 'he that increases knowledge increaseth sorrow.' then Hodge was a happy man for he had little knowledge. But, for all that, he had a wisdom which is sadly lacking nowadays and which taught him where to look for true happiness and content.

East Anglian Customs in the early 20th century

Miriam Sykes (c1954), Illustrated by Joan Pickford

I WONDER if there are many - and I often think there must be - who, like myself, regret the passing of time honoured customs that were once a great feature of East Anglian life.

My childhood was spent in the Norfolk village of Walpole St Peter and I have vivid recollections of the excitement and pleasure which the observance of these customs occasioned amongst us.

To me the May Day visit of The 'May Ladies' was a joy second only to that of Xmas. Little girls working in pairs would make house-to-house calls, carrying between them a large linen basket, lined and covered with a sheet or tablecloth, the cover being supported by bent willow withes. Arriving at a house and setting down the basket they would knock and when the door was opened would shyly ask:

'Would you like to see the May Ladies?'

Then turning back the cover they would reveal the interior profusely decorated with flowers, two or three dolls, wreathed and garlanded and, in the centre, a money box. After gazing for a few minutes at the pretty sight we would place a coin in the box and the children would replace the cover and depart. They would be followed at intervals by others throughout the day. I do not know how much money would be collected by this means but after May Day many little girl would appear at Sunday School in a new frock or pair of boots.

May 29 was known as 'Royal Oak Day.' Being the birthday of King Charles II and the anniversary of the Restoration, it was marked by the wearing of oak leaves and woe betide the boy or girl who went to school without a favour. They would have their ears and noses pulled and their toes trodden on and would be called 'Roundhead.' The origin of this custom is not far to seek and would seem to indicate that the merry monarch had many loyal supporters in this part of the country.

If May day was exclusively a girls' day, the boys came into their own on 5 November. When darkness fell, bands of little boys with soot blackened faces, wearing the raggedest clothes they could find, many of them carrying 'hobby lanterns,' would parade the village, calling at houses and chanting this foolish old ditty:

'Please to remember the fifth of November,
When poor old Guy, he went to the war, he got a black eye.
With a hole in his stocking and a hole in his shoe,
Please can you give us a copper or two?'

Hobby lanterns, I should explain, were made from mangolds, the insides of which had been scooped out and holes made to represent the eyes, nose and mouth with a lighted candle inside, they presented a weird and fearsome sight in the darkness.

The money the boys got would be spent later on fireworks at the village shop, open till 10 o'clock in those days.

An incident occurring one Guy Fawkes night stands out clearly in my memory. Hearing some boys arriving, I went to the door and on opening it noticed that one boy was not in keeping with the rest.

'Why haven't you blackened your face?' I exclaimed.

'His mother would not let him,' chorused the rest.

'There's a bag of soot in the coalhouse over there,' I said thoughtlessly and instantly there was a scuffle and a stampede towards the shed, the unfortunate boy was pushed head downwards into the sack and the soot was rubbed well and truly over his face, into his hair and down his neck. Finally the sack was picked up and the entire contents emptied over the boy. As I feared the poor boy got a thrashing when he went home. I felt partly responsible and bought him a bag of sweets next day (a rare treat in those days) but he never forgave me and always put his tongue out at me after that.

AT Xmas the waits would travel round in farm wagons and sing carols beneath the bedroom windows. It was usually about 2 or 3 o'clock in the morning when they arrived at our farm and we children would be awakened by the noise and the lights of the hurricane lanterns and would watch the singers from the windows, afterwards dropping money into the boxes held up to us. As the wagons rumbled away our parents would call to us to stop talking and go to sleep again. This, however, was not too easy when the stockings left hanging limply over the bedrail a few hours earlier were now bulging with exciting mysteries.

On New Year's Eve 'the ringers' would come. These were the men with the handbells. They would file into the kitchen and taking up their positions round the table would play appropriate tuncs finishing always with 'Auld Lang Sync.' After that there would be food and drinks for the men. As our farm was outlying and almost the last call and as they had the same generous reception at many other houses before reaching us, few of the ringers were strictly sober when they arrived and would depart with laughter and song and great merriment.

I wonder what became of those handbells and if anyone ever plays with them now?

A wedding would have seemed incomplete with-out a visit from the 'rough band.' Lads and girls equipped with mouth organs, combs, kettles, tin cans, pot lids, etc., approached the scene of rejoicing, usually after dark, making a great noise with their band and after 'playing' for a minute or two would begin shouting for 'a penny to go in the next street.' They got their pennies and usually refreshments as well, then took their departure and marched all round the village playing their band and gathering more pennies as they went along.

A strawberry tea was held each year in the rectory grounds. Ladies who had undertaken to 'give a table,' took along their best china and linen, silver teapot (if they had one), cakes and pastries of their own baking and of course an immense supply of strawberries and cream. I helped my mother several times with her table and it seems to me now, on looking back, that the sun always shone on those occasions.

I think it was the 1914 war that put an end to all those practices, whch had survived so many other wars. We turned our attention then to Zeppelin raids and songs about the Kaiser and after the war to armistice and peace celebrations and the new generation knew nothing of May Ladies and strawberry teas and certainly never thought of rejoicing because a king long dead 'came into his own again.'

A Farthunth of Sherbert
E. A. H. Ward (c1959)

ON a warm summer evening last year (1958) the silence of the road in which I now live was disturbed by the tinkling of a bell - a handbell wielded by the driver of a gaily coloured motor van boldly inscribed 'ICES'.

Hardly had the van made its entry than, as if by magic, children appeared at windows, at doors, from gardens - a whirlwind descended on me as my small daughter rushed in for small change. Then all of them dashed in hot pursuit of the van and its contents.

Watching them go, I mused that the days of the town crier may have gone, the cry of 'Blowers' or 'Water CREESE' no longer heard (all of which I remember in our quiet Suffolk street years ago) but here surely was a worthy successor to those picturesque characters of the past.

Here was the Pied Piper with all his power - for I am sure the children would have chased his van to the world's end if he had not stopped.

Rather a sinister looking man, with a long black beard, was he who called 'Water CREESE' as he trudged with his basket along the path. I concluded that my mother was mistaken in referring to water cress: this impressive man actually had the stuff in his basket so he *must* know what it was called.

Only a Suffolker born and bred could understand just how the call 'Blowters' sounded. The vowel 'o' bears no resemblance to the vowel sound in 'blow.'

I mused, too, that it does not seem that children value money nowadays. I remember in the years before the First World War, when summer days were an endless serenity of glorious sunshine (official records notwithstanding), we children knew nothing of ice cream. Instead, in my street there lived one Mrs Turpin, a kindly, lovable old soul even when she looked severely at us over her nickel spectacles: slow moving she was - not surprisingly so in view of her considerable girth and the fact that her 'front room' was crammed with boxes of sweets and - oh, scrumptious stuff - sherbert. (She it was who, in her homely style, cut down my trousers from father's almost as fast as I wore them out.)

'A farthunth of sherbet, please, Mrs Turpin' . . . and what a generous bagful she handed out. Then to a quiet corner, where the choice lay simply between putting the tongue direct into the paper bag or, less favoured from the point of view of economy, dipping in wet fingers.

How well I remember the day when (I expect as a privation of the early days of that war) she sadly replied that she was sorry, she couldn't make a farthunth any more, but only a ha'puth.

She had a son, Freddy, at whose head she aimed a slap every time he came near her, probably regarded mutually as on account of his past or future misdeeds. But she was so slow moving, her slaps never made contact - we always said that he had time to put on his cap and be half way up the street before the blow fell . . . But, knowing her gentle nature, perhaps she intended it so.

Near our parish church there stood the Penny Bazaar in which interest was allowed to centre near birthday time. What an exciting variety of good things in that tiny shop (I realise now that it was but a single room of a small house). The choice (and what agony it was to make the choice) ranged from tops, whips, whistles, walking sticks, to pistols with rolls of caps, masks and those streaky marbles that remind one of rock.

Speaking of rock, at our school, at playtime, there came the 'hot rolls' man from a nearby bakery, and those strong and lucky enough to get near him and to be in possession of a ha'penny could buy a hot roll or a small stick of rock. In those days it was 'rock *or* roll'. Typically, today youngsters expect both.

The Ferry, the Armistice & A Day with Cousin Grace

Barbara Smitherman (c1951)

EVERY year from about 1906 to 1914 our family spent most summer months at Felixstowe Ferry. Since those years included the year of my birth my earliest recollections are of the ferry in those golden days.

I cannot honestly say they are the happiest of memories for one or two incidents were rather alarming and that is no doubt why they were so clearly imprinted in the mind of a child of two or three years of age.

Those who knew the ferry then will remember the old high breakwater, on the low side of which ran the ferry itself - some of it was still there a few years ago (before 1951) - and they will be able to picture a small boy and a small girl in dark blue 'fishermen's' jerseys throwing stones over the high side into the water beneath them. The boy excelled himself - and accidently followed his stone. His sister has forever the picture of a frightended face beneath the clear water and of a maid and an elder brother jumping into a boat moored nearby and pulling out the screaming boy!

She also well remembers the feeling, unusual for an only daughter, of being completely unimportant as she trotted behind the couple as they dragged the bawling boy back to the cottage behind the Ferry Boat inn.

Earlier - and before I was born - the village postman was one day attracted by something red in the water and as his son wore red he went down to the edge of the water and found my elder brother floating out to sea supported by his petticoats and scarlet-caped coat.

August 1914 brought soldiers to the door of the cottage at five o'clock one morning with orders for us to leave the coast immediately. I can recall being dressed that early morning. I was far too young to know the meaning of it all. I was more interested in a large black village dog that went by with its foot bandaged - Suffolk's first war casualty? Later, as we drove back along the marsh road, we saw troops digging trenches near the beach.

Another war memory is recalled by the Zeppelin L48 which was brought down at Theberton. I was taken to the window of our house in Ipswich (being already awake because of whooping-cough) to see it burning in the sky. I thought it was a second moon. When I was taken into Ipswich to see the lights and jubilations when the war was over I cried at the noise: 'I don't like peace. Take me home!'

IT must have been towards the end of the war years that I used to visit Falkenham with my grandfather 'to spend the day with Cousin Grace.' First there was the train journey to Trimley, then the seemingly endless walk across the cornfields - tedious for me because I couldn't see over the top of the ripe corn. At any rate, all I remember are the varieties of little paths, their ups and downs and now and again the excitement of a stile.

At Falkenham, Cousin Grace, Cousin Jim and their daughter would be waiting. I would be handed over to Dorothy, a young woman my own age who was fairly dancing with excitement at having a visitor. How I envied her her pinafore with its frilled shoulders and embroidery. A snapshot shows us looking very much town and country cousins, her dress being six inches longer than mine. None of the old fashioned charm of her dress distinguishes the village child from her town counterpart these days.

Firstly we visited the fruit bushes. Oh, the

'None of the old fashioned charm of her dress distinguishes the village child from her town counterpart these days.'

delicious scent of sun-warmed currant bushes! Further down the garden there was a trap for birds - a kind of cage - easy to enter, impossible to leave. I was horrified and let go one sparrow accidentally on purpose.

The E.C. (Elsan closet) was an extremely fascinating place. It had lovely white-scrubbed wood and was, I believe, a three-seater.

Back to the house we went for dinner. I cannot remember the kind of food we had except that it was some sort of cold meat and there were mounds of potatoes. But the huge plates and tureens fascinated me with their old brown patterns of flowers, and best of all were the knives and forks with their horn handles. How my cousins questioned me and how they piled my plate. Because I was smaller than 'Dot' I think they thought I wanted feeding up.

29

In the afternoon we went to see the horses down near the marshes. Cousin Jim would call them and up they would trot, a dozen or so beautiful Suffolk Punches - a perfect picture.

Then, after Cousin Barbara had been suitably paraded to satisfy neighbourly curiosity, came tea and time to leave. Sometimes it meant the dreaded walk but once, at least, Cousin Jim got out the horse and trap. 'Dot' and I were lifted on to the back seat and secured with a blanket while Grandpa and Cousin Jim sat in front with their backs to us. Off we went in the evening light, over the white, dusty roads and sandy, rutted lanes to the station. A solemn handshake for Cousin Jim, a peck on Dot's cheek and off they drove, leaving us to stare back at the few other passengers who waited, holding their bunches of homely cottage flowers.

The train was never full and we travelled in comfort to Ipswich. Then the tram - lovely slatted seats outside, which you reversed when the tram turned and, inside, long smooth seats of golden wood.

So, home to Brook Street, my white muslin dress smeared with a hundred dead thunder flies and, all unknown, in a small child's head a hundred ever-living memories of a visit to 'Cousin Grace.'

Whitsuntide at Wendling

Godfrey Windham (c1952)

MY native village, Wendling, lies along the highway that winds its way from Yarmouth to Kings Lynn. There is nothing to distinguish it from any other village and the traveller may well pass through it without being aware of its existence. Yet in my youth it was my world - and not a dormant world, particularly at Whitsuntide, when lilacs and laburnum were in full bloom and the lanes were perfumed by the smell of hemlock and sweetbriar. In the evenings, bells from a dozen churches rang out their joyous peals over meadows carpeted with buttercups which left a deposit of gold on the boots of the labourers returning home.

On Whit Sunday, the chapel held its school anniversary in a neighbouring barn. For weeks past the children had practised their songs and 'pieces' waiting impatiently for the day when they could put on their new suits and summer frocks and, standing in front of the platform made from sheep hurdles and wooden planks, display their knowledge of elocution.

Each year a favourite local preacher was invited to conduct the anniversary services. One year it was George Langdon, a huge, bearded man with beaming face and thunderous voice. He had walked some three of four miles from his little farmstead. On entering the barn, he removed his bowler hat. Wiping the sweat from his brow, he said how glad he was to be with his Wendling friends again and announced the first hymn. After the hymn, George knelt on the platform and prayed a long and ardent prayer and when he rose tears streamed down his face. For no good preacher could pray without emotion and the depth of his emotion was the standard by which he was judged. He wiped away his tears and his face transformed immediately into a beaming smile. He called Winnie Walker to say her 'piece.'

Winnie was four years old and in a lisping voice began: 'God who made the daisies and all the pretty flowers . . . ' But at this juncture some of the boys at the back of the platform started to giggle and, in attempting to smother their merriment, over-balanced and sent the form on which they were sitting crashing to the floor. This commotion was too much for Winnie. Wth her little face sad and puckered she burst into tears and ran back to her place.

The next item George announced was the anthem by the choir. Now for a small village the choir was well trained and sang in perfect harmony. There was a hush over the con-gregation as the anthem swelled out:
'Send us thy light and thy truth:
Let them lead me,
O let them lead me; O let them lead me to Thy holy hill.'
Loud and soft, soft and loud, the words were repeated with growing fervour until the whole place seemed inspired and infused with the very presence of the Eternal God. There is no one who, having experienced such moments as these - in which earth meets heaven and the spirit of

man links up with the Heart of God - can return to the daily round and common task without being influenced thereby. Neither is the influence fleeting, for it lingers over the years and is a sure and certain anchor for a faith which may be torn and shaken by the winds of time and chance.

The afternoon service ended, George Langdon tramped home to milk his cows and back again to preach the evening sermon. This was a repetition of George's usual discourse, without reason or cohesion, but eloquent in its sincerity and moving in its direct appeal. When he had ended, he carefully wiped his eyes and said: 'Now my friends, I expect you would like me to sing.'

It was characteristic of this tireless man that, after preaching, he must sing a song which he called 'Exalted High.' All the boys knew George's song and used to imitate his manner of singing it, to the amusement of their elders.

With handkerchief in hand and head thrown back, he would close his eyes and begin, very softly:

'Exalted high, at God's right hand,
Nearer the Throne than angels stand
With glory crowned in white array
My wondering soul cries: "Who are they?" '

The first two lines were sung slowly and the second two equally fast and so on, over and over again, first repeating one line and then another until, mopping his beaming brow, he would work up into a crescendo of excitement which stopped suddenly at the last line. And then came the answer:

'These are the saints, beloved by God,
Washed are the robes in Jesu's blood.
With angels, clothed in spotless white
They shine in uncreated light.'

It was a storm at sea, with the winds lashed up into a fury and then dying down into perfect calm.

Such were those men whose hands were rough and hardened through wresting a living from the land, whose clothes were course and badly fitted, but whose faith burned within them like a living fire, a fire which consumed all petty jealousies, all desire to ride roughshod over the feelings of their fellow man in pursuit of their own ambitions, and brought into their lives a peace like the whispering of leaves in a summer breeze.

On Whit-Monday the Band of Hope annual fete (or treat, as it was called) was held in a meadow adjoining the barn. Wendling boasted a vigorous Band of Hope and this treat was a highly organised affair. To begin with, the Salvation Army band from Dereham headed a long procession of blue ribboners who marched and sang around the village. Hale and hearty fellows were those bandsmen, particularly the drummer who, in the pauses between playing, would take off his red cap and wipe his perspiring head. It so happened that he had a particularly shiny bald head and, much to the amusement of his pals, one of the small boys called out: 'Coo look! Ole Harry 'a bin usin' metal polish.'

After the procession had returned to the meadow, an ambitious sports programme began. This included tug-of-war, pole-jumping, pillow fighting on a greasy pole, and egg and spoon racing for the children.

At one side of the field a cricket match was held between teetotallers and beer-drinkers. The captain of the teetotallers was a tall and rather handsome young man called Fred Butcher. Bill Bradley was the beer-drinkers' captain (both on and off the field). These two wore cream shirts and trousers but most of the players were in their black Sunday suits, starched collars and bowler hats.

The beer-drinkers won the toss and batted first. Bill Bradley took the first ball, which went miles wide of the stumps, beat the wicket-keeper all ends up and produced two easy runs. The next ball was a full toss, which Bill swiped into the field with a resounding smack. It sped towards the fieldsmen head high, and smashed into the bowler hat of a short fat youth of twenty, named Charlie. A roar went up from the onlookers. 'Good ole Charlie. Keep yow yar hat on bor. Yow'll catch him out if he send yow another like that there!' And so the game went on; full of fun and everybody in a good humour.

At the end of their innings, the beer-drinkers had managed to knock up 56 runs and by this time tea was ready in the barn. Everyone in the village who could walk came to this tea. They sat on long wooden forms on either side of trestle tables covered with plates of ham sandwiches and fruit cake. The tea was free for all, provided out of the Band of Hope funds and, for the older folk, was the event of the day. There they would sit and talk about their rheumatics to their hearts' content. The children competed one with another in the number of sandwiches each could consume, dodging under the tables to avoid the restraining influence and admonishments of their parents.

WHEN the tea was over, they rushed back to the meadow, most of them stealthily darting behind the bushes to prevent themselves from bursting with tea and lemonade. Games were resumed and the teetotallers began their innings on the cricket pitch. Five wickets fell for 14 runs and things looked bad. But at this stage Alfred Butcher and Maurice Carter made a stand, bringing the score to 38. Then the beer-drinking bowler took off his hat and coat, rolled up his sleeves and called out: 'Yow're bin in there long enough tergether. I'm agoin ter git one on yer out or I'll eat my hat.'

So saying, he walked back about 20 yards behind the wicket and, turning round, loped back again, gathering speed all the time. His hairy arm went over and, an instant later, so did Alfred's middle stump. It was soon all over after that and the honour of the beer drinkers was upheld by 13 runs.

By this time the evening shadows were extending from the towering elm trees and, over the little stream which wound its way along the far side of the meadow, a film of mist was rising, forecasting a fine day on the morrow. As soon as the sun had set there was a sudden swish like the hissing of escaping steam and, high above the heads of the happy crowd, a cluster of multi-coloured lights spread out like a gigantic fan. The firework display had begun. Children clapped their hands and danced with glee and old men stared with mouths wide open.

When the display was over, there were cries of 'Come on Willie . . . Harbut . . . Gordie, tha's time we wurra goin' hoom' and, one by one, the little family group disappeared into the quietness of the night. For youths and maidens the fun was not over yet. Linking their hands together, they formed a circle and began the age-old game of kissing in the ring. Three boys and three girls started walking round the ring, the boys in one

direction and the girls in the opposite. Each had a white handkerchief and dropped it on the shoulder of a willing victim. Then began the chase. Girls ran giggling and screaming in all directions, each followed by an eager male. The first chase was a long one for as yet there was no competition. Each had chosen his or her favourite and the boys made sure that the girls reached the extremities of the meadow before they were caught. Then, with arms enfolded around each other, they kissed and sauntered back to the ring. From now on there was competition for the prettier girls and more handsome boys but, as time wore on, none was left out of the game.

ON Whit-Tuesday, Wendling was the centre of attraction for a host of people from all parts of the county. Posters printed in red, white and blue advertised a grand sports meeting which included trotting matches, hurdle races, and cycle handicaps. Large refreshment booths were provided and innumerable side shows. The meeting would be attended by the band of H.M. Norfolk Regiment which, by kind permission of Colonel Trollop, would play selected musical items. Special trains were run by arrangement with the G.E.R.

The meeting was held on the village common, by the side of the turnpike. In the morning the common was the scene of feverish preparation. The competitors' ring was roped off and the racing tracks mown and rolled. Marquees and stalls sprang up more quickly than mushrooms ever did and an air of cheerful expectancy prevailed.

The proceedings were timed to start at two o'clock and at half past one the first special train steamed into Wendling station which, strangely enough, was in the centre of the village and quite close to the sports meadow. The station road joined the main road opposite the chapel and, although there was a strong puritanical disapproval of this meeting among the chapel elders, they saw no harm in diverting some of the devil's money to a better cause. So all day long the chapel was open, not for prayer, but for the provision of light refreshment at modest charges.

The chapel yard formed an excellent vantage point for watching the crowd of spectators on their way from the station to the meadow and there was much friendly banter between the local young folk and the visitors. Some 8,000 people came to Wendling sports every year. This was verified by William Green, whose house adjoined the chapel; all day long he sat at his window and counted them as they went by.

Great excitement arose when the trotting ponies were detrained and led to the meadow, followed by the little machines to which they would be harnessed. These were drawn by stable lads in jockey caps and racing colours. A corner of the field was reserved as a paddock and the race meeting atmosphere was completed by the bookies, wearing loud check suits and brown bowlers. There was Jack Lees of Norwich, Tom Smith of Yarmouth and a host of others, each having an enormous Gladstone bag and his own little stall. These soon got started with their business. 'Who says a bob on Black Jack?' 'Two-to-one happy Lass,' Fools and their money are soon parted.

The first race, a trotting match, started promptly at two o'clock and there were six runners. Spectators surged towards the ropes, jostling each other vigorously for the best positions. From every corner there were shouts of 'Go it, Black Jack,' 'Come on Merry Weather,' 'Let him have it Davy bor,' 'Look out Sam, George is arter ye.' It happened that one of the horses was observed to be breathing very loudly. He had a broken windpipe and was breathing through a tube protruding from the middle of his neck. An excited voice called out: 'Wur look at that, Charlie, that airn't a hoss, thas one of ol' Johnson's traction ingines.' The race went off without incident and sure enough the traction engine won.

THE next event was a cycle race and this aroused more local enthusiasm for Jim Barton, a member of the chapel choir, was a favourite competitor. For weeks past Jim had been racing along the local roads and his speed was the talk of the village. But now he had to compete with some of the best riders in the county. Round the course he raced, down the slope towards the railway and up the other side, riding for dear life. Soon it was over and the stately bellringer announced: Morton first, Chaney second, Wharton third.' Murmurs of sympathy for Jim were mixed with caustic comments from the locals. One boy called

out: 'Yow'll hetta pull yar socks up afore yow ride agin, Jim.' Someone clipped the lad over the ear and the next race began.

The sonorous voice of the ringer rose above the chattering crowd. 'Heer ye, heer ye, heer ye. Two hundred yards obstickle race is now agoin to start.' There was a rush towards the rope to see the fun. The two chief obstacles were a stack cover, under which the competitors had to crawl, and the usual suspended barrels. Big Bill Bradley was one of the runners, but Bill had spent most of the time before the race in the refreshment booth and was not in the best of condition. The pistol shot cracked out and the dozen runners lurched forward together. As they came to the tarpaulin there was a scuffle for the outside places and Bill was wedged into the middle. There were moving bulges corresponding to the individual bottoms of the competitors and that of Bill Bradley was gyrating round the middle of the sheet. The crowd roared and egged him on. 'Wur, whatter yow arter, Bill? Yow're goin' the wrong way. Git yow back agin, bor.' And so Bill struggled, first one way and then the other, until he finally collapsed inside the sheet without seeing the light of day. They pulled the cover away and a dejected voice called out: 'Where's that there boy who told me to go t'other way? I'll what yer call lather him.'

Meanwhile, the older members of the crowd were regaling themselves with saucers of cockles and plates of shrimps, according to their taste. Here and there would be seen little groups, pouring out their beer from brown and white stone bottles covered with wicker basket work. These were the days when beer was beer and potent in its effect.

The sports ended at six o'clock and the chapelites hurried to their observation posts to watch the crowds go home. The greatest sport was taunting the drunks who spewed their way along the roadside. There would be outpourings against drunkenness at the next Band of Hope meeting and extra fervour put into 'Hold the fort, for I am coming.' But there was no questioning that beer drinkers and teetotallers alike had had a wonderful Whit-Tuesday.

Chilblains, Gleaning and Lamb-Tail Pie

Emily E. Gray (1952), Illustrated by Mary Jarvis

I WAS born 80 years ago (1873) on what at that time was called an 'offhand' farm, almost away from civilisation, in an East Anglian village. My father was a 'working steward.' We lived in half of a rambling old farm house and the horseman lived in the other half. The horseman's wife was my mother's sister. They had six children and there were six of us too.

A 'working steward' lived rent free - but didn't he have to work ! He was resposible for everything on the farm. Also, my mother had to do the washing for the grown-ups in the farmer's family. Washing really was washing then. The clothes were all frills and embroidery and they had to be done up to laundry standard for sixpence a dozen articles. My mother had to rear the poultry, too, and she received a penny for every score of eggs she collected. My parents did all this work for the privilege of living rent free and for sixteen shillings a week in wages.

My earliest recollections are of when I started school. We lived over 2 miles away and I started school in the winter-time. The weather was bad and I got chilblains and I used to cry as I walked. I was the only girl going to school from the farm among six boys, and the boys would not stop for me. But just up the road was a small cottage and the little boy who lived there also had chilblains and he and I went many a day to school hand in hand, crying and comforting each other as we walked.

We had no such thing as rubber boots. We had to sit in school with our wet shoes on and the floor used to run with water when the snow on our shoes melted. We took our dinner with us. Very often it consisted of home-made bread with pure pork lard and brown sugar on it. We loved it.

And when we went home in the afternoon our eyes would shine if we smelled the smell of bloaters. If mother could afford it she would buy three-pennyworth from the bloater man when he came round. For threepence you could get six bloaters. And then she would cook a large saucepanful of potatoes and mash them as only she could. They were lovely. That was a special treat for us.

WE children were never dull. We had a large bedroom in the old farmhouse. There was only one bed in the room but it was a huge four-poster with curtains all round. In the winter, after we had had our tea, my father would make a huge fire in the old-fashioned bedroom fireplace with old stumps of trees. Often the fire did not go out for a week. How we enjoyed ourselves in that bedroom! The boys would play marbles or horses and one game we all used to play was pretending we were gipsies in a tent: and we would jump out to frighten the children, for in those days children were terrified of gipsies.

When we grew bigger we used to have to work in the winter evenings. There was a big back-kitchen in the farmhouse which also had a huge fireplace and burnt the same big logs. We would draw up before it a deal table and - this was before the time of machinery - sort corn, parting the good corn from the bad. We sorted peas and beans, too. The bad ones we put into a pail and we used to see who could bang them in the hardest. We were paid one shilling per comb of four bushels for the beans and three shillings for the peas. Sometimes it would take a week to sort a sack of peas. They would then be ready for sowing the next year.

The only sound we ever heard in the winter evenings was the sound of one farmer going home from market on Tuesdays about 5.30. On Saturdays my brother and I used to go to the little market town, over three miles away, to do the shopping. We took a little old wicker pram to bring the things home in. Sometimes, as a great treat, we had a ha'penny to spend between us - but we always had to take a sweet home for each of the little ones. I remember mother used to go over her shopping list three or four times to see if there was anything she could do without.

But we had our fun, too, and there was much to interest us. Early in the new year there used to be great excitement when we saw the shepherd getting ready for the little lambs. We already knew when they were coming. First of all the men took the hurdles which had been stacked up ready from the previous year and threaded them with straw to make 'folds' in the fields near the stackyard. Then a hut on wheels came along and we waited to get a peep inside (thought the shepherd soon sent us off if he saw us). There were two wooden benches along each side and a cupboard, and under the benches were cosy little boxes filled with straw - here they put the sick little lambs and fed them from a bottle.

Lambs are born with very long tails and when they reach a certain age the shepherd chopped them off. And - would you believe it? - we used to have the tails and make lamb-tail pie. It was lovely.

Straw stacks had a great attraction for us. We would put the ladders up one side and slide down the other. If we were caught we very soon made ourselves scarce. Then

again, on Saturday afternoons, we would take the old wicker pram (which had two wooden seats without upholstery and wooden wheels with iron tyres) with the baby in it and wheel it up and down the country lanes. My brothers pretended to be a pair of horses and I was the driver. I expect poor baby was sore the next day!

THEN there were the harvest holidays. We children took meals into the fields to our father - the men worked from dawn to dusk - and when the corn had been carted we went gleaning. What a happy pastime that was for us children. We took our meals and went for the day. I well remember one boy from a large family who used to bring bread and mustard sandwiches - and eat them with relish. Our mother used to have the corn ground and then made bread with it. Sometimes we got enough to last us a month. If harvesting took a long time we had another week's holiday for the gleaning.

Sunday was, of course, a special day. We lived over three miles from the church but we were always there by 9.30. The service was at 10.30. We took our dinners and ate them in the large vestry and there would be about 60 of us.

Sunday school was held again at one o'clock and then came the afternoon service. There would be about 130 children present. The boys sat on one side of the church and the girls on the

other and we were kept in order by teachers. An old superintendent used to sit with the boys and if they didn't behave themselves he came and shot them behind the ear with his thumb. It didn't half sting. The boys called it 'Old Tye's shoot.'

But the real high spot in our lives was the Sunday School treat. It was held in a big park. It nearly always rained and often the anticipation was more enjoyable than the actual thing. But one year we went to Felixstowe which was a very small place then. We went in farm wagons, which had no springs, and we decorated them with flowers. We went merrily and when we got to Martlesham heath, which was heath in those days for miles and miles, the drivers made the horses trot. We bumped up and down but it was great fun and we went along singing. We had better draw a curtain over how we felt next day but we thought we had a wonderful time.

It was a happy childhood and I wouldn't have it changed for the ice creams and cinemas of today.

Yellow Boiled Pudding and a Day on Grandpa's Farm

Evelyn Barrett (c1954)

M ANY years ago when I was young we used to be taken just before harvest time to Priory Farm, Toft Monks, the home of my grandparents. We always looked forward to this outing and I cannot remember the weather ever being other than warm and sunny.

We four children would watch out of the front window about 10 a.m. for the horse and cart to arrive. It would be driven by my grandfather, a dear soul with a large white beard and a rosy face. He was always punctual. The cart would pass the house and turn round at the corner.

My mother and father would mount and sit on the high seat in front with Grandfather, and my little sister would sit on a stool between them. We three others - my two brothers and myself - would sit on a form at the back of the cart with a fine view of receding traffic. The farm was over three miles away and the journey was packed with jolts

and thrills. We loved every minute, especially as we passed through Gillingham and saw the village children being marched off to church while we had the good fortune to be missing it.

After about an hour we would drive up the lane to the farm amongst the trees. And my grannie, very small and bent through years of hard work, would open the top half of the kitchen door to greet us. She never came out. As soon as we all reached the doorstep she would shout: 'Feet! Feet!' as a reminder to wipe our shoes on the sack before entering and then again on the mat inside.

In a twinkling we would take off our coats and run outside again to the orchard, where Grandad had always fixed up a swing for us on the branch of an apple tree. The apples were soury-sweet and delicious.

About one o'clock we would be called in to dinner. We children always sat at a little round table in the brick-floored kitchen while the grown-ups sat at the big table near the window. It was a huge kitchen and had a big sink with a pump over, a big brick oven and two coppers. On the fire Grannie would have a large black saucepan from which she would produce a lovely yellow boiled pudding which was sliced and put on plates with gravy and vegetables while the grown-ups had meat in addition. After that we had mixed fruit pie and custard.

When dinner was finished we children and my father went for a long walk over the farm with Grandfather. He would take us all round the fields and stackyards and then back to the garden to see the beehives and to have swings again until teatime. The tea was laid in the parlour and we all sat round one big table. There was home-baked bread, farm butter, stewed apples, honey, baked custard and loaf cake.

About seven o'clock Grandfather would get the cart out and after stacking our pockets with apples and pears he would take us home, very tired but happy.

I shall never forget those annual treats nor the two dear souls who now rest in the village churchyard.

Fretwork, Liquorice & The Band of Hope

Arthur H. Pye (c1951), Illustrated by Nancy Blyth

ONE often hears the question: Are children of today happier than those of past generations? Certainly they have more reason to be, and they enjoy many things denied the youngsters of years ago. Nevertheless, in the past, there were many games and pastimes which have now very largely become obsolete.

In the winter, for example, there was fretwork and the making of cork picture frames and wool mats. In spring and summer there were tops and hoops, conkers and 'pussy cat,' three varieties of the game of marbles, ('big ring,' 'three hole cramper' and 'bibble hole') and during the break at school such pastimes as 'Spanish fly,' 'toot' and 'challey wag,' all of which entailed jumping over other boys' backs and then performing acts of agility.

An interesting occupation was the making of watch-chains from hairs plucked from the manes or tails of horses, and if you were lucky enough to obtain hairs from a chestnut, a white and a black horse, very pretty chains could be braided.

Musical tastes were catered for by an occasional German band or a barrel organ with a monkey perched on top dressed in a scarlet uniform and holding a collecting bag. The appearance of a dancing bear at the end of a long pole, held by an individual dressed like a Russian who chanted some gibberish to the bear which was supposed to make him dance, was an occasion of great excitement.

Of course, money was scarce, especially among children. But then, lots of things could be had for a farthing. A penny was riches. Many a time I have gone into a shop and asked for 'a ha'porth of sweets and a ha'penny out.' About a yard of some stuff called 'liquorice bootlaces' could be purchased for a farthing and a large bag of popcorns for a ha'penny. A Christmas tree could be decorated for half a crown and would have plenty of sugar mice and sugar pigs at eight a penny.

There used to be a popular sweet about the size of a two shilling piece on which was engraved a coloured motto. Some of them were in the shape of a heart and bore the words I LOVE YOU. These were surreptitiously passed by the boys to the girls, who might return another sweet bearing a message not quite so loving.

I knew a little old lady who sold what were called 'alli-ca-pa-nies.' (I don't know whether that is the correct spelling but that is how it was pronounced). They were made of sugar and treacle and eight of these delectable lollipops, served on a strip of brown paper, could be obtained for a penny. They were vulgarly called 'gob stoppers.' One of them would last for at least an hour.

ST. Valentine's Day provided an opportunity for an amusing, though to the victim a most annoying, trick. It was known as 'snatch' Valentine. A bundle of paper containing nothing whatever was attached to a long piece of string and then placed on someone's doorstep. The door was then loudly knocked. When the occupant had opened it and picked up the parcel a strong pull on the string by the perpetrator - well out of sight - caused the package to disappear from the hands of the astonished and sometimes frightened individual.

Magic lantern entertainments, visiting shows such as Poole's Diorama and Pepper's Ghost provided other sources of amusement and thrill.

I wonder whether youngsters of today are capable of appreciating how much very real pleasure could be obtained for a very small outlay. I remember an occasion when I and two chums spent a very happy bank holiday at Yarmouth at a total cost of not more than half a crown each. Railway fare was a shilling. A dinner at Foulsham's, consisting of roast beef, Yorkshire pudding and two vegs., followed by a sweet, cost tenpence. A shrimp tea could be had for sixpence. This left a penny for an ice cream and a penny for a donkey ride.

But it was the annual Sunday School treats which were the crown of the year. Seventy or more years ago (1880s) the Church of England Sunday School in my native town had between 700 and 800 scholars. These young people, accompanied by the rector, the superintendent and the teachers, with numerous banners and flags flying, would parade through the streets to the castle meadow where the afternoon and evening were spent in games, races, scrambling for sweets and nuts and in sitting on the grass doing justice to a sumptuous tea. Large crowds of parents and the general public would line the streets to watch the happy children pass.

The Congregationalists had the next largest number of Sunday School scholars - 300 to 350 - and they, too, followed the same procedure, had the same rendezvous and passed the time in the same manner.

Theological or ecclesiastical divisions made no difference to the children of that age. They were quite generous in their patronage of the various religious bodies. I knew of some families who considered themselves very slow if they could not qualify for at least two treats with different denominations.

One boy I knew managed to engineer three such outings. At that time Sunday Schools met both in the morning and the afternoon and his method was to attend one school in the morning and another in the afternoon or, alternatively, devote one whole Sunday to one school and the next to another. If he were asked where he was the previous Sunday he would present a cherubic look of innocence and reply: 'Please, sir, I wasn't well.'

BUT the really high spot of the year was the Band of Hope outing to Southwold. This brought unbounded happiness to many children and indeed remains a cherished memory to me. Early on the morning of the long-awaited day the adults would be up to decorate the miller's wagons which were to convey the party to its destination. These wagons were each drawn by a pair of sturdy cart horses which jogged along at a steady pace, taking about three hours to do the twelve mile journey. Shortly after nine o'clock the children were assembled and packed into those festooned wagons. With excited cheers and shouts they started out upon what to them was a day of adventure. The long, winding country lanes, devoid of all motor traffic, bordered by thickly foliated and untrimmed hedges covered with pretty pale-pink wild roses; the beautiful avenues of massive trees; the scent from the blossom of the beanfields and the new mown hay; the interchange of greetings from the villagers . . . these were sources of unspeakable delight. The children certainly were intolerant and intemperate little teetotallers, for they felt it incumbent upon them to boo loudly every public house they passed.

Then there was the eager look-out for the first glimpse of the sea, and the clambering down from the wagons of some of the older boys who went racing off to see who would be first over the little bridge which spanned the tiny stream marking the boundary of their destination.

'The little tee totallers felt it incumbent upon them to boo loudly every public house they passed'

On arriving at Southwold, each child was presented with a bag containing a huge meat patty almost the size of a teaplate and a bun of similar size. Tracks were immediately made for the beach where the repast was enjoyed. The remainder of the day was spent in paddling in the sea, searching for amber, climbing the lighthouse or playing games on the common, while the elder boys and girls chummed up and made excursions to Walberswick.

Late in the afternoon all assembled in the church hall for tea. Then, very tired but singing happily, they began the homeward journey.

Rabbiting, Popguns and Boxing in the Barn

W. F. Turner (c1954)

I SHALL soon have spent 50 years as scholar and teacher in West Suffolk schools. I often look back and compare my school days with those of the average schoolboy today (1954).

In my boyhood, spent at Brent Eleigh and Lavenham, the various games and occupations came round as regularly as the seasons themselves. Winter saw us playing football, arranging our own road races, slipping off on a Saturday to the local farm and helping prepare cattle food, hoping against hope that the farmer would get finished in time to go rabbiting with us, when to carry the ferret box was bliss indeed.

The long winter evenings were spent in many ways. Fretwork with its alluring patterns and plans was always a good stand-by. Music practice, card games and, most exciting of all, making 'cock birds' in preparation for warmer days. This game of marbles and cock birds has completely gone and what a pity! To make a 'cock bird' was a very fine art and to do it one had to find a soft red brick, or better still two soft ones. One face of each would be carefully rubbed against the other until they were both level and fitted together perfectly. This had to be done out of doors or there would be trouble from mother as brick dust even in the kitchen was not acceptable. The next stage was to get an old penknife and, working from the edge of one of the bricks, sketch on it and cut out to a depth of about one eighth of an inch the 'bird' itself which took many forms according to the artist's imagination - a swan, a fox, a dog, a horse, a tree. The two bricks were then clamped together and now the real excitement began. An antiquated iron spoon was filled with lead, inserted with great care into the fire and melted and most carefully poured into the mould. There was a moment of anxious waiting, then the bricks were taken apart and there, silver-like in its newness was the model.

Some were indeed very beautiful. By the end of the winter I had often made as many as 40 or 50 and waited patiently for the day when 'marbles' started. Then forth I would go armed with three or four of my precious cock birds. Break time came and after the mad rush into the playground I, and the other owners of cock birds, would stand them against the school wall, scrape a line with the heel of a good hob'nailed boot and from this line other boys would bowl their marbles in an attempt to knock over the bird. He who was fortunate and skilful enough to do so claimed it, whilst the owner claimed all the marbles which were unsuccessfully bowled. This was a very popular game if a little dangerous, perhaps, in the preparations with molten lead (and sometimes even before the lead became moulten some risk had been run in obtaining it!).

SPINNING tops went out as the motor car came in. Those lovely 'jumpers' could no longer be whipped along the dusty roads. Marble alleying along the roadside on the way to school suffered the same death.

In the spring, when the sap was rising, we made ourselves whistles somewhat similar to tin whistles but instead ours were made in this way: a piece of ash about half an inch in thickness and a foot long was cut from the hedgerow. At one end the mouthpiece was shaped and at regular intervals round holes were cut in the bark. The piece was then very carefully tapped all over and round and round until with gentle force the bark could be stripped whole off the wood. The mouthpiece was fitted and there was the whistle.

Pop-guns were made from pushing the pith out of a straight piece of elder, thereby leaving a hole right through the centre. A rod was made to fit this hole and then the fun began. Paper was chewed to make the first wad which was carefully pushed to the very end of the hole, thereby sealing it. Another well-chewed wad was inserted in the other end and with a sudden thrust of the ram rod a considerable bang was made. Again our own work.

Another game we enjoyed was 'up against the wall' - one demanding considerable toughness and agility. We split up into teams of five. One team took up positions against the wall with backs bent one behind the other and clingling tightly to the one in front. The one next to the wall would face his mates and stand upright. The second team had all to leapfrog on to the backs of the first team and stay a few moments. As jump succeeded jump so the backs would gradually straighten until the five jumpers could no longer cling on and they then had to take their stand against the wall. Some of the leaps were very spactacular.

Cricket, bathing in the local stream, birds' nesting and butterfly collecting kept us as busy in the summer. Our knowledge of butterflies and birds was considerable.

The autumn brought conkers, nutting, gleaning and on Saturdays particularly 'driving' - this was walking with the beaters putting up game for the guns. And, speaking of guns, there was, of course, Guy Fawkes' day when we really set to work with a will. We knew our penny-a-week pocket money would not buy a very great deal, so it was a case of 'God helps him who helps himself.' Red-headed matches were the vogue then and we found them very useful. We obtained a hollow door key and found a nail which fitted into it. We then ground down the point of the nail to make it flat ended. The key was tied to one end of a piece of string about a yard long and the nail to the other. Several match heads were scrapped into the key, and the nail pushed in and then holding the string at the centre the nail and key were swung sharply against the wall - a fair explosion was the result. Into empty tins with a small hole driven into the lid small pieces of carbide were placed, water added and a match put to the hole - and thus we had another firework. Mangolds and swedes were, of course, hollowed out and candles inserted and eyes, mouth and nose cut out. These we carried by means of a small piece of string. The bonfire and the roast potatoes were religiously kept for the fifth itself.

Boxing and gymnastics in a barn lighted by a suspended paraffin oil hurricane lamp were much indulged in and greatly enjoyed. Sometimes when one's boxing opponent was lucky enough to get into the shadows he delivered a good straight left or right while he was momentarily unseen. It was reckoned just the luck of the game. Good sportsmanship was bred here. The village blacksmith made the iron rings for the ropes. We ourselves made the horizontal bar. We also made a punch bag. We made and erected our own diving board for our summer bathing and the remains of it I saw standing only two or three years ago in the stream near my old home at Brent Eleigh. Paper chases we organised ourselves. We were in fact almost independent of adults. We had to be, for in our youth there were few half days for any workman. In the country the normal man spent practically all his time at work, either on the farm or in his own garden. When he had finished the day he wanted the fireside of his own home or a game of cards or a drink at the local.

Today there is so much organisation, so much watching and so little doing; so much copying and imitation, so little originality. Catch phrases, hit songs, queueing at the turnstiles to watch a football match, queueing on Saturday mornings, of all times, to see a film show at the children's own film club! I know one boy who, some eight years ago at the age of seven, took his tea with him to the local cinema, going there at 2.30, sitting in the front row and staying until the end of the evening performance. A rare case perhaps but true!

My Picture Gallery of Childhood Memories

The Rev. C. E. Woode (c1951)

AS we grow old, the private picture gallery we all have, of which memory is the caretaker, grows longer, and the pictures hung there in youth are, I think, the most vivid and perhaps the most interesting. Recalling them gives me a pleasure which I hope may be shared to some extent by those who care to read them.

The earliest recollection of my childhood days are centred in the village of Bures on the banks of the Stour. My father went there as curate in 1875 when I was two years old. The Rev. Arthur Hanbury was rector of the parish and held the living for some sixty years. But at the time of which I am writing he was quite incapacitated, and it was practically a sole charge - a sole charge helped enormously by the prestige and generosity of the old rector. I can just remember him sitting in the rectory pew with his benevolent face and his white hair surmounted by the black skull-cap he always wore.

In the main street was a public house called 'The Angel,' which, strangely enough, was in those days kept by a 'Pilgrim'. It gave me, as a small boy, a somewhat incongruous idea of a pilgrim, for this Pilgrim was a man of substantial build who seemed to exhale the spirit of well-being and good cheer.

One vivid memory of those early days is that of a violent earth tremor which did considerable damage in the district around Colchester and Wivenhoe. At Bures it cracked the Waldegrave monument in the parish church from top to bottom.

The Waldegrave family lived in Elizabethan times at Smallbridge Hall, which stood in the parish and which was one of the many houses where that energetic queen is said to have stayed. It was built on the banks of the Stour and was surrounded by a moat, which consisted of the river on one side, and on the other of a deep and wide excavation, which left the river above the house and returned to the river below it.

When I knew the hall a family lived in it with whom we were very friendly, and many a game as a small boy have I played in its panelled rooms and quaint passages.

Another recollection of those days is of going with my father on Wednesday afternoons to a little service known in those days as a 'cottage lecture'. It was held in one of the cottages which happened to have a good-size sitting room and was attended by several aged women and one old man.

On one occasion my father was describing in a graphic way 'the fall' and the tempting of Adam by Eve and the dire consequences that followed. And I remember how the old man, thoroughly roused, at last exclaimed: 'Why dint he *hide* the bitch?' I have no doubt it was a remedy he himself had found efficacious when his own better-half had been cantankerous.

I am afraid that in those days there were to be found people like himself who believed in the old saying:

'A woman, a dog, and a walnut tree -
'The more you beat 'em, the better they be.'

AND that reminds me of a story current in the countryside in those days. It was one of those narrow winding lanes which are so common in Suffolk and along it was proceding the low, four-wheeled carriage of the rector. It was drawn by a sleek cob and contained the rector and his autocratic wife.

Coming down the lane in the opposite direction was a loaded wagon drawn by two powerful Suffolk Punches, led by a stout and sturdy team-man. It was impossible for the two vehicles to pass in that part of the lane and the rector, who rejoiced in the ecclesiastical Christian name of Theodore, realising the position, said: 'My dear, we shall have to back down the hill.'

'What are you thinking of, Theodore?' asked his stately spouse. 'Of course we shall not back. The man with the wagon must do that.'

'But, my dear,' said the more reasonable Theodore, 'we cannot possibly ask the man to do that up the hill and with a load like that.'

'Impossible or not,' replied the lady, 'I refuse to allow you to back the carriage in that undignified way.'

All the time this argument was proceeding the wagoner was looking on with a sympathetic feeling in his heart for the rector and he at last broke in with the remark: 'Niver you mind, Reverend, I'll back my hosses. I've got just sich another varmint at hoom!'

Another picture comes into my mind of the same parish. It is that of the village barber, addicted by absorbing more liquid refreshment than was good for him. He had a mother-in-law living about half a mile away and between him and that outspoken lady there existed a mutual and deep-founded dislike. I remember how on one occasion, when the mother-in-law had called to commiserate with her daughter, it came on to rain heavily. Now, among other sidelines, the barber re-covered umbrellas and generally had one available minus its cover.

On this occasion he walked home with the mother-in-law, carefully holding the framework over her, serenely oblivious of the soaking he himself was getting, in the ironic pleasure he enjoyed in thus scoring off the old lady.

ON the death of the aged rector, we moved into West Suffolk to a village situated on chalk hills about six miles from Bury St Edmunds. It had a large village green surrounded by houses and a few shops. On to this green our new home looked out. Here again, in a very large rectory near the church, lived the rector, old, infirm and a widower. He was of a type long since vanished; very wealthy, as may be judged by the fact that he kept seven servants in the house and three men in the gardens. In his younger days whenever he went away to stay (usually at some big country house) he travelled in his carriage hung on leather springs and took his own feather bed with him!

At the rectory, broth, wine and brandy were freely dispensed by the cook who ran the house.

My father did the rector's correspondence for him and always used envelopes that were fastened with wafers, for the old gentleman never would use an adhesive envelope. He considered it bad manners to *lick* an envelope and send it to another gentleman.

One interesting and amusing feature in the village life here was the genuine old village concert held in the 'reading room' on the village green. Only local talent appeared on the platform on these occasions. The concert was usually opened with a pianoforte solo by the caretaker's wife. She was a woman of generous proportions and could always be relied on to give a vivid rendering of those musical masterpieces, 'The Blue Bells of Scotland' and 'The Watch on the Rhine.'

This turn was generally followed by a humorous song from the head gardener at a neighbouring hall, a genial old gentleman with a merry twinkle in his eye. He disdained any piano accompaniment because, he said, 'it always put him out!' His favourite mannerism was to twiddle one thumb round the other as he sang.

One song of his was always well received and the chorus especially was very popular:

That's the way to the zoo.
That's the way to the zoo.
The monkey house is rather full,
But there's plenty of room for you!

Make haste and ketch th' evening bus,
To Regent's Park afore it shuts,
And I'll come down on Sunday next
And bring you sich a lot of nuts!

There was one gentleman in a front seat whose countenance Darwin would have hailed as a triumphant argument for his great theory and on him the singer would turn a humorous eye to give point to his songs. More humorous still was the whole-hearted way in which this member of the audience joined in the chorus, oblivious of the innuendo.

And those concerts remind me of a still more homely affair when one of the servants at the doctor's house, which stood on the other side of the green from us, had a birthday.

This occasion was usually celebrated by a high tea and sing-song in the kitchen, to which the doctor's groom and the boy who helped him in the stable would be invited.

The doctor had several young sons who were great pals of my brother and myself and it was the custom for this graceless bevy to conceal themselves at some point of vantage near the kitchen where they could hear the proceedings without being seen.

After the tea was over, Old Scott, the groom, would open the sing-song with a pathetic song of many verses describing the hopeless passion a butcher's boy had conceived for the squire's daughter. The more hopeless this unfortunate love affair became, the more pathetic the verses grew - until at last came the tragic ending where the devoted boy committed suicide with a meat skewer and the last verse ended with the sad refrain:

O lady, lovely lady, whatever have you done?
You've killed the finest butcher-boy
That ever the sun shone on!

the two last words being repeated to indicate that the song was finished. Of course there was always an encore then Scott would respond with a rollicking hunting song.

AFTER a few years in this village, my father moved to Culford, on the other side of Bury St Edmunds, where the Earl Cadogan, who at that time was holding the important position of viceroy in Ireland, had purchased the estate, rebuilding and adding to the old mansion in the park.

The original house had been the home of the Reverend Benyon, who had also built the beautiful little church of St Peter's to serve an outlying part of the parish known as 'Seven Hills'.

One of the inhabitants, the last in my picture gallery of memory, is the dear old lady who for many years had been mistress of the school on the heath. She was a fine old Christian who taught the children not only the three R's but a love of the Bible stories and the religion which stood for so much in her own life. I think many an old man of that part of the village has looked back with gratitude and affection to the time when he attended the school which she conducted.

When this old school mistress was on her deathbed, Queen Alexandra was staying with the Earl and Countess Cadogan. My father, being the earl's domestic chaplain, went to the hall every morning to take prayers and in that way the queen heard of this old lady and of her great sorrow that she had not had the chance even to see her. Her Majesty at once said that she would go to the school house and visit her. It fell to my father's lot to have the honour of showing the queen to the old lady's house.

Arriving there, Her Majesty said that she would go in alone, which she did. After the visit, when the queen had returned to Culford Hall in her carriage, my father went in himself to see the old lady.

Tears were in her eyes as she told him of Her Majesty's kind and sympathetic talk with her and she murmured: 'Lord, now lettest Thou Thy servant depart in peace, for mine eyes have seen the Lord's anointed.'

The Village Doctor

Phyllis Pearce (c1954), Illustrated by Andrew Dodds

EVERYONE knew him, from the oldest inhabitant down to the five-year-olds trudging their muddy way along the lanes to the village school. In those early pre-war days there was strangely little traffic to be seen on those country roads out there in the quiet Suffolk villages only a few miles inland from the sea. The rumble of farm carts was still the most familiar sound. But in sunshine or rain, driving snow or howling wind, the chug-chugging of the doctor's motor-bike was as familiar to us all as the landscape itself. We children held him very much in awe. I think it highly probable that our elders did as well.

As we scuttled hurriedly to the side of the road and took shelter in a friendly hedge, we watched him pass, his typical black doctor's bag strapped firmly on behind. Out of that bag came the pills we knew so well, the magic 'listening in' apparatus, the small wooden spoons for peering into our unwilling throats. Inside there too reposed, as some of us were told but few of us believed, the babies which from time to time arrived at our own or our friends' houses.

A small, erect little man was the doctor, with something of a military air, closely clipped moustache, precise manner of speaking and keen eyes surmounted by light shaggy eyebrows. On looking back it seems to me that he must have been clad summer and winter alike in an old fawn trench coat, cycling leggings and tweed cap, for I never remember seeing him in any other attire.

He was the sole hope and support in times of illness and trouble of at least seven widely separated villages, not to mention numerous outlying hamlets way out over the nearby marshes or tucked away in the wooded heathland further inland. Then there were, too, the dozens of remote cottages built for no apparent reason in the most inaccessible spots imaginable.

Those were the days when the capable figure of the district nurse had not yet become an essential part of village life - at least not in that district - and there was no one to stand as it were between us and the doctor.

'Good-day. Good-day' was always his somewhat staccato greeting as he walked unannounced in through the back door and straight up into the sick room. All parts of the day and night were alike to him, he always said, so 'good-day' must do for them all.

He had been there a long time, as long as many folk could remember. He had brought us into the world

and carried neatly filed in his head our various ailments and troubles. He was quite clear, too, on all matters concerning which members of this family had married that member of another. In fact the doctor could tell most people in very few but none the less forceful words more than they knew about themselves or their family.

HOW was it, I wonder, that with such a widely scattered practice he answered all our summons for help so promptly? I never remember hearing of any genuine case to whom he refused his services or to whom they were niggardly given. With the help of his motor-bike he would be there - and no time wasted en route either. In fact the speed at which the doctor travelled was a matter of mild concern to the police constables of every village in the district. For not one of them felt equal to the task of bringing to justice someone as useful and as important as the doctor. But there was one occasion, I understand, when his speeding was so bad that one worthy constable took it upon himself to suggest to him in a very polite and friendly fashion, that perhaps he ought to have a speedometer fitted. This mild rebuke so astonished the doctor that he followed the constable's advice and thereby shocked himself as much as he had previously shocked the villagers.

Of course, sending for the doctor in those days was not the casual decision it sometimes is today. Often it entailed a two or three mile walk or cycle ride to the nearest phone, usually to be found at the local post office. In many cases it meant a five or six mile walk to the surgery itself. At best one watched for the doctor when he came to a nearby cottage. Visits to the house, too, were accompanied by the words: 'Send for the medicine this evening' - and so the weary miles had to be cycled or walked again. Perhaps this all tended to weed out the less serious cases who were doubtless treated with the traditional remedies so beloved by the genuine country dweller. Many were the tallow plasters we endured as children, the home-made salts we swallowed and the home-made ointments we smeared liberally over our broken knees. 'Excellent. Excellent. I've nothing better in my surgery,' I remember the doctor saying once when he chanced to call at the house of an elderly woman busy making up the family supply of salts and ointments.

He was not always so precise in his speech, however, and many were the tales the local people could tell of his violent and highly coloured language.

At the outbreak of the First World War his patriotic fervour was intense. The sight and sound of newly born females goaded him to outbursts of fury. ' - - - !' he would cry. 'It's boys the country needs now. Boys!' And away he would stamp, leaving the unfortunate mother to a feeling of failure and disgrace.

BUT it was in the surgery at the back of his house, where his explosive language came into full play. At the end of a busy day he would arrive back, often wet through, to face a roomful of people. Most of them had cycled or walked several miles. They came from lonely places and here, seated on the hard wooden forms, they sought to while away the waiting time with a neighbourly chat, the exchange of news of local happenings or a bit of mild leg-pulling. Then the fun would begin. Crash would go the little sliding wooden partition through which from time to time appeared the healing bottles of physic. And there, glowering at the now silent gathering, the doctor would pour forth a stream of violent language guaranteed to quell the strongest heart. For the rest of the surgery hour the atmosphere in the room became as uncomfortable and unyielding as the wooden forms on which the patients sat.

I remember hearing of one such occasion. The room was packed. Men, women and children were chattering away happily and the hubbub rose higher and higher. Suddenly the partition slammed back and the doctor's wrath descended. So violent was this outburst that for the rest of the surgery time no one dared say a word - not even to mention the name of the patient for whom they were fetching the medicine.

Now country families were large in those days. Older children fetched cough medicines for younger brothers and sisters; grandchildren for grandparents, nephews for aunts and uncles. The whole arrangement must have been something in the nature of a human jigsaw to the doctor, who on such an evening had put himself on non-speaking terms with them all. One by one each person meekly approached the hatch. After one glance from under those shaggy eyebrows a bottle was filled and labelled and handed over and not a word was exchanged on either side. Considering the extent of the practice and the size of the families this was no mean feat even for one who knew his people so well.

Much has happened since the days when the old doctor battled his way down muddy farm lanes, over sandy heath tracks and across marshes on his motor-bike. The National Health Service surrounds us with its protection from prenatal days to the time of our death and does so most efficiently. But there are times when the most efficient 'scheme' can leave one nostalgically longing for the days of the old-fashioned family doctor, be he rather a peppery one at times!

Memories of a Kitchen Maid

Kate Elizabeth Chapman (c1956)
Illustrated by Beryl Irving

MY father was a tradesman in a small East Anglian town and when I was 18 years old he became bankrupt. This meant that I had to earn my own living and as I wanted very much to learn how to cook I applied for a situation as kitchen maid.

It was a lovely day in June fifty years ago (1905). I walked across the park to the nearest hall in answer to an advertisement in the local paper, was interviewed by the lady, and engaged.

They took me into a lovely little study where the roses came creeping in through the French windows. 'This is lovely,' I thought. 'I shall like living here.'

A few days later my box and I were collected by the coachman in the luggage cart. My first job was to skin a hare for roasting. It was very 'high' and had an awful smell and was full of maggots. After skinning it I was pumping water on to it to get rid of the maggots and blood when cook came running towards me shouting:

'What are you doing? I want that blood for a pudding.'

I thought: 'If that is the sort of thing they eat here I don't think I'm going to like it.' I liked it even less when I saw some of the maggots in the gravy.

After the hare, I plucked some game and was then shown my other duties. Three mornings each week I had to be up at five o'clock to clean out a great 'Eagle' cooking range. The nights before those mornings I did not take my clothes off for fear of being late. I had a very long stone passage to sweep and scrub, a gun room to sweep and dust, and two large front doorsteps to clean. Then I had to sweep and dust the servants' hall, lay the breakfast table and cook bacon and eggs, or whatever there was for breakfast, for the staff of 15 by 7.20, also to call cook with tea and hot water.

After breakfast, kitchen and larder tables and floors had to be scrubbed. Then I had to help with the dining room breakfast, make fancy butter, toast, decorate the cold dishes and be out of the kitchen by 10 o'clock, at which hour the lady of the house came to give her orders to the cook.

There were three cooks in three months. The third, an Irishwoman, was a good cook but very extravagant - and very bad-tempered. I expect I tried her patience by doing things wrongly. For example I remember rubbing through the sieve some fillets of veal which were intended for one of the entrees for about 10 people. Rubbing raw meat through a sieve is a hard job. The trouble was I should have dealt with only the odd bits in this way, not the main fillets. Didn't I get told off!

COOKING in those days was luxurious. We hadn't heard of margarine. We had farm butter all the time. But potted eggs were, I suppose, known, for the gamekeeper came in to ask how many eggs were required from the cellar. I heard him say:

'How many today, cook? You know you've had 400 this week already?'

'I'll 'cook' yer. Just you call me Mrs Donaldson - and mind your business about how many eggs I've had.'

There was, of course, a huge garden. But every now and again a large basket, as big as a large laundry basket, arrived from France. It was full of lovely fruit - huge pears, big black and white grapes, plums, pineapples. I was given a dish of these fruits to peel, pip and cut up for fruit salad. How they made my mouth water. I daren't eat one, as cook stood the other side of the table.

This salad, with maraschino added, was one of the three sweets for dinner that night. The other two were a champagne jelly and a rice cream decorated with crystallized fruit. I remember it was a nine-course dinner - hors d'oeuvres, soups, fish, two entrees, game, a hot sweet, ham with green peas, sweets and savouries.

But what was left of the dishes came to the servants' hall table where a few tradesmen from the town had been invited to supper (making about twenty altogether) and to play cards with the upper domestics.

About seven o'clock I was told to put an apple tart and a rice pudding in the oven. I wondered why. I soon found out. I, as the lowest domestic, and the footmen were the last to be served at table. The first to be served were the French ladies' maids, then the English ladies' maids, then the

house maids, and so on. In great perturbation I watched the sweets go round and when it came to the footman's turn and mine there was nothing but the apple tart and the rice pudding. I was so bitterly disappointed I could hardly keep from crying.

We 'under-ones' were not allowed to speak at table. The butler asked the footman what he would like. 'A small piece of duck, please,' he replied. The butler gave him a whole carcase. I giggled and so did the footman and we were told to take our suppers into the scullery. We didn't mind a bit. We could laugh there as much as we liked.

The footman and I were great pals. I well remember the day he arrived from Herefordshire. I determined that I would at least be clean. I was usually grubby from my work. So I went to my bedroom, tip-toeing past cook's door, to put on a clean print frock and apron. I had just taken off my dress and soaped my face and hands when the door of my room opened and there was cook shouting: 'What are you doing?'

I began to cry. She stamped her foot and demanded again: 'What are you doing?' and stood in the doorway holding out her arm as Hitler did.

She said: 'Put those clean things in the drawer.'

By that time I was howling. I dried myself and put on the dirty dress and apron again and passed under her arm and went downstairs. As I was going she said:

'Now go and ask that footman what he'd like for his tea - cold beef or boiled eggs.'

I could have knocked her down, as my eyes were red by then. But I went and asked the footman what he would like. I was still weeping a bit and by the time he told me he was crying too. We were good pals.

I USED to like to watch the 'Victoria' go out. The coachman and the footman wore green livery, gold buttons and cockades in their high hats, black patent leather top boots with about nine inches of pink patent leather round the tops. How smart they were - and woe betide me if the cook caught me wasting my time watching them.

Of course, I never finished my work. There was always a job to be done. Supper in the servants' hall was at nine o'clock. Afterwards the sinks would be full of saucepans and it would be 11.30 or 12 o'clock before I could go to bed. There was no wire wool or 'Vim' in those days - just an old knife and some sand. But my friend the footman used to say: 'I'll dry the tumblers and put the plates in the rack if you'll wash them.' Several times after cook had been grumbling at me, telling me that I was neither use nor

ornament, I sent a note asking my mother to come and take me away. Then cook would be a bit kinder and I would meet mother in the drive and tell her I'd decided to stay after all.

All the time I was learning. And now, though I am getting old, I can cook almost anything from turkeys (boning, stuffing, trussing and glazing) to sprats (which if properly cooked would be more popular than they are today).

My wages in those far-off days were £6 10s a year, which included beer and washing money. We could buy beer from the butler. I did not like it, which was a good thing for, of course, I could not afford it anyway.

The Lost Art
of Contentment
R. H. Futter (c1952)

HAPPINESS and contentment are relative terms and the present generation, which turns a pitying eye on past eras for their lack of amenities and amusements, forget (or if it does not forget, entirely ignores) the certainty that succeeding generations, who for all we know may regard weekend trips to the moon more calmly than old Giles contemplated his 'Trip to London,' will be entertaining the same contempt for what is now regarded with satisfaction.

Is there any reliable evidence that people at the end of the last century were any less happy and contented than they are today, in spite of the blessings - save the mark - of football pools, dog racing, cinemas, television and the almost universal system under which the public acquire all kinds of fixed and portable property by mortgaging their future existence on the 'never-never-system,' known as 'ten bob down and ten bob a week for the rest of your life.'

I doubt it. And I ought to know because I lived in the days when amusements were scarce and almost entirely homemade. But the fact that they were infrequent made them all the more appreciated. Remember that happiness is a thing quite distinct from mere pleasure and has this advantage, that one can never have too much of it, while a surfeit of pleasure is as bad as, or worse than, none at all.

Take an average East Anglian village in the 1880s and 1890s. All the inhabitants could look forward to in the way of amusements was an annual concert in the schoolroom, an equally inevitable Sunday school treat at the rectory, perhaps a fair somewhere in the neighbourhood, harvest suppers (which were pretty general on farms of any size), a cricket match or two and the junketing at Christmas when:

Christmas told the brightest tale
Christmas broached the mightiest ale
And Christmas gambols oft would cheer
The poor man's life thro' half the year.

I well remember those cricket matches, which were as exciting as a test match to the locals. One member of our team was an ex-blacksmith and the star bowler was the chimney sweep. The blacksmith had but one arm, having lost the other in an accident at his trade. As he was used to handling a 7 lb. hammer, a bat was no more than a feather in his mighty fist and if allowed to stay there for a few overs he would hit sixes all over the place. The outfield, a few yards from the pitch, was plain meadow and you had to lift 'em to score more than singles. One could occasionally sneak a couple if, as not infrequently happened, the ball fell in a cowpat, because it was regarded as a distinctly unfriendly act to return the ball to the wicket keeper before wiping it.

The sweep, who used to make every praiseworthy effort to wash his face for a match, without any notable success, cared nothing about in-swingers, out-swingers or leg theories. He just slung 'em down as fast and as near the wicket as he could, a sort of rural demon bowler. He wore a deerstalker cap, a la Keir Hardie, and an old pair of dress trousers which someone had given him. Pads were scarce and the rector, who kept wicket as he had done years before for his college, was the only man seen in a pair. I played a lot of better-class cricket in later years but got no more fun out of it than out of the encounters on the village green in schoolboy days.

I HAVE said that our amusements in those days were homemade and one has to confess that practical joking contributed more than a fair share of

them. A good leg pull was the source of amusement for weeks while the tale went round.

There was an old skin-flint down our way who always took a leg of mutton home from Norwich market on Saturday night for Sunday dinner and always pulled up at the Dun Cow where he treated himself only to a jorum of hot gin. He had never been known to push the boat for anyone else and it was therefore much to his astonishment that he was invited one Saturday night to a dinner party.

The jokers told him that a birthday was being celebrated and he, as the oldest farmer present, was required to take the chair. Something for nothing was always good enough for old Dick, who was filled up with more 'unsweetened' while the dinner was cooking. The joint came from the old man's gig. He carved the mutton, ate his full share and being towards the end of the feast what used to be called 'market merry' even sang a song.

The fat was in the fire when he got home and his wife, who was a lady of vitriolic temper, looked for the joint. Old Dick was ordered to go back and find it. He roused the inn-keeper only to

49

be very cross, she would kick up and shoot the old man out. She treated the cooper to this experience and then discovered that she had the right horse but the wrong cart and man.

HARVEST suppers, alas, have long gone to the limbo of forgotten things but they were pretty general in the 'bad old days.' My father always entertained his men in the old barn to a feast which began with Norfolk dumplings, went on to beef and pudden and ended with plum duff, topped of course with home brew. Such suppers would be scarcely possible now when the relationship between the farmer and his men is nothing like so close as it was in those times.

Some of the songs, which were remarkable for their length more than anything, had a distinctly Rabelaisian flavour and one old reprobate I remember who never took the floor till my father and the women had left went by the name of 'padlocks.' He acquired this sobriquet through his vocal contribution which related certain precautionary measures which the squire took to protect, or maybe restrict, his wife and female staff during his absence abroad after big game.

An unpopular young officer who lived in the nearby market town had his leg so badly pulled and was so laughed at about it that he soon after asked for and obtained a transfer. He was told confidentially that a well-to-do resident in our village had a dog for which he had no licence. Now this villager who was advised of the plot, had a very pronounced stutter which became particularly virulent if he were very annoyed or highly amused. Along came the excise man, knocked at the door and out came old John L. The following conversation ensues:

'I understand you have a dog, Mr L.?'

'Ye-ye-ye-yes, I've got a dawg.'

'And a licence I suppose?'

'N-n-n-no.'

'Can I see the dog?'

'Cer-cer-certainly. C-c-come this way.'

They went through the house and into the front garden where old John pointed to a stone dog on the rockery.

'Th-th-th-there's my d-d-dawg,' said he. 'Wh-wh-when he ba-ba-bark I'll pay for him.

learn that he had carved and helped to eat his own mutton. He never gave the jokers a second chance at his Sunday joint.

A couple of old toppers who lived in our village were the victims of an amusing prank. One of them, old Charlie L., used to peddle hundred-weights of coal from an ancient cart drawn by an equally ancient horse which knew the way home without any guidance. This was just as well, for old Charlie always fell asleep in the cart and never bothered about the road. His crony, known as a cooper, had a similar outfit from which he used to peddle taps and crockery. They invariably finished the day at the Maltsters Arms and stayed till closing time, when they tumbled into their respective vehicles and promptly fell asleep.

One night when they were having the last pint, some jokers changed the horses. Old Charlie woke up to find himself at the cooper's steading while his crony encountered old Charlie's wife, a lady of vinegary aspect, whose habit it was to take the horse out and stable him leaving her somnolent spouse in the cart, which, if she happened to

Memories of Mendlesham

W. Tye (c1950)

MY wife and I sailed for New Zealand on 11 September 1913. I took the services at St Mary's church, Mendlesham, the Sunday before I left the village, all the family being present to hear my last sermon in England.

The day we left Kersey's Farm I rose early to have a last look at the farm buildings, the old pony and the familiar fields around the house. I felt it likely that I might not see the old place again, and now it looks as if it is so.

The week before I left Mendlesham I took my wife with me to see some of the places I knew so well - Palgrave Barn where I was born and which was recently (1950) burnt down; the ancient flint-stone chapel at Gipping; the plantation where I had followed a squirrel to the topmost branch of a tree (it escaped by jumping to the ground); the Chapel Green where many an after-school fight took place with varying results; Old Newton school where that vivacious Mr Blackman more than did his duty to us; the rookery of Mr Scotchmer, where he caught me up a tree after his young rooks; Garrod's Farm whose dog my father (tinned)! when its attention to our bitch became too frequent; orchards and gardens too numerous to mention, where we had little regard for the eighth commandment so constantly drilled into us both at school and at home.

I doubt if it ever occurred to us that taking gooseberries, apples, pears and walnuts was wrong, or the turnips and swedes that we found juicy and exciting after our mid-day dinner of dry bread and cheese at school. I had a great surprise one day when old Tom Woodward, a well-known farmer and school manager, walked hurriedly into school shouting out: "Blackman, where are the boys who stole my turnips?" On hearing this I thought it best to divulge that I was one of the culprits. So I stood up and said: "It's me, sir." He was flabbergasted and, after a moment's hesitation, asked for my name. Then he quietly intimated that he would speak to my father about the matter. I heard no more of it.

My most outstanding performance at school, I think, was when I enlivened a reading lesson on a drowsy afternoon in the porch by giving a vigorous representation of a fisherman shouting "Yarmouth bloaters, four a penny." The headmaster immediately went into action by saying: "I'll give you Yarmouth bloaters." He did. Three strokes of the cane on each hand. But did I catch a look of amusement in his eye? However, there was no further attempt on my part to hawk bloaters in school.

I remember, though, what a feed we used to have when father brought six pennyworth of herrings from Stowmarket. Six pennyworth provided two herrings each for the whole family, and with father and mother there were ten of us. What a treat it was to get a herring with a soft roe - a real delicacy.

GIPSIES often camped in the Hundred Lane that ran past Palgrave Barn. That remote green lane was a favourite meeting place for well-known gipsies such as the Lees and the Robinsons. Grandmother Lee had quite a reputation in the district as a fortune teller.

I bore no hatred towards those Romanies, feeling that they were in the same trade as we boys. I often watched them from a distance, especially in late evening when they had finished their day's rounds. It was a picturesque sight when they gathered around the fire at nightfall, the men busily preparing linen pegs for the morrow, the women cooking. The old woman would be sitting in front of her caravan, surveying the scene and smoking her clay pipe that was yellow and black with age. The lurcher would stretch out on the grass, head on paws, tired by his day's exertions but obviously still alert.

And what a delicious meal those Romanies seemed to provide. If smell is any criterion then it was indeed good. Very rarely did they go short of a rabbit or a hare - or a chicken. They always had plenty of skins and feathers for sale. They also had a liking for hedgehogs. These they encased whole in clay and threw into the fire to bake.

After supper, the elders smoked while the children played. What a carefree life they led. George Burrow and Hindes Groom may well have been attracted to them.

On the whole they behaved well when camping

An old view of Front Street, Mendlesham

Photograph: Tudor Photos, Ipswich.

in our lane - at least as far as we were concerned; they seemed to regard us as understanding, though temporary neighbours. On one occasion only do I remember them stealing any of our possessions and that was during a very dry summer, when they took a truss or two of hay.

They didn't stay long as a rule. After a few days they would harness their piebalds, collect their hens, goods and chattels and move off to some other lane in East Anglia.

They must have made a deep impression on me as a boy. For many years my dreams had a Romany background. My most common dream was that I had upset a saucer of ketchup when passing through their camp and that an infuriated gipsy woman chased me gasping down the lane. Fortunately, I always reached the back door of our house before she caught up with me.

NEXT to rooks and gipsies I miss the windmills. Our little Palgrave Barn farm sloped down to the Gipping, a narrow stream and, I believe, the source of the Orwell. On the opposite bank stood Bendall's windmill, which I was never tired of watching. My brother Alfred, when working in the fields, often used to coo-ee across the intervening lowland to Sutton Bendall, the dusty young miller, standing on the stairs surveying the countryside.

Almost every farmer, as well as the gleaners, sent their corn to be ground at the windmill. Altogether, Mendlesham then had three such mills, and they, when there was any wind at all, were always busy. It is hard for me to visualise what Mendlesham looks like today without those windmills.

But what I have missed more than anything else since coming to New Zealand are the bells. The only church here where a peal of bells is rung is in Christchurch. As a boy, living at Roper's farm, Mendlesham, quite near that magnificent St Mary's church, I was vastly interested in the bells.

Every Tuesday night, when the ringers met for a practice, I used to watch those serious looking men as they handled the ropes with such ease and dexterity. Sometimes they allowed me to try my hand at chiming before the bells were pulled up for a peal. Later they encouraged me to try to pull the big tenor bell up, ready for Arthur Clements, the leader, to take over.

Very rarely did those men, such enthusiasts, miss attendance on Tuesday night. As for missing on Sundays, or on any important festival - that was unheard of. I can still see those men handling the 'sallies,' as they sometimes called them.

Arthur List, the shoemaker, rang No. 1. H. J. Weintz, the young schoolmaster - he was a real enthusiast - often took No. 2. Fred Keeble, a farmer's son, and later landlord of the King's Head, was invariably at No. 3. No. 4, a slightly cracked bell, was usually handled by another Keeble, known as "Sunny" - he always had a smile, even when ringing. Last of all, the great tenor was rung by Arthur Clements, the veteran leader. No-one ever disputed his leadership or decisions. He was willing, however, to take suggestions from the young schoolmaster whose knowledge of mathematics gave him a privileged position when discussing the possible changes on five bells. His successor, Mr Arthur Mayfield, later wrote a very interesting pamphlet on the Mendlesham bells. I have a copy still, and treasure it.

On a quiet Sunday evening on our way to church we could often hear the bells of some half dozen neighbouring churches, all calling their people to worship. It was not till we entered the village that our own bells obliterated the sound of others.

THE tenor bell at Mendlesham was usually rung to call the people to prayers. Mr Jackaman, the village shoemaker, tolled this bell, as well as blowing the organ. When someone in the parish died the same bell was tolled, once for a child, twice for a woman, and three times for a man. With regular intervals this was repeated for an hour. As the village was very much like a big family, everybody on hearing the bell, would pause to count the strokes. If they did not know of anyone being seriously ill, then enquiries were made of neighbours, and men in the fields would leave their work to ask a passerby.

At one time (I do not know when the change took place) the passing bell was tolled when the doctor had given up all hope of recovery. But, while there's life there's hope, and the time came when it was decided not to toll the bell until life was declaired extinct.

A sobering experience it must have been to hear the passing bell; and more so to those who felt and saw in themselves the obvious signs of decay.

The same tenor bell tolled again on the day of the burial. As soon as the funeral procession came in sight of the church the bell was tolled more frequently, finishing with three quick strokes just as the churchyard gate was reached.

Whilst feeding cattle at Roper's farm nearby, I often listened to the service at the graveside. Though now so long ago the words and voice of that much loved parish priest, Mr Randolph, are still music to me.

I heard the muffled peal at Mendlesham only once, when the Duke of Clarence died in 1892.

THE bells at Mendlesham were nearly always rung on the occasion of a local wedding, or when a well-known parishioner was married away. All of our family but one were married away from the village. But this made no difference. The event was always celebrated by the ringers. My mother always sent them five shillings by way of appreciation. After a peal, Arthur Clements would conduct his ringers to the Royal Oak where they drank to the health of the bride and bridegroom and "the old lady." Five shillings seems a small sum these days. But it went a long way then. With this now paltry sum they could then buy five gallons of beer made from the best malt and hops. This was ample to quench the thirst of the five ringers and the two or three learners. Whilst enjoying their drinks I've no doubt they talked the while about the affairs of the family concerned - dwelling mainly on their good points!

At Christmas, the ringers made a special effort to keep alive the true spirit of that most important festival of the church. Early on Christmas Eve, soon after tea, they assembled at church and rang out a short merry peal. This was a hint to the village folk that they could soon expect the ringers with their handbells. They had a special liking for farmhouses, where the best home-brewed was on tap.

I well remember them calling at Kersey's Farm. Sitting round the kitchen, looking solemn and stolid, they played us several Christmas hymns and carols. For a few minutes the whole house reverberated to the music of those small bells. Liberal helpings of Christmas cake, mincepies and home-brewed were at intervals handed round. They said but little by way of conversation, but their faces were a true indication of their feelings. With good wishes they left quietly by the back door discussing amongst themselves their next place of call. I think, too, a little money changed hands, for the leader usually called out: "Oh, thank you mum. We really didn't expect this."

OF all the days of the year in Mendlesham, I have the most vivid memories of Christmas Day. Early in the morning we could hear the bells of the church calling us over the frosty air. And a visit there on Christmas morn was certainly worth while, if only to see the decorations. For every benchend and windowsill was decorated with holly and mistletoe, with white cottonwool snow as a background. Countless stars of Bethlehem peered out from every corner.

Apart from the Christmassy atmosphere, the service itself was always memorable.

As for the rest of the day, this was even more memorable still. Turkey, roasted chestnuts, snap-dragons, Christmas games. How home-sick we were that first Christmas in New Zealand! For dinner we had ham, new potatoes and green peas. So hot was it that perspiration dropped off our faces on to the plates. We tried to be Christmassy by singing a few carols. But in the end we gave it up as useless, and went early to bed. Having no ice, no snow, no holly, we thought it best to forget it all by going to sleep.

Our Changing Village

J. A. E. Kitchen (c1955)

WE were waiting for the train which was to take my weekend visitor to Marks Tey and then back to London. The end of the platform, reached by a long flight of stone steps, gave us an almost bird's-eye view of the village. We could see the distant gleaming thread of the river Stour that laps in a single stride to the Suffolk bank, where the square-towered church seemed to nestle among tree-tops, like an old grey hen with her brood about her. For all around and clustering almost immediately below us were tiled or slated roofs, while a clean hard road twisted away under a bright expansive sky, piled high with those big fleecy clouds such as Constable captured with his brush in the 1820s.

It may have been those clouds which caused my friend to remark: 'A lovely little place! And nothing ever changes, I suppose?'

Just then we saw the ten-twenty-two, drawing its three coaches and throwing out puffs of steam, coming round the bend from the direction of Cambridge, and there was no time to answer his question. But there have been changes - many changes - as subtle as the transformation of increasing age . . .

I well remember my first arrival, proposing to rent a modest cottage as a sort of retreat where I could do some swotting and writing. The air was sweet after a summer shower and as I stepped out of the car a very shy little girl with a cardboard tray and finger in mouth asked me to buy a flag for the church restoration fund. I was so relieved to see a human face again, even a very small one - for I had been hopelessly lost in the meandering byways between Halstead and Lamarsh - that I did so willingly and then, to make sure of things, went into a rambling old grocery store on the corner to make further enquiries.

A bell jangled. I entered to a delicious odour of coffee, bacon, a touch of paraffin oil - and cheese! Ha, that cheese! They specialised in cheese. In fact, I took a huge chunk of it back to town with me, causing my friends to ask: 'I say, old boy - where on earth did you get this cheese?'

I used to put on a knowing and superior air, saying: 'Oh, a little place I happened to strike down in East Anglia . . .'

What a shop that was! Balls of string and rabbit snares hanging from the old beams, huge tea chests decorated with coloured scenes from China and Ceylon and rows upon rows of little drawers containing pepper, cloves, starch and spices. Later on, when the grocer and I became better acquainted, I went all over the place. Upstairs were huge oak beams carved with mulberry leaves.

There were unexpected steps up and unexpected steps down, so ingeniously arranged that in avoiding knocking out your brains against some low doorway you stepped on nothing and nearly dislocated your spine! All the same, it was a fascinating old place - although the very devil to keep clean.

Legend had it that a tunnel led from under this shop to the reputedly haunted rectory at Borley. But how the priestly tunnelers managed to get under the bed of the Stour en route I could never work out! However, there it was - ramshackle, crooked and with a quarter of an acre of slate and tile roof badly in need of repair.

Is it still there? In substance - yes, but you'd never recognise it. It is bright and clean under coats of cream and green paint. The counters and nests of drawers have gone and in their places are shining urns and glass shelves. It's now a cafe, where cyclists in shorts and fishing parties for the river can gaze out upon a village that for them, no doubt, is still 'one of those old places that never change . . .'

JUST opposite used to be a derelict butcher's shop almost hidden under a mantle of red creeper. They knocked that down so that motorists coming along the road from Colchester could see what they were likely to hit unless they slowed up.

A few yards further up, on the other side of the road, facing the blacksmith's, one could see the weatherbeaten sign of 'The Eight Bells'. In the old days - that is to say, only some ten years or so back (1940s) - the landlord used to point to stains on the glazed wallpaper of the large but somewhat dingy public parlour at the back, where the waters from the Stour used to flood in the winter months.

But has 'The Eight Bells' gone too? Not exactly - but the brewers have 're-done' the place. It is now panelled and, although the several bars are lit by iron lanterns containing electric light, looks much more Olde-World than ever it did. It's very nice - very cosy - but I did like to hear the old landlord, now gone to his rest, telling us about the floods, illustrated by the wallpaper.

Incidentally, they seem to have got the Stour into shape too - with the aid of lock gates and a board of some kind. It still turns many fields along its banks into lakes in the bad weather but it appears to behave itself better than it did - which is, I suppose, something to do with 'man's conquest over nature' in a small way.

I HAVE been asking myself how, or at what point, more insidious changes - and these are numerous - really began in our village? I have a whimsical idea that it started at the little newsagents and confectioners shop that used to be kept by two dear old ladies on the Suffolk side of the bridge and facing the church. It seemed a tiny place when they had it. Three customers and it was crowded out! They also ran a lending library. But it was so dark in there, you could never see the titles of the books. Eventually it was sold, goodwill and all, and after that an American bulldozer got out of control and smashed the front in. From then on, after the rebuilding, it has gone from strength to strength. Show cases with inside illumination, a refrigerator dispensing ices, fancy goods - and fluorescent lighting. Indeed, one might imagine that the very walls had moved politely outwards to accommodate the new proprietorship.

Subsequent to that there appears to have been a positive eruption of fluorescent lighting. In the butchers, the grocers, the chemists, we all assume the hue of corpses under the blue, glowing tubes, looking vey much like players in a film studio before the advent of gas-filled lamps.

Apart from the butcher who must inevitably deal in his pounds of flesh, the nature of consumer goods has changed too. The chemists, which has also swopped ownership since I first knew it, no longer wafts an odour of liquorice and scented soap, but more subtle perfumes bearing exotic titles announced by three-colour pictures of languorous ladies, usually brunettes, wearing the sheerest of evening gowns and a seductive look. Gone forever are those cards which used to bear, stuck upon them, little boxes of salve for chapped hands or tiresome corns. In their place is make-up a la Hollywood, perm lotion as used by the stars, and lipstick invulnerable to the usual tokens of affection.

SIMILARLY, in the drapery and haberdashery department of our 'central' grocery store, are other symbols of the march of progress. The wax-faced window models, apt to wilt in summer heat, have given place to featureless objective outlines in chromium. Red flannel, thick stockings and sturdy shoes have given way to celanese, rayon and nylon; stockings as fine as spider's webs, wedge-soled footwear for every-day occasion and dainty things, shaped like lilies, in gold and silver for dancing.

Dancing! Ha, now that's where you can observe the change, if you are in a position to make comparisons. I have a vivid memory of the first village hop I ever attended - that atmosphere of newly washed linen, all those pink faces and a few shiny noses in the bargain. The young men in their best suits and with their heads well oiled looked a trifle awkward, eyeing the opposite sex across the floor as though they'd like to know them better. And when the piano struck up - a round dance to get them acquainted - such a stamping and pounding you'd think the floor might go through. Hop, jump, hop. The faces of the males grew redder still, they breathed heavily, their throats gripped by unfamiliar collars, while the girls seemed to creak as they capered - which was probably excitement rather than corsetting!

But does one ever see a shiny nose at the village hall these days? The girls are cool, well poised, with uplifted eyebrows, even a touch of aloofness that fences well with the self-confidence of their partners, who perform all the modern dances, from the samba to the creep with the style of so many Gables, Kayes or Grangers. Some of the lads wear tuxedos and many of the girls wear evening gowns - one of them a strapless creation, displaying shoulders which a society lovely might envy. Modern dress, modern music - supplied by our one and only radio dealer - and, of course, fluorescent lighting. This was last winter.

Needless to say, there were the shy and old-fashioned ones. Those we shall have always with us - bless 'em. Here and there, among those seated, one heard:

'Whatever made yer such a while Sarah?'

'Owd Mr Cutter hollared owt to me as I c'm paast. "C'm yow here, Sarah," he saah . . .'

But I don't hear much of that kind of dialect among the new and young East Anglians these days. Nor does one see, in our village at any rate, aproned housewives at front door of house or cottage to eye the stranger with half-shy curiosity; but neatly dressed women, carefully coiffeured, wearing a gay print pinafore (or slacks) with a quick and ready smile of welcome.

Communal life widens. If some of our teenagers want to go to a Saturday night dance or social a few miles out and can't get back by bus, they hire a taxi between them. It's only the older generation we see now foot slogging it in their Sunday best from an outlying area for some 'do' or other at the village hall. For we have two garages - and how they have changed.

One resembles a rusty nissen hut with a bad leak. The other was little more than a hut and a pump on a piece of waste ground. Ye gods! you should see them now! Half a dozen petrol pumps glittering like a scene in pantomime; a pagoda-like structure to shelter them from the rain; illuminated signs at night assuring you that every oil and fuel is superior to the other - and the staff in uniform overalls, provided, I believe, by some arrangement with the oil companies. Once upon a time, if you called at the rusty nissen for a job to be done, it was just as well to take a packed meal with you. You got something like this:

'Charlie! Come out a minute will yer?'

Voice from depth of nissen hut, hot as an oven in the mid-day sun: 'Hullo - what d'yer want?'

'Have a look at this steering will yer . . .?'

Then the first man would go away to discover why Charlie didn't come and you'd be left in a peaceful humming silence to admire the fields opposite or to do a bit of nature study to fill in the time. And when at last Charlie did come, he would have to get flat on his back and ease himself inch by inch underneath your car. Then he'd want a spanner or a drill and would emit muffled cries for the other fellow, who couldn't hear him. Proprietor and staff were able and obliging chaps but they lacked equipment.

THERE are other changes which a mere visitor could not be expected to know, however observant he might be. On the Suffolk side of the river, for instance, only some 12 years ago (1943), there used to be a saddler's shop. But Whitehall put

'Half a dozen petrol pumps glittering like a scene in pantomime and a pagoda-like structure to shelter them from the rain.'

Photograph: L. Sewell

paid to that. In the frenzy of war, some brass hat, at the War Office presumably, decided that if the Germans landed and eventually decided to cross the Stour by our bridge, it would be a good idea to open fire upon them from the rear. So they requisitioned the saddlers, mounted a gun inside and, to make a blockhouse of it, filled the place so full of concrete that it would cost more than it's worth to chip it all out again. Its a sad little ruin now, with an old poster and a few dead flies in the window - where at one time a much respected old gentleman used to work at his craft behind a display of halters, harness polish and a few bottles of Seven Oils Liniment.

Contemporary with the saddler was the cobbler, in a little combined house and shop right down on the river bank. I used to see him at work in the autumn evenings - an oil lamp with a white shade in a wall bracket shining upon his perfectly bald head. He wore iron-rimmed glasses and a leather apron and had two passions - betting and Strict Rotation! If Farouk in person had taken a pair of shoes into that shop they would have gone to the end of the bench to be dealt with in strict rotation - or, if you like, according to the principles of true democracy. The new owner has put machines in, so that

even if S.R. be still observed, you don't have to wait very long.

LITERALLY a stone's throw from the shoe repairers, as it is now called, stands the church and outwardly that has altered too. In the days of the saddlers and the oil-lit cobblers, we had a big hearty looking vicar who used to stride about the village wearing his biretta and cassock or stand with his arms folded talking to the characters like the cure in a small French town. Now we have a much younger man who came from overseas - and at once had all the massive overhanging trees cut well back, so that we can now see only the ancient grey walls but the face of the clock too! On a warm day one may sometimes see him in shorts, shoving a lawn mower among the tomb stones and unless you are wary he is apt to corner you and start off: 'I remember once, when I was in . . .'

A good man and an energetic and sincere Christian but, alas, there are no characters left for him to talk to as did his predecessor. We had three outstanding types up to about 1940 but - well, one was found dead in his hut in a wood, poor chap; another decided to go further afield, into Norfolk; and the third, I believe, went to live with a married sister near the Seven Sisters Road - which shattered my illusions about characters forever!

The same village and yet a changed and changing village! Odd isn't it? This train of thought started in my mind as my visitor settled himself in a corner seat and I endured those ridiculous moments when you expect the train to start and it doesn't - because there's a crate of chicks or a bush with its roots wrapped in sacking to be stowed away in the guard's van. But at last the whistle blew, I waved farewell and ran down to the wide, sanded space before the station entrance. And as I turned my steps to the road, a little dark-eyed girl with a tray approached. But this one wasn't shy and she didn't have her finger in her mouth. She said pertly: 'Will you please buy one of my flags for the church restoration fund?'

Sunday - How it has Changed

Arthur H. Pye (c1951)

OF the many changes in the habits and ideas of the people during the last 100-150 years none has been more striking than the attitude towards the observance of Sunday.

The Sabbath or Lord's day used to be looked forward to as a time of rest and respite after a long and laborious week of toil consisting of 70 or 80 hours with no half-day's holiday. In all the towns and villages of East Anglia the Sabbath was strictly observed. It was indeed a day of rest. No work of any description was allowed to intrude upon it. All the material needs of the day were prepared on the Saturday. Clothes to be worn were already laundered and repaired. Boots and shoes had to be cleaned and polished before the Sabbath eve.

This strict and narrow observance of Sunday sometimes resulted in acts of cruelty and injustice which had on the victim the opposite effect to that intended. A case that came under my notice was that of a minister in the village in the north-west of Suffolk. His small sons had neglected to clean their boots on Saturday after playing football. They were not allowed to clean them on Sunday so were compelled by their father to attend chapel in their dirty boots and listen to him expounding the gospel.

All food necessary for Sunday was prepared and cooked the previous day and cold collations were accepted as a holy rite. No toys or games were allowed to be seen. Little girls were not even permitted to play with their dolls.

Reading was confined principally to the Bible, Bunyan's 'Pilgrim'sProgress,' Foxe's 'Book of Martyrs,' Richard Baxter's 'Saints Everlasting Rest,' Thomas a Kempis' 'Imitations of Christ' and certain weekly religious periodicals. Novels were taboo.

For the children there were such books as 'Jessica's First Prayer' and 'A Peep Behind the Scenes.' The overpowering sentimentality of these works brought copious tears to the eyes of the young readers.

There were no Sunday papers and all shops, except public houses, were closed. Whistling, even in the home, was forbidden and running in the streets, even though one might be late for church or Sunday school, was considered unseemly.

Of course there were no buses or motor cars and everyone walked everywhere, except those who drove in from the country by pony cart to attend places of worship.

THE day began early. There was no such thing as breakfast in bed or arrival downstairs just in time to partake in the mid-day meal. The children had to be prepared for Sunday school, which began at 9.30. After their departure the parents prepared themselves for the morning service at 10.30. And what a preparation it was! Father would be arrayed in a black frock coat, a silk top hat, a gold watch chain festooned across his waistcoat. He would carry his kid gloves and an ebony, gold-mounted walking-stick and would most probably sport a choice buttonhole.

Mother would adorn herself in her rustling silks and satins, flounces and laces, and would wear a bonnet gaily decorated with coloured ribbons and flowers. It was considered most immodest for a married woman, however young, not to wear a bonnet.

We youngsters did not find the day at all dull. We looked forward to meeting our friends and acquaintances at Sunday school to chatter over experiences of the past week. There was no such thing as grading in Sunday schools at that time. All except the infants met in the large hall for the opening exercises and then repaired to tiny classrooms for the Bible lesson. Most of the teachers were very young although they appeared to us youngsters to be somewhat ancient. But there were generally one or two greybeards with very stern visages.

A story used to be told of a superintendent walking round the main hall one afternoon and hearing a tremendous noise going on in one of the classrooms. He opened the door and seized the biggest lad by the scruff of the neck and planted him down on a chair outside, commanding him to remain there. On passing this same classroom some minutes later the superintendent was amazed at the ominous silence which prevailed.

So opening the door once more he demanded to know what was the matter. 'Please, sir,' exclaimed one of the lads, 'you've got our teacher.'

Morning school ended at 10.30. We were then shepherded into church, from which there was no escape. Herded in the gallery at the back of the building we had inflicted upon us a service lasting at least an hour and a half in which we had no part or interest whatever. The 'long prayer' lasted twenty minutes and the sermon from three-quarters of an hour to an hour. Should an irreverent youngster dare so much as to raise his head during the prayer he received a crack from the walking stick of one of the accompanying teachers.

Almost everyone went to some place of worship. All the churches and chapels were full. Those who did not conform to this custom were considered to be lost souls. A good deal of snobbery existed, however, among professing Christians of that age. The 'working classes' were patronisingly tolerated. In the Non-conformist chapels the ground-floor of the building was occupied only by the well-to-do, the 'employer class' or tradespeople. The working people and servants were relegated to the galleries. One concession, however, was made to them. No collection was made there.

The preaching was that known as 'literalism' or 'fundamentalism.' Often the sermon consisted of a string of isolated texts with utter disregard for their context, quoted to bolster up a preconceived theory of the preacher. Conversions were often the result of the reaction from fear of some possible disaster in a future existence or the longing for a state of everlasting bliss as a reward for good behaviour while on earth.

BEFORE the introduction of a musical instrument in the Non-conformist chapels, the singing was led by a deacon who sounded the note on a pitch-pipe and read out the verses one by one. The reason for this was that many of the congregation were unable to read or could not afford to buy a hymn book.

Much controversy was evoked by the introduction of the pipe organ into some of the chapels. It was considered to be the instrument of the devil; and the singing of 'amen' at the end of the hymns raised protests on the grounds that it savoured of Roman practices.

At the close of the morning and evening services, and weather permitting, a walk round the town or a visit to the local cemetery was the chief form of exercise for the day. The visit to the cemetery was actually a morbid ritual. All the latest graves were inspected, the wreaths and flowers admired and the captions on the attached cards eagerly scanned. Comments, adverse and favourable, on the departed individual were freely exchanged. All the relatives of the deceased person, dressed in deep mourning, would gather round the grave.

Perhaps the most enjoyable part of the Sabbath day came after the close of the evening service. Our parents would invite some of their friends to our home and we would sing unaccompanied a number of our favourite hymns. It was a fitting close to a worshipful and busy day, for we sincerely believed that:

A Sabbath well spent
Brings a week of content.

A Village Without a Future

Keith Irvine (c1950)

BURIED in the leafy West Suffolk country- side, four miles east of Lavenham, stands the village of Kettlebaston. A village of a mere 90 inhabitants, it derives its strange-sounding name from the Old Norse "Ketelbern's Tun." Of all the 534 villages in the broad-acred county of Suffolk, it must surely be one of the most backward and derelict.

Market towns such as Thaxted or villages such as Kersey are often cited as evocative of "mediaeval atmosphere." Yet, as one glances at the carved beams and quaint pargetting of the old half-timbered houses, one is struck by the unnatural silence. Our nearest contact with the mediaeval men who created the atmosphere, and belong in the houses, comes when we gaze over the wall into God's Acre and see the long grass sown with their tombstones.

Yet, at Kettlebaston, one cannot help entertain- ing illusions that the inhabitants of the old

cottages, the majority of which are "condamned" as well as thatched, belong to some such bygone age. Speaking of them, it is not hard to imagine that one is listening to the last surviving men and women who think and speak as man thought and spoke in those legendary mediaeval days.

It might be questioned whether a village inn has a civilising influence. Yet it must certainly be admitted that it has a socialising one, for if Kettlebaston had possessed such a thing it would diverge less from the arch-type of the Suffolk village. As it is, however, no traveller, full of city conceit, has the chance either to instruct the yokels in his opinions, or to explode their deeply-cherished illusions. In place of the inn, the street is the villagers' forum, and the church their centre.

The village sign, erected at the coronation, resembles that of an inn. It commemorates the fact that in 1445 Henry VI granted the manor of Kettlebaston to William de la Pole, Marquis of Suffolk, to hold in return for the service of carrying a golden sceptre at the coronation of all future kings of England, and an ivory sceptre at the coronation of Margaret of Anjou, and all future queens.

Our sign is the sign of the sceptre and dove.
A token of purity, mercy and love.
Should you chance to be thirsty,
There's nothing to pay
And our "Public House" stands over the way.

So runs the rhyme, which proclaims that pump water is free, and that spiritual refreshment may be sought at the church opposite. However, the ignorant "foreigner," mistaking the sign for that of an inn, and reckoning nothing of William de la Pole, frequently applies to Church Farm, which stands just behind the sign. The tenants of the farm have learnt to support these enquiries very well, but become peevish when wayfarers walk in, seat themselves in their dining-room, bang on the table and call loudly for beer.

But, although away from the world, the social revolution wrought during this century has made itself felt, today it would be unthinkable, even at Kettlebaston, to have a girl cow-herding through- out a long summer's afternoon in return for a helping of rice pudding in the rectory kitchen at dusk. Yet such, in the "old days," was considered a fair return for her work.

In the "old days," too, to be socially acceptable you had to be born a Kettlebaston person, and marry another, otherwise you would bring a foreigner into the village - and they were found to be never satisfactory.

With no convenient cinema, only the ubiquitous radio provides Kettlebaston with entertainment. For the most part, people are thrown on their own resources. Consequently, much of their amusement lies in telling the old tales.

These are mostly concerned with personalities of bygone days, tales of "my father's day," or that

The village midwife, "Ria" Manning, who lost but few babies and never once a mother.

still more far-off epoch "my grandfather's time." Beyond that, history is the domain of the rector, and is confined to dates and Latin names. The rest is silence.

The legendary personalities of these stories were invariably born and bred in the dearly-loved village, the best in England. Like the listeners, they too were born with the secret of love for each hedge and well-known wall, each inch of the village street. They, too, were "Kettlebaston."

Such a one was Maria Manning - midwife from 1865 to 1880. Known to the village as "Ria," she never lost a mother, and few babies. She started housekeeping with a silver spoon, found in a muck-heap by her husband, George. Together they raised a family of seven children.

The eldest girl, aged 11, ran away from her first "place," arriving home at five on a winter's evening. Mother pulled a small twig from a faggot, and drove her back a matter of five miles. Father remonstrated: "Why, Ria, let the girl have some tea," but mother was adamant. "I warrant she 'oont try that game on agin," said she, returning home.

People were more neighbourly in Ria's day. If anyone was knowing to be dying, the whole village would assemble at the house to show their sympathy. Two kept watch by the sick-bed, so that the moment of passing should be known, while downstairs the remainder made numerous brews of tea, and told tales of the deaths that they had witnessed.

"We was just having a cup of tea," related one old wife, "when Liza came to the top of the stairs and called out: 'Come on together - there's a change.' We blundered upstairs, and was just in time to see her go. She went off like a bird . ."

An official of the Royal Society of Psychical research commented that there are few ghosts in Suffolk. "Most of our work occurs in the Celtic fringe," he remarked. Yet, although the county as a whole has a reputation for hard-headedness, Suffolk has always been a "wonderful" place for witches - and so, too, has Kettlebaston. By all accounts, quite a colony of "witches" throve there in the nineteenth century, and some of their exploits are still recounted with awe by the older folk.

It would seem likely that these old ladies encouraged the discreditable tales which circulated concerning them. Trading on their age and bad temper, they gained a prestige and consideration to which they could never otherwise have pretended. Nevertheless, the impression that they left behind them was deep, and contemporary villagers believed implicitly in their powers.

One of the most notorious of these characters was called Mumpshy Brett.

"I remember Mumpshy Brett well," said one village ancient. "She loused my grandmother - covered her from head to foot with lice. Another time Mumpshy's husband wanted to go into Bildeston, but she forbade him to go. Still he got out the pony and trap, so she transfixed them in front of the house. They were there all day - the pony and cart, and him in it - and they couldn't move a hand or foot. That's as true as I'm standing here. People were afraid of witches in those days. But now it's different."

Mary Howe, suspected of witchcraft and who died about 1887. Nothing was proved against her.

With the drift from the land, there are few strong young arms left to trim the hedges, dig the gardens, or clean out the ponds. The old-world cottages, too, are slowly tumbling into decay.

Were it not for the church, the village would seem doomed to extinction. The older generation, with bright memories of their own young days, cannot understand what is happening to their world.

Harkstead Memories

George W. Giffen (c1960)

I OFFER some memories of the days when I lived in the village of Harkstead, immediately following the conclusion of the First World War.

I am reminded of the Church of England school which served Erwarton and Harkstead villages. Principal Smith was a conscientious tutor who grappled bravely with the unmanageable Bugg boys from Erwarton and lent me *Wulf the Saxon*, which I read six times. Finally Mr Smith married the assistant teacher and retired to Higher Holbrook.

Gardening was one of the subjects taught, and the basic training I received useful years later when I married and cultivated my own plot. I had not encountered a gardening course at any of the several schools subsequently attended and came to the conclusion that the science was one which you were expected to acquire from your parents.

I wonder if the villagers of Harkstead still share the allotments that used to run up to the main street? And the common at Lower Holbrook?

As a boy of eight my congenial pursuits included making popguns from alder branches, birdnesting and gathering winkles for sale, letting sheep out of the fold, hawking Victoria plums from door to door, learning how to set snares, and carrying ferrets for old man Firman when he went rabbit hunting with his dog and gun.

Other occupations I regarded as chores at the time included gleaning wheat fields owned by squires Allan and Richards, picking acorns to sell to the Sucklings for their pigs, fetching drinking water almost daily from the spring on the road to Lower Holbrook (was it opposite Stackhouse Cottage?), and gathering sere wood for the fire.

The only organised sport among the villages

was quoits, but young folk never lacked things to do.

THE big thrill was the once-a-year trip to Ipswich in the back of the Grimstead van. There were two benches in the back of the van and a horse in front. We made the seven mile trip to buy boots and clothes and to see a distant relative who lived in the great town on the Orwell. The van left every week and the Grimstead family had the status of world travellers in our eyes.

We divided time happily between the attractions of the country and the shores of the river Stour. The tide was a beautiful cleansing agent which washed and remade the shores twice a day, sometimes forcing us into the reedy marshes, sometimes tempting us to venture out half a mile between tiny quicksands, pieces of shell-encrusted wreckage and seaweed.

We tested the banks for sandpiper nests, the ditches for hedgehogs, the 'tip' for rats and the skies for seagulls, safe from our slings. Heavily laden barges crept up and down the river, how propelled I still know not. Vaguely we talked of Harwich and Shotley, places remote and awe-inspiring.

The 'tip' is the word I recall we used for the garbage dump and I do hope that is a rodent-controlled operation by now. Also I hope that there are septic tanks or sewerage disposal systems that eliminate the need for little boys to walk a mile on a frosty morning with two gallon cans to be filled up at the well. We did have a community well in those days of course but it was reputed to be the Valhalla of cats and my people would never use it.

In my day the men of Harkstead worked in the fields - except, of course, Mr Firman and the keepers of The Baker's Arms and The Fish and Fiddle.

One made one's own social life in such circumstances. Most of mine lay on the water-carrying route which took me past Mrs Suckling's rhubarb field. For occasionally buying twopennyworth of rhubarb I got a job in the fields picking potatoes or helping to stack turnips in the field pits for the winter. I still have some twists in my fingers from chilblains - an occupational hazard for that area, I imagine.

Also on my route was a kindly nonagenarian who liked to chat with children and a retired gentleman whose similar bent was rudely ruptured when I awakened him at 6.30 a.m. one day for a chat while on my water-carrying chore. Having made the acquaintance of the gentleman the previous day I had taken too literally his invitation to drop in at any time and had hammered on his front door until he thought his house was being broken into.

The rector of those days was a Mr Berners whom no one in my circle had ever seen. Reputedly bed-ridden for years he was represented in the parish by a succession of curates until one day I and other choirboys assembled in the churchyard for the final obsequies.

The church played an important part in our young lives. We were allowed to ring the big bell in the steeple for Sunday School and I remember deputising for Rose Thurlow in the dedicated function of pumping the church organ. That was when I learned that pumping was not done in time with the music.

What would Harkstead be like to come home to now (1960) after all these years? In my mind's eye its rural charms linger as attractive as ever.

Winnifred Lambert of Colchester responds:
HARKSTEAD has changed very little.

We often used to go to Ipswich in Mr Grimwood's cart - one of my sisters was always sick in it.

I remember Ria Tillet who was a cripple. It was said her mother let her paddle when the tide was going out. She used to crawl around indoors surrounded by chickens.

And poor Silly Billy, who used to come to the door and offer my mother a piece of string.

Then there was Georgie Lockwood who lived for several years in Chelmondiston in a wooden hut. He used to ride around in a little cart with a scraggy white pony. When the poor thing died, he was heard to exclaim: 'Dropped down dead in the road, he did. Niver done such a thing afore in all his life.'

School Days

A Village School is Born

Rev. J. R. M. Wright (c1960)

TODAY, quite rightly, education is a national concern. The provision of adequate buildings, the training of teachers and the extension of the services, absorbs a good deal of the national income. The cost of education is measured in millions of pounds.

Just over a century ago (mid-19c), things were very different. Then, education was the concern of a very few enlightened people, eager to do what they could in their own area. One of the registers of the parish of Barrow, near Bury St Edmunds, tells how the school came into being.

It was in the year 1845 that a new rector came to Barrow. He was the Reverend William Keeling. During his first year, he took steps to establish a school in his parish. He persuaded the Marquess of Bristol to give half an acre of land and then set to work to find the money needed for the building. The subscription list totalled £308 10s., of which Lord Bristol gave £100, the Rector £127 and the widow of the former incumbent £30. Grants from education societies totalled a further £159. The parishioners voluntarily arranged for the carriage of the materials needed.

The school, together with the master's house, was built and equipped for £467 10s. The first stone was laid by the Marquess of Bristol on 5 October 1846 and the school was opened on 5 July 1847.

So Barrow obtained its school, which remained substantially unchanged until two years ago (1958), when extensions and modernisations were carried out by the West Suffolk County Council at a cost of £10,000.

WHAT of the first scholars? The same register contains a list of rules, drawn up when the school was first opened, some of which would today horrify the National Union of Teachers, the parents, and the children. Here they are:

1. Children residing in, or belonging to, the parish of Barrow, may be admitted into the school at 6 years of age, if they can say the alphabet and point out the letters. (The age was altered to 5 in 1848.)

2. All the children admitted into the daily school will be required to attend the Sunday school also; but children will be allowed to attend as Sunday scholars who do not belong to the daily school.

3. Each child belonging to the daily school will have to bring each Monday morning Twopence in payment for the week which is begun, except where there be more than one of the same family in the school. If two, or more, of the same family belong to the school at the same time, the payment will be:

Two children of the same family 1½d. a week or 3d for the two.

Three ditto, 1d a week or 3d for the three and so on, one penny being charged for each additional child.

4. The children are required to be at the school by 9 o'clock in the morning and 2 o'clock in the afternoon, of every day, except Saturday, which will be a whole holiday.

5. All the children will be required to walk two and two, in an orderly and quiet manner, from the school-house to the Church on Sundays, and other days when desired, accompanied by the Master and teachers, and to return in the same manner to the school-house, where they will be dismissed.

6. The children must always come to the school neat, cleanly washed, and with their hair clean and plain.

7. The children are forbidden to talk or be noisy during school time; to use bad words; to call each other names; to quarrel; to behave rudely to each other, either in or out of school.

8. The children are required, at all times, to behave respectfully to, and obey the orders of the Master, Mistress, and assistants.

Barrow School - A class of scholars in 1900

9. Two girls in the First Class will, in their turn, be required to sweep, or clean, the school-room daily, on weekdays, after school hours in the afternoon, for which they will each receive two tickets on the following Monday morning.

10. The girls will be taught needlework and knitting, and will, at all times when required, be expected to work for the benefit of the school.

11. Two reward tickets will be given on the Monday in each week to every child in the first and second classes of the daily school who shall have attended regularly, have been diligent at lessons, and well behaved in all respects in the previous week.

12. A ticket will at once be forfeited for being too late for prayers, for talking, or playing, during school hours, for coming to school unwashed, and for carelessly damaging the books, slates, or other property belonging to the school.

13. Rewards of clothes or books, according to the number of tickets gained, will be given to the children at the end of the year. Rewards of the same kind will be given to the most deserving children who belong only to the Sunday school.

14. Parents cannot be allowed to interfere with the Master, Mistress, or teachers, otherwise their children will be at once dismissed.

READING these rules, we may smile at the simple belief of those who framed them, that rules would produce perfect little ladies and gentlemen; we may be infuriated by the way in which the school was used to force people to go to church. yet, whatever their faults, the Reverend Mr. Keeling and his friends realised that knowledge mattered and they were prepared to pay out of their own pockets that education might come to a small country village. Other groups of people were doing the same. From their efforts, the mighty education system of today has sprung.

The Story of a Village School

Walter Tye (c1955), Illustrated by Mary Tye

HERE is the story of a Suffolk village school during the 1870s and 80s, those two critical decades following the introduction of W. E. Forster's Education Act of 1870 which sought to provide elementary schooling for all children in England and Wales. The facts in general are collected from the school's log book, supplemented by a few personal recollections of nearby schools in the late 80s. Incidentally, it is hoped that a definite effort will be made by all concerned to preserve the oldest of the school log books which present such an accurate and illuminating picture of our schools in those far off days when our educational system was undergoing its birth and growing pains.

The village concerned is situated in the heart of Suffolk, not far from the Norwich turnpike road and only a few miles from Eye, which for centuries has boasted a grammar school and which in Victorian times was well patronised by farmers in the Hartismere area. From all accounts this little village school was built by the lord of the manor, keenly supported by the rector of the parish, a member of a well-known clerical family. The school, as originally built, was unpretentious and small, containing but one room and a vestibule and covering in all some 800 square feet of floor space. And there in that confined area the mistress for two or three years had to teach some 50 to 60 pupils. Where she placed her desk and blackboard and easel is a mystery. Maybe, like the maps, 'conscience clause', ball frame, etc., it was suspended on the school wall.

Although built in the 1860s, the school did not receive any government grant until 1872, when it began to function under 'government principles'. Actually grants had been available as far back as 1833, when the 'huge' sum of £20,000 was set aside by the government for educational purposes. Grants, however, were made only to schools where attendance and general attainments satisfied the inspectors. Under these circumstances the rector realised it was useless to apply for financial aid, knowing quite well he would receive but little support, as regards school attendance, by either farmers or parents.

Readers, however, should not blame them unduly, for agriculture at that time was on the verge of a deep depression which culminated in the 90s when wheat was sold for as little as 7s. 6d. a coomb. Hence the crying need those days for cheap labour, including the employment of children.

Although the children did not attend school regularly before 1872, most of them apparently had learned to read. This was largely due to religious zeal and rivalry. Both churchgoers and chapelgoers considered it most essential their children should learn to read, so that in reaching mature age they would be able to interpret the scriptures for themselves. Thus whilst most of the village people could read during the 60s very few, excepting farmers, could write. A glance at the marriage registers in the church verifies this. Despite their inability to write, however, the local farm labourers and domestic servants had a considerable reputation as good workers, for right up to the 70s employers came in from miles around to secure their services on the annual 'Michaelmas hiring day'. This practice apparently petered out when the Education Act came into force in 1870.

THE school was opened under government control on 8 January 1872 when the teacher, a fully qualified certificated mistress, made the following entry in the log book: 'Admitted 31 girls, 16 boys. Examined the children in arithmetic and found them backward in numeration.' The girls evidently were keener on schooling than the boys or maybe the boys were in greater demand on the land, where they could earn a few much needed pennies to augment the family income. The entry also indicates the teacher's high regard for arithmetic in the school curriculum. Barely a fortnight later she again alluded to the pupil's backwardness in this subject. 'Children who read well can scarcely write or make a figure.'

This weakness was by no means exceptional for on enquiry into the general standard in Suffolk schools at that time it was found only about one in ten satisfied the government inspector. This was mainly due to the backwardness of children in writing and arithmetic. It may interest readers to know that as far back as 1850 there were approximately 1,000 schools in Suffolk, including

grammar, denominational and 'old dames' and of these only 100 qualified for government aid.

The first term was spent in grouping the pupils, arranging cumbersome desks, finding accommodation for piles of slates, enrolling new scholars and in general giving the various groups a rudimentary acquaintance with arithmetic and writing. Copying from the blackboard and the memorising of 'tables' were the order of the day. The new mistress seems to have been popular. No fewer than 14 extra pupils were enrolled during the term, some being only three years old. The parents evidently were glad to be relieved of the toddlers. The rector went in daily to take the religious instruction, as well as helping in other ways. Strangely enough none of the Nonconformist parents, many of whom were strict Baptists, are recorded as having taken advantage of the Cowper-Temple Conscience Clause, which gave them authority to withdraw their children from religious instruction. As for the school managers, most of whom were farmers, they were divided in their loyalty between farm and school. This was in accordance with the times when farmers often said: 'Schooling can wait for the winter but farming for the rest of the year comes first.' In general the term passed quietly and satisfactorily. The only cloud that appeared on the school's horizon was the falling off in attendance before Easter, when boys were wanted 'to take father's dinner or go bird-scaring and stone-picking'.

IT did not take the mistress long to learn that her job was by no means a sinecure. Managing and teaching some 50 to 60 children of varying ages and intelligence in two rooms was no easy task and neither was it well paid, for she would not recieve more than £40 a year and even that was considered a good wage for a teacher those days. As one school manager on a nearby school is reported to have said: 'Why, that's more than I pay my cook.'

But the greatest drawback of all was the constant strain of having to prepare the pupils for the annual examination, on which the school grant entirely depended - and incidently the teacher's reputation and salary. Realising all these difficulties, the rector and his wife, like scores of other clerical families those days, did their best to help - not only with religious instruction but in any subject where help was needed. Thus the entry for 15 January 1872: 'Mrs. X attends to the needlework class every afternoon. The needlework consists of shirts, ties, aprons and darning stockings.' Then on 29 April 1872 it was further recorded: 'The rector gave the First Class boys a dictation and arithmetic lesson.'

Even so the teacher's job was hard. She endured it for a time but by the Xmas holiday her patience was exhausted. On 6 January 1873 she made a pathetic and urgent appeal for help: '56 children in the Registers, no assistance yet. Rector and wife still helping in all subjects.'

This entry must have been noticed by the sympathetic H.M.I. for soon after his visit on 27 May 1873 the managers decided to appoint a monitress, a promising young girl in the school. This was in full accordance with the monitorial system of the time, originated by Bell and Lancaster. Anyhow, the managers evidently considered that the monitress in question was quite capable of teaching the infants the A-B-C., how to read and write three-lettered words and do little sums involving not more than three figures.

The mistress was well satisfied with her new assistant and more pleased was she still when the managers decided to add a new classroom to the school so that the little ones could be better taught. Unfortunately, however, it had no heating, a bone of contention between H.M.I. and managers for many a year.

THE school curriculum in the early 1870s was narrow but intensive, the time being entirely devoted to religious instruction, the three Rs, singing and needlework. Grammar and geography were added a few years later. Thus, apart from the scripture lesson, the children were puzzling their heads almost all day long over reading, writing and counting, with a break on one or two afternoons in the week for singing and sewing. Whilst the girls were using their sewing and darning needles, the boys had to fill in the time with transcription or 'chanting' out loud the multiplication tables. One can understand why boys those days so often truanted.

The singing lesson was usually spent in trying to sing up and down the scale in the tonic-sol-fa modulator, a trying ordeal, especially for the teacher with a musical ear. What with the intricacies of tones and semi-tones, the grunts and groans of 'tone-deaf' pupils and the general lack of interest, the lesson was painful indeed. Only occasionally was a new song or round introduced by way of variety. Well might H.M.I. in his annual report say: 'The singing was very inferior and my lords will look for a better report next year.' This comment seems to have disturbed the rector, who soon after presented a harmonium to the school. Whether he thought it might drown the singing or keep the children in better tune, the log book does not reveal. 'All's well that ends well.' And so must have thought the rector, when he recieved the next annual report which opened up with the comment: 'The singing has considerably improved.'

The learning of geography in the 80s was largely a matter of memorising long lists of capes, bays and rivers, as the teacher pointed them out on the map and always in the same sequence. I well remember being taught the geography of Great Britain in this manner in a nearby school in the late 80s. Starting with Flamborough Head, Spurn Point, the Naze, North Foreland, etc., we gradually made our way round the coast, chanting out aloud their names in true Suffolk sing-song style. And so the lesson continued till we had exhausted the physical features of the country, generally finishing with hills and mountains. One thing can be said in favour of this obsolete method and that is we never forgot. I wonder how many pupils leaving school today can recite the names of all the counties of England and their capitals! This was a common performance then.

As for instruction in grammar, the children were first taught the various parts of speech, beginning with the noun in Standard I. Then when adjectives, adverbs and verbs, had been exhausted the top standard proceeded with simple analyses of sentences and parsing. Thus the mistress, with apparent pride, made entry in the log book: 'gave Std I a lesson on the idea of a noun. The result of the lesson was very successful.' And some years later: 'Gave the First Class its first lesson in parsing.' This method of instruction evidently satisfied H.M.I., who reported: 'Grammar has been well taught and the boys answered creditably.'

away for weeks on end. Then no sooner had they returned to school than the winter set in, with its impassable roads, floods and epidemics, including measles, scarlatina and a strange disease called 'rose-rash'. These conditions prevailed year after year till the late 70s. Then on 14 January 1878, to the delight and relief of the much harassed mistress, a new official arrived, known as the school attendance officer. Incidentally, this date marks the time when school attendance first became compulsory, and prosecution for prolonged absence, legal. For a time attendance improved, but even the attendance officer soon found that indifference to schooling as hard to combat, especially amongst the farmers. Readers may well be wondering if the children of this remote little country school ever needed punishment and if so, the form adopted. From all accounts the boys were often unpunctual and occasionally lazy and rebellious. The girls, too, were sometimes stubborn and sullen, even 'refusing to read or speak when spoken to'.

In the early days the mistress ruled by persuasion, cajolery, reprimand, scolding and the everlasting 'staying in'. Later, sterner measures were adopted such as sending naughty children home or even expelling them. These methods, however, proved distastrous for nothing suited boys better than to be 'sent home'. At last a teacher of the Amazon type was appointed, who evidently knew how to wield the cane to good effect - so much so that in a matter of weeks good order and discipline were restored, thereby gaining favourable comment from Her Majesty's inspector in the next annual report. The following extracts from the log book will tell their own story:

Incidentally, this was the only occasion when the boys seem to have surpassed the girls - they evidently had a more analytical turn of mind.

FOR many years bad attendance and late-coming caused grievous trouble to the mistress. In the spring the older children were needed on the land for stone-picking, bird-scaring, bean-dropping, etc. Then in summer there were the Sunday School treats, visiting circuses, flower shows and an occasional village auction which no child could resist. The worst period, however, was the autumn when gleaning, picking acorns, keeping hogs and 'brushing' kept the older boys

'Fourth Class kept in this morning to learn how to count up to 50, as they had been troublesome.' 'Kept 1st Class in for staying too long on the ice.' 'M.F. played truant three days this week and spent his school penny. Reprimanded.' W.C. was kept in for looking over another boy's diction.' 'Kept in whole school till five o'clock for creating a disturbance in the road the previous evening.' 'Bad Lad. W.F. left school today to attend one under a master.' 'W.B. was expelled by the mistress. Most unruly. He is not a fit companion for other children.' 'Three boys . . . came to school at quarter to 3 this afternoon (Friday). Had been playing. They were punished and sent home again.' 'Four boys . . . came to school at 10 this morning. They were caned and kept in as punishment.' H.M.I. reported soon after: 'The discipline is now quite satisfactory.'

No mention was made of any physical training until 21 January 1882 when the whole school turned out for exercise. As no more was heard of such a lesson for many years it can be assumed that 'forming fours, wheeling and dressing' in so small a playground was not to the liking of either teacher or pupils. In general, however, they were not lacking in exercise. The boys had their seasonal games such as marbles, top-spinning, bowling hoops, hide-and-seek and following the hounds, of which they never tired. The girls, too, were quite happy with their five-stones, skipping ropes, rounders and, best of all, the playground singing games in which they took an endless delight. One rarely passed a country school playground those days without hearing the strains of 'Poor Mary lies a-weepin', a-weepin', a-weepin'' or 'Now you're married you must be good. Make your husband chop the wood.' Alas! those lovely old singing games are no more! The gymnasium and organised games have killed them.

DESPITE poor facilities and inadequate staffing the school, by the year 1893, when it officially came of age, had made considerable progress. The curriculum had been broadened and the general standard of work improved. Almost every successive year saw a better report from H.M.I., which was always made with sympathy and a close understanding of prevailing conditions. Probably the best report of all came from the South Kensington Science and Art department in 1893, which stated that the instruction in drawing was excellent. April 28 1879 must have been a proud day for the school, when Henry and James Dean and George Lummis passed the 'Labour Certificate Examination,' which qualified them, at 12 years of age, to leave school for work on the land.

The happiest day for the school in general seems to have fallen on 5 October 1891 when the mistress gave notice that the 'school penny' would no longer be required. The most outstanding year as far as the teachers were concerned, was 1890, when individual examinations in all standards were abolished and government grants in future were to be based on general attainment and not on individual results as hitherto. And so passed away the teacher's greatest bugbear.

The School Down the Lane

Godfrey Windham (c1952)

MORE than fifty years have passed since I first trudged down the winding lane from my cottage home in Wendling, Norfolk, to the village school. Amongst my earliest memories is one of a boy in a brown corduroy suit and celluloid collar, swinging a brass-edged bell just outside the school gates. At the sound of the bell, children of all ages between four and fourteen would scamper along the lane towards the iron gateway.

The little ones were shepherded into the porches by their elder sisters and thence into the infants' classroom. The older children formed into lines and marched into the main classroom with the orderliness of soldiers on parade. Having taken up their appointed places at the long wooden desks, they would start whispering and shuffling as monitors brought out piles of books for the first lessons. Suddenly, the teacher would call out: 'Be quiet!' And all the eyes would turn towards the door. The great moment of the day had come.

The door would open with a flourish and the children would rise with a concerted chorus of 'Good morning Governess,' as a lady of middling height and indefinite age entered the classroom.

She wore a straw sailor hat with a black band, securely fastened by a wide silk scarf; beneath the hat, a narrow-waisted full-skirted costume, relieved by a white ruffled blouse with a black bow under the collar.

When she had taken off her hat, her firm pale face was framed by a mass of very black hair. She was the type of woman who commanded respect without inspiring fear. Judged by the standards of her day, Mrs Boddy was an extremely efficient governess, with a strong flair for discipline and a passion for music and for her beloved Scarning church. Each morning, she would sit at a wheezy old harmonium and, swaying from side to side, create an atmosphere of rapt attention throughout the school. If by any chance she discovered inattention, she would spring up from her cane-bottomed chair and, crashing a blackboard pointer on to the table beside her, cry out: 'Silence.' For a moment, she would stand poised and threatening, then the lesson was resumed.

Part songs were her obsession and, even now, after years of satiety in music good and bad, I recall with nostalgia the sweet voices of children taking up in turn:

White sands and grey sands
Who'll buy my white sands?
Who'll buy my grey sands . . .

IN winter the schoolroom was draughty and very cold. A cylindrical slow-combustion stove warmed the area around the teacher's table but children seated at the back of the room shivered in bleak discomfort. On the coldest mornings, we warmed ourselves by stamping on the floor for five or ten minutes to the rhythm of arithmetic tables. This practice had lasting effects. It consisted of endless repetition of multiplication tables and, because of it, I for one have never had to pause when making mental calculations.

The curriculum of the school was limited but clearly defined. Each subject was taught with a thoroughness which appears to be lacking in many modern schools. In evidence of this, one has only to consider the number of children who now leave school without being able to spell quite simple words correctly, who funk problems involving mental effort and who are reluctant to shoulder responsibility as they grow older. It may well be that much of this is due to external influences over which the school has no control. The fact remains that the modern child at school-leaving age lacks ability to write, spell and calculate correctly and in this respect is less well equipped for a career than were his forebears.

Scholars and staff at Wendling school 1906. The author is in the middle row (wearing a bow), and Mrs Boddy, who was still playing the organ in Scarning church at the age of 97, on the left.

I LOOK back with gratitude upon the tireless effort of teachers who were ill-trained, ill-paid and ill-equipped but who, by perseverance and thoroughness, made sure that their scholars were well grounded in the fundamentals of English and arithmetic. They also taught them to appreciate all that is beautiful and deprecate that which is vile and ugly.

The pity of it was that the social system prevailing at the time was such that scholarships were almost unknown at village schools. This was not surprising, for two reasons. First, most of the children's parents were incredibly poor, the farm worker's wage being not more than fourteen shillings; it was thus inevitable that parents encouraged the natural desire of all teenage children to earn their living. Secondly, the schools were managed mostly by local farmers who wanted the boys on the farm and the girls in the household. This applied to their own and their workers' children. I have no doubt that many of my readers will question the accuracy of this assertion but I cannot recall, up to the time I left school myself, a single instance of a child passing on to a grammar or high school by means of a scholarship. I merely record the facts, in the sure knowledge that these things are no more.

It is often said that the old days were the best. I believe that in some respects they were. The school down the lane certainly imposed greater discipline and encouraged greater effort from the scholar. The essential difference lies in that the door of opportunity is now wide open. The inference is that those who pass through it might well be better equipped with a sound knowledge of the fundamentals.

That Very Remarkable Headmaster

F. C. Oakley (c1951), Illustrated by Andrew Dodds

I HOPE I may be reckoned an East Anglian. I am a Cockney by birth, but at the early age of four my family removed to an obscure village on the Suffolk border of Essex and from then to five years ago I have lived in Essex, Suffolk, Cambridge or Norfolk - mainly Norfolk - except for a break during the Kaiser's War.

I want to write something of my own schooldays at the end of the last century. My first school was the Fauconberg School, Beccles. I have read very little about it in print and

nothing of its very remarkable headmaster, the Rev. John Hardy Raven.

I came in for the end of his long reign and stayed on with his two immediate successors. Time has dimmed my memory of him a good deal but I must try to give some idea of his personality, which I see now must have been quite outstanding.

Owing almost entirely to his sterling qualities the Fauconberg School must have been unique. At the time of my sojourn there the number of boys was about eighty, about half of them boarders who came from all over England. The school was run on the lines of a big public school, except that the numbers did not allow for its being divided up into houses: day-boys v. boarders was the natural division. The teaching, organisation and tone of the school certainly compared very favourably with those of the large public school to which I afterwards moved.

The headmaster was small of statue. But he was in every respect a Victorian 'character,' such as is seldom found in later days. His name was appropriate, for he had a beaky nose, liable to become purple with emotion, and wearing his cap and gown had something of the appearance of a bird of prey. His hands always seemed to be chalky and we irreverent schoolboys affirmed that when a piece of chalk broke on the blackboard he went on writing with his finger.

He was very musical (he was joint editor of an edition of Hymns A. and M.) and we poor little trebles were the weekly victims of his vituperative sarcasm at Glee Club practices. Fifty years later (1951) I can still sing the treble part of 'O who will o'er the downs so free' absolutely correctly in time and notation. I remember singing the three words 'light I'll set' continuously for a quarter of an hour until Mr Raven was satisfied that we had mastered the tune. At evening prayers we boys were encouraged to suggest what hymn we should sing. But we had to be wary. One boy spoke up for 'O Paradise, O Paradise,' and was promptly told to write out a hundred times the line: "No healthy-minded schoolboy longs for Paradise!"

As a teacher he was rather terrifying to a small boy. His methods would be absolute anathema to modern educationalists. But they delivered the goods. He was too fond of the cane - at any rate to our thinking. I remember him seizing an unfortunate boy (his own nephew) and beating him round and round the classroom. Yet I never heard of any bad feeling resulting, either with boys or with their parents.

In his form some such dialogue as the following was a commonplace:

"Now, boy, what is the meaning of 'delubris'?"

Silence and the head hung down.

"Did you look it up, sir?" "Please, sir, yes, sir; but I've forgotten it, sir."

"Stand up on the form, boy, and repeat: 'Formula Number One - Gottles!' and go on saying it until I tell you to stop . . . Now you, Jones; what is the meaning of 'delubris'?"

"Please, sir, I haven't got so far."

"Stand up on the form, boy, and repeat:

Formula Number Two - Gottsofar'!"

One wonders what a stranger would have thought had he come suddenly into one of Mr Raven's classes. He would be sure to find one or two boys lying flat on their tummies on the forms, having been told: "Go to bed, sir, and get up when you know the answer!" There would also be at least one pupil standing on the form, slowly revolving, and repeating over and over again: "The non-possession of pencils on the part of the pupils is penal." I do not believe that ever in my life since my acquaintance with the headmaster could I have been found without a pencil in my pocket. But woe to the miserable youth who dropped his pencil in form! "Pick it up again, sir!" And then would follow some eccentric punishment.

Yet he was extremely popular, if not actually beloved, because we boys knew instinctively that his whole heart and life were devoted to the school and our well-being. I do not suppose that the boys were so well fed at any other school in England. Many were much better fed than they were at home. In the season the boarders were given 'strawberry feasts' - huge plates of strawberries with lashings of cream. Both the headmaster and Mrs Raven were generous to a degree and we all appreciated the fact, in spite of his little foibles in the classroom - not that they were confined to the classroom.

We also knew that in his palmy days he had been a first class batsman who had played cricket for Kent. He could therefore be forgiven anything. And we all loved Mrs Raven, who was at the same time a gracious lady and a motherly woman - a somewhat rare combination. When we little boys were occasionally relegated to the sick room for a spell, Mrs Raven saw to it that we never missed our mothers or felt home-sick. There are few stronger tests of feminine character than that.

LIFE at the school was very jolly for us boarders. There was an excellent bathing-place on the banks of the Waveney and we all trooped down there on summer mornings. We were woken by the school porter who walked down the dormitory ringing a hand-bell and crying: "Five-and-twenty to seven, gentlemen! Bathing: sixty-eight." The last figure, which varied, told us the temperature of the water. If it was below fifty, there was no bathing that morning.

The dormitory was built in L-formation, with no wall or door dividing the arms of the L. I have never been able to understand why our dormitory games before lights out did not more often bring us into severe trouble, since the noise was terrific and the whole building used to shake.

There was the towel game, for instance. A towel was twisted up and the object of the game was to prevent your opponent from touching the wall with it at your end of the dormitory, while at the same time trying to reach your opponents' end with it. There were no rules: It was an all-in scrap. Most of us smaller boys spent the time lying on our beds with a big boy sitting on our heads. And the big boy had to 'ware teeth.

A still more noisy and boisterous game was chariot races. A small boy sat on a blanket and a big boy dragged it along the floor. Three chariots raced abreast up the dormitory and round the corner to the other end. As there was barely room for one - the washing stands stood at the end of the beds - the resulting chaos can be imagined. Yet everything was always straight and tidy and we were all half asleep in bed when the master came up to turn out the lights.

The school, although small and unadvertised, was consistently fortunate in its staff. This, although we did not know it, was another tribute to the headmaster's character. In my memory two men are outstanding: E. J. Llewelyn Davies, who grounded me in the classics and to whom I probably owe more than to anybody else for my education; and F. F. Edwards, who taught me enough French to enable me to get along. These two also spent an immense amount of time coaching us at cricket and generally licking us into shape. Mr Davies eventually migrated to Elstree, and Mr Edwards to Dulwich. And there were others, such as 'Beefy' Bowers, to whom we owed much.

But perhaps the most remarkable was 'Daddy' Soanes. He was not a regular member of the staff but used to come and lend a hand in case of vacancy through illness or any other cause. He was 'one of the people' and took classes in Latin. There was nothing the matter with his discipline and he taught us boys by his example that being

a gentleman has nothing whatever to do with social classes - a very salutary lesson for us at that time.

Prominent among my memories is Mr Edwards, who had a small sweet-shop in the town and brought a selection of his wares on a 'grub-cart' after school. The barrow became the centre of a howling mob but Mr Edwards was equal to the occasion. Not so his son who occasionally deputized for him and was apt to lose his temper. However, we were chronically short of cash and often had to turn sadly away when Mr Edwards demanded: "Show me first your penny!"

Going through my mother's papers after her death, I came across two picture-postcards written to her by me from Beccles and apparently treasured ever since. The first informed her that we had all been asked to subscribe a shilling to a fund for the wounded in the Boer War. The second ran something like this: "Dear Mother, thank you very much for the 1s. I think I shall give 3d to the wounded soldiers."

I WELL remember the school glee club and certain other musical occasions. Besides full-dress concerts given by the glee club, there were also more informal musical evenings rather like smoking concerts (without smoke) after supper on special occasions.

The Toy Symphony was a popular number and so was a special school march which had been composed by Mr W. Warder Harvey, at that time organist at the parish church. For this effort Mr Edwards played a French horn, to the admiration and envy of the boarders.

But the vocal items at these concerts were the chief attraction. The headmaster usually managed to have a male voice quartete - Mr R. H. Craze, who afterwards took holy master tenor, and boys for the alto and orders, *basso profundissimo*, the head-treble parts. Mr Raven used to become worked up to the height of enthusiasm, his face purple, perspiration streaming from him, gasping, spluttering and gesticulating, as the quartete rendered a setting of 'Peter Piper':

Where's the pepper,
The peck of pickled pepper
Where's the pepper Peter Piper picked?
If the occasion was the end of the summer term

Mr Raven insisted on everybody joining in the 'horkey' song:

We hev ploughed; We hev sown; We hev repp;
We hev mown; We hev gott In ther corn;
Now we croy *(f f f)* HORKEY!!

This triumphant finale would always find the headmaster weak with laughter and mopping his face with an outsize handkerchief.

Besides the assistant masters I have mentioned there were others who were usually birds of passage, not staying long enough to make much of a mark. I have a very shadowy recollection of 'Ziph' Turner, who retired very soon after my arrival. (I do not wish to imply that this was due to cause and effect.) Why he was called 'Ziph' I have no idea.

Ziph Turner would allow little boys to leave the room only if they could swear that the matron had given them a rhubarb pill the night before. If it was a case of necessity and the boy had had no pill, he had to write out a hundred times: 'I must not leave the room in class.'

He had a remarkable system of marking essays. He counted the number of words in the first six lines, took an average, and multiplied that by the total number of lines. Then he awarded a mark for each word. I once scored over 1,000 marks for an essay on flowers. 'There are many different sorts of flowers: the daisy, the buttercup, the bluebell, the daffodil . . . ' and so on till I had exhausted the list of flowers known to me. I then went through the list again: 'The daisy is white, the buttercup is yellow, the bluebell is blue, the daffodil is yellow . . . ' and so on quite literally *ad nanseam*. The reader will now be able to spot the foundation of my literary style.

Schooldays at 'Hunston'

Fred D. Cross (c1959)

THE advertisements of the Great Eastern Railway used to call it HUNSTANTON - ON-SEA, but if you are an intimate acquaintance, regarding it, as I do, with affection, you will probably end by calling it HUNSTON. And if you travel from Liverpool Street to this corner of Norfolk, you may be sure your train will stop there, for Hunston is a terminus; British Railways can carry you no further. Had you wished to visit the coastline beyond, you would have changed trains at Heacham. But that is another story.

When most people travel by road, it may seem odd to follow the railway but years ago it was not so; we travelled by train. It was by train I first came to Hunston. Nearly 50 years ago, before the First World War, motor cars were a rarity and Hunston was smaller, quieter and more secluded, a snug little town of cragstone houses, bright when new and weathering to warm dark brown; a little gingerbread town, spreading up from the Station, framing the Green, climbing up to the High Street and spreading to right and to left. Eastwards it went to the cliffs, where near the end was the lighthouse, immaculate in its livery of white and black, with a broad red band on the lantern tower.

Below the Green ran the old promenade and over it the iron pier stretched out to the sea. But the sea played tricks with the pier, retreating beyond it twice every 24 hours; such are the tides of the Wash.

Hunston air is bracing and invigorating; breezy, sometimes boisterous; undeniably a healthy place. Perhaps this accounts for the half dozen preparatory or boarding schools which flourished there in late Edwardian times. It was to one of these schools that I was sent. Despatched would be a better word, for with a label attached to the lapel of my coat (term had already started), I travelled in the guard's van in the charge of the guard. He delivered me safely, along with the other baggage. It is a good thing the small boy is adaptable, for he needs to be. But given a week or two to settle, he usually accepts boarding school life with surprising cheerfulness.

IT was a small school - not more than 50 boys. It was a strict school, with plenty of discipline. Maybe we were none the worse for the spartan life; we accepted it and managed to enjoy ourselves. My first surprise was financial. We arrived with purses of pocket money but whether they contained £5 or 5s. mattered not at all. The purse was surrendered. And on Saturday mornings we were paid our weekly allowance: one penny. This may sound a small sum today but if shops are avoided, there is no opportunity to spend. Besides, we had our own currency: fanshells picked up on the beach. The same rule applied to tuck. This was impounded and distributed in small daily doses. The two sweets you received so eagerly were hardly ever yours.

We seemed to be always walking. The Hunston air was free, it was full of ozone, so when not at our lessons, we were taken for walks. We walked to the promenade in the early morning to play football on its hard unyielding concrete. One goal was under the pier, the other less well defined. Two boys patrolled the beach to throw the ball back.

Incessantly we walked down Lewis' Lane which led to the Downs. We knew every inch of it but never did we discover who Lewis was. There was cricket of course and we were peculiarly addicted to 'bat and trap'. I do not think we took sport very seriously.

So much has changed, perhaps most of all the traffic on the roads. Then it was the horse-drawn vehicle and the bicycle.

One remembers those rare early cars; the Darracqs, the Alldays and Onions, Napiers, and the little de Dion Boutons. We knew them all and watched them trying valiantly to climb the hill from the station. How often it proved too much for them. But the seashore does not change, neither do the tides. Beaches are unaltered and of all the beaches of East Anglia - to me - Hunston's is one of the loveliest.

Past the lighthouse, just beyond where the cliff slopes down to the beach, the school owned two beach huts; one large and plain, for the boys; one small and elegant, for the staff. An ideal spot. On fine summer days we would camp there, bathing, playing and enjoying ourselves. These expeditions were on half holidays. Off we would set about mid-day; up on to the High Road, past the water tower. This tower had a strange fascination; we imagined it to be literally full of water and there was speculation about what would happen if it burst. Once on the cliff, two hefty boys, giants of 11 or 12 years, would be chosen to 'fetch the drinking water'. With an outsize water can they would make for the coastguard's

cottage to fill it, whilst the main body would round the lighthouse wall by the cliff's edge. Then down the rough cliff path to the very end, where we slipped and slithered down the sandy slope to the beach. A few yards away stood the huts.

It is strange how things stick in the memory. Today, a round red Dutch cheese reminds me of these picnics. We always had thick wedges of it to eat with our bread and butter 'doorsteps' - and a little sand thrown in too. Then the long trek home by the cliffs in the late afternoon and, when we arrived, that special meal. It was known as 'meat tea'.

IF one's parents were willing to pay, you could learn to dance, improve your deportment and acquire polish.

The dancing class was held on Saturday mornings at the Town Hall, overlooking the Green. Amongst the boys there was no great eagerness to learn but to attend had one great advantage, one got out of morning school. Whether the select band who attended benefited from their endeavours was not clear. They certainly appeared no more graceful than the rest of us.

Sunday is supposed to be a day of rest but our Sundays were the reverse. It was a day of Eton suits and high collars. It is true we had no lessons but we still had our tasks. One, I remember, was to learn, and in the afternoon repeat, the collect for the day and two verses of a hymn. Until this feat was accomplished, all other diversions were banned. Before morning church there was the annointing of heads - no delicately scented unguent but an oil labelled 'Pure Lucca'; and normally used for salads. It imparted a shine but we smelt slightly rancid. Then we were inspected, finger nails examined, handkerchiefs checked and, when at last pronounced sartorially correct, given our penny for the collection. In this state of unusual cleanliness we would set off.

Two by two in crocodile formation we would go, large boys in front, small fry to the rear - our course set for the old village church. Sometimes we would meet the High Road School boys as they too converged on our objective. On their youthful heads were not caps but real top hats; a splendid sight. We sat on the left and they on the right of the aisle. And during service it was common for us to faint. It may have been the walk, the tightness of the Eton suits, the high collars or perhaps the scent of the Lucca Oil - no one knew. The casualty would be revived in the porch; we others enjoyed the commotion. But fainting was frowned upon. It was our own fault, they would say. If we would stand on two legs instead of one, these calamities would never occur.

Our Sundays ended with hymn singing to the tintinnabulation of the schoolroom piano, and when the last hymn had been sung and the piano lid closed, off we would troop to bed. It was nearly seven o'clock.

Life on the Farm

Nehemiah Looks Back

R. H. Futter (c1957)

AS one gets near the bottom of the hill and looks back on a fairly long life, there is a tendency to get rather impatient with the younger generation who know all about the 'bad old days' and compare the present 'welfare state' with conditions prevailing at the end of the last century very much to the detriment of the 1880s. One has, however, the satisfaction of knowing that time will correct early impressions and that there is nothing so futile as making any comparisons of that nature. Like many a one before them they will come to see that 'black's not so black nor white so very white'. It is impossible not to look back with longing for some of the things of the past.

I recently met a real survivor of the 'bad old days' who revived all sorts of nostalgic memories. Like myself, he had known the time when a harvest field smelt like a harvest field and not like the forecourt of a garage, when corn was cut with a scythe, when the almost universal dress for 'Hodge, the poor, honest country wight', was a

'Like myself, he had known the time when a harvest field smelt like a harvest field. . .'

77

pair of cotton cords and a sleeve 'weskit'. Those old cord breeches used to smell a bit in church on a hot Sunday afternoon. They were, however, the best thing for the job but, like the 'weskit', have long since passed into the limbo of forgotten things.

This old chap, like most of his contemporaries, had a biblical name - Nehemiah - and once I had drawn the cork of a barrel of memories I found he had forgotten the disadvantages of life on 10s. a week and remembered only the satisfaction of a job of work well done, the close relationship of the farmer and his men and the practical joking which supplied a good proportion of the amusements of those days. He took a rather dim view of modern life and manners in the rural areas in spite of the cinemas, football pools and the 'never-never' system of buying things necessary and others not so necessary. He even cast some doubt on the advantages of piped water which he said 'don't fare to have no body in it'. No doubt he and his forebears had their water from a pond but it must be added they never drank it, except in the form of tea or beer which they largely brewed themselves.

HE recalled that he had started work on 1s. 6d. a week and was startled one day when his master said to him: 'Miah, I'm a-goin to hain you.' His hope of a substantial rise was, however, rather dampened by the news that he was to get another sixpence a week - but for that he had to work Sundays. This he thought poorly of so went fishing and his first voyage earned him £10. 'Coo,' he said, 'I thowt I'd niver want no more money.' Subsequent fishing ventures, however, were not so good and he spent the rest of his working life behind one of the old wooden-beamed swing ploughs and a pair of Suffolks.

Speaking of horses he said: 'Hosses are gone off the farms now and I notice one thing about it. It ain't no use hollerin "hold ye" to a tractor or "whoa". He oon't start nor stop unless somebody gits on. Thass where the hoss war better at cartin' corn or muck. No hosses now and no hossmen. They're all farm engineers now and wear out the seats of their "britches" stid of their "butes".'

I said: 'You must have come across some characters on the farm in your life.' 'Aye,' he said, 'just as now, they all had their little owd ways. I mind owd Ephraim the shepherd up at the hall. His missus was a proper owd vixen and her great trouble was Ephraim wouldn't fight. When she got proper mad he just went on wi' his dinner. She'd then bounce outdoors and say she was agooin' to drownd herself. Ephraim never paid no regard so she had to come back. One time, however, she din't come back and owd Ephraim began to think perhaps there was a wolf this time. So he went out and took a peep round the cowshed. There, sure enough, was owd Sairey up to her knees in the hosspond. Ephraim, he took one look at her and said: You'll ha to put t'other end in Sairey. Yew oon't drownd like that." Then he went back to his dinner and Sairey come back too. She didn't try that on any more. She give owd Ephraim best.'

'I mind a time when one of these 'ere temperance lecturers come along and said we could work better on cowd water or tea than what we could on beer. Tim Wade, a great black-bearded feller, was there and he challenged the chap to pitch wheat agin him for a day - the temperance man on water o'course. Tim was one of these bull-headed fellers as would stick his fork in a stack of hay if towd he couldn't lift it. O'course it won't fair on the temperance bloke who was soft-handed while Tim was hard as nails. Anyway the thing was arranged on 10 acres of wheat on farmer May's place. Tim did his piece, then went to help t'other chap who was properly done up, hands blistered and sweat a-droppin' off 'im. There may be one or two left who remember this.

'One time when we was down to marsh' - 'mash' he called it - 'at Haddiscoe, the landlord of a little pub on the river played a fine joke on some Broadland holiday-makers. We was down there hay-making and some of us din't go hoom at nights and went to the pub for a pint.

'When the bar was pretty full of boys and gals from the boats the landlord, owd Jack Boast said:

' "Would you fooks like to see my hotter?" ' (It appeared later on in the story that the 'h' was deliberately employed.)

' "Hotter?" said one guest. "What's that?"

He spent his life behind a plough and a pair of Suffolks

' "You know," said Boast, "water hotter out of the river. I've got a big one out in the yard."

' "Oh, ah, an otter. Yes, let's have a look at it," says one.

'Well, away they all trooped, up the pub yard. On the way an old ostler chap, who had been well briefed, was told to get out the 'otter which was said to be housed in a big dog kennel at the end of the yard.

' "No, marster," said this worthy, "I ain't a-gooin' nigh 'un. He was suffin savage when I fed 'im this mornin' and if you want un you get un out." '

With that the landlord proceeded to the kennel from which a long chain fastened to a stake protruded. Clutching this the landlord proceeded to haul out whatever was at the end of the chain, making pretence it was a tough job. There was a scrabbling sound from the interior and at length out came a bundle of straw and then a huge iron kettle which had apparently been at the bottom of the Yare for years and been hauled up by some fisherman.

'There,' said the landlord, 'I'll bet you fooks have never seem a bigger water hotter than that.'

The visitors looked at one another for a minute and then one of the girls began to laugh and they all roared with laughter. Admitting that they had been well and truly had, all trooped back to the bar while the landlord re-kennelled his hotter for the next batch of victims.

Old Nehemiah chuckled over his practical joke and I left him to his meditations on the 'bad old days'.

Life as a Farmworker's Wife in the late 19c.

Mrs Scarfe Webb (c1946)

EVEN despite present-day shortages (1946), I am sure that everyone will realise that things are better now than when I was young - for the housekeeper especially, who has to lay the money out. I do hope we shan't have to go back to anything like our parents experienced when bringing up their families in those days - anything from a dozen to eighteen.

Most of the people who lived in the villages were landworkers, whose wages were very small. Ten shillings for full-time workers if they were agricultural labourers. I think the men who looked after the horses and stock got about two or three shillings more as they had to put in extra hours, but anyhow I know I have seen my father come home many a Friday night, when the weather had been bad, and they had nothing that they could do in the barn, and lay six or seven shillings on the tray to keep a family of seven for a week. That included father, mother and five children.

I often wonder how they did it, and out of that small amount, the school pence used to come, for four of us, every Monday morning. My Godmother paid for me, and I used to go and get it every Monday morning. That was one thing I did not like at all, and once I told my mother I wouldn't go after it, because it was begging, and she had always told us we were not to ask anyone for money. But she told me it was a different thing to begging. My Godmother was giving me this education so I could go out into the world with what knowledge I could get while at school, to fit me for whatever lay before me. When I went out into the world to get my living, I should be glad I had gone to school. When that time came, I knew my mother was right.

NOW we look back at the hard work that had to be done in those days. There were no labour-saving devices for housework as there are today. Not many homes had covering for floors - just an old sack for the hearth, or a shred rug, and another old sack laid at the door to wipe your boots on. Twice a week those floors had to be scrubbed by clean and tidy people. Some who didn't like a scrub brush used to put clean sand down every now and again. That saved a lot of hard work. Most of the floors were bricks, and you could not find many boarded ones, so that those that were scrubbed looked very clear because they taught us it was not the scrubbing, but the clearing of them with plenty of water after you had used your brush, that mattered.

Well, now we come to the wash tub. There were not many easy ways of washing as there are today. Most women rubbed every bit of their linen. It went through two waters, what they called the first and second, before being put into the copper to be boiled. After it had been boiled it was taken out and put through two more lots of water, which they called sudding and rinsing. Today many of us possess nice little mangles, but there were not many of those about then. I can remember what they called the box mangle. It was a great huge thing, weighted with stones, and it was very difficult to put the linen round the rollers to get pressed, and they were no use for wringing the water out of the clothes.

On a baking day, the bread used to be laid in the putch and put to rise. When you baked a big batch to last a week, it took a long time before it was ready for the oven, especially if the yeast was not fresh. We had to make our bread with

brewer's yeast in those days. I used to fetch it. Our mother used to say, "Don't you bring me Porter yeast, do you can take it back." No gas ovens or cooking ranges in those days. If there were any ranges at all, they were in the trades-men's houses, who paid for them in their rent. Our ovens were of brick. You had to heat them with bush faggots, and have a long pole to stir the ashes about. When you saw the bricks were white all over, you knew you had got a nice oven for your bread, for that was what the ovens mostly contained. There were not many cakes and pies. Sometimes we had a pumpkin pie in winter, but that was a luxury. I have heard the old ladies say they were more tired after baking day than if they had stood at the wash tub for two days.

WHEN harvest came along there was the brew-ing to do. There was water to fetch - many had to go a mile or more to get it as the ponds were dry in summer. There were not a lot of pumps or wells for cottages. People that had them were exceptionally lucky. I myself was brought up on pond water, and we had to make spare in the sum-mer when more was wanted for everything. I have often thought when I have gone to my pump or tap, how different it is from the old days, when I had to go with my father and brother to help push the water up-hill. We had a huge cask on iron wheels, and we used to take a wooden bucket to get the water from the spring, and a funnel to put it into the cask. We had a good mile or more to go before we got to the spring, where the water was always running. At harvest time it was needed for brewing. Of course the more malt that was being brewed, the more water wanted fetching.

THE corn is cut and tied up by machinery nowa-days, and there is not so much hard manual labour attached to it. But when I was a child, so many men undertook to do the harvest, and mowed it down with their scythes, one behind the other. All the wheat and oats were cut by the men, though sometimes their wives used to tie up for them, and when they carted the barley, that's where the women came in again. That could not be done without every man that was in the harvest having his own gaveler, which means someone to take a rake, and rake the barley on to the side of the stetch, so the wagon could get up in the middle of two rows of gavels. Then the men could load it with the forks. So it fell to the lot of the man's wife to gavel for her husband, and if she was unable to do it, he had to pay someone out of his harvest money to do it for him. This sometimes did happen, and it made a hole in the money which was badly needed at home, as the rents were paid yearly out of harvest money. I can tell you harvest meant a month's hard labour for the wives in those days. Many a time have I known my mother to be in the field all day and then stay up all night to wash or bake or brew, and go into the harvest field again next day to do her job there. Sometimes she did not see her bed as many as three times in a week.

AFTER it was all gathered in and settled up, they had something to look forward to. The good Roast Beef of Old England, and plenty of vegetables and plum pudding, and plenty of home-brewed beer. It was their harvest supper, and they used to invite their friends, and they had a jolly good time. After supper there was singing and dancing, and a good old accordian to accompany them.

Then came the kiddies' treat. It was the Largess Spending. On the farm where my father worked, and a good many more, their employer, whom the men always called 'Our Govner,' used to let the men have a wagon and horses. Everybody who worked on the farm and their families were able to go to the seaside for the day and have a jolly time. Again there was not much pleasure for the women, with all the food to pack up for the day, and the children taking advantage of their parent's purse for the pretty toys that were to be seen. And if the penny was not forthcoming you heard plenty of yelling from them, and I have heard the mothers say to each other coming home, "Thank God this day is over. It is worse than hard work taking these children out."

Well, I think there is another woman's job we don't see done today. That is putting the pork down into the pot, when the pig in the sty is fatted and killed. If a neighbour said his pig was fat enough to be killed, there would be three men buy one quarter each, and he would keep one

quarter for himself. The quarter of pork was weighed and taken where the people lived. Next day was a busy day, salting it and putting it in the pork pot, which was weighed with huge stones, to keep it covered in the brine. Then the lard and pork cheeses were made, pigs bellies cleaned and laid in salt and water. I believe they call them chittlings today. There was nothing wasted from that pig which was good for human food. You don't get pork like that today. They used to let the fat be in the pot till it was red, and it used to be beautiful. You want to hear what some of the old people say today about the pork.

NOW one word or two on how we used to spend our pennies. If we ran errands and got anything from a little farthing to a penny given us, we used to take it home and put it in our money boxes. When we wanted boots the money was taken out to help buy them. Sometimes we had sweets, a quarter of a pound of large pear drops broken up and put into a bottle, and shared amongst five. That was our allowance for a week. I remember now the words on my money box which my Godmother gave me:

Not for to hide it in a hedge,
Or for a train attendant,
But for the glorious price,
Of being independent.

I do think we are blessed today in many ways. We have our National Health Insurance, which provides for maternity. There is not the worry of getting it put by out of the week's money. Then the Public Assistance is providing well for people that had to call on the Parish in days gone by. In my time the Relieving Officer used to come to you after you had made an application to call on the Parish, and if you had anything worth selling in your home, you had to sell it. Then until your money was spent you did not have any help, and then it was only about a stone of flour and a shilling.

I have lived in this old village for many years, and here I mean to stay. We've lived in troublesome times, with Huns and bombs about. But all the time I knew they couldn't drive me out.

The Changing Years

Godfrey Windham (c1947), Illustrated by Bernard Reynolds

IN the very heart of Norfolk, there lies a village in a valley, on either side of which the cornfields spread out over gentle slopes, crested by isolated woods. I worked in this village forty years ago), in an era when tractors, motor coaches and crooners were unknown. Then the only sign of mechanisation was the steam-hauled threshing tackle which, as it travelled from one village to another, rolled along the turnpike with a metallic ring, the noise of which rose and fell with the changing of the wind. The hardy labourers clothed themselves in corduroy and "drabette"; strapped up their trousers below the knee and plodded their way across the meadows with hazel staff in hand and frail-basket slung behind the back.

There was regimentation amongst the workers in those days - steward, team-men, cow-men, yard-men and labourers, and rarely did a man pass from one category to another. Children tramped through muddy lanes to schools where fiery-tempered mistresses taught little, but taught that little well. Scholarships were unknown and, at thirteen, sons of labourers followed in their fathers' footsteps, whilst their sisters slaved in the dreary kitchens of isolated farmsteads, sitting out the long winter evenings in the company of purring tabby cats, their loneliness accentuated by the hooting of the barn owls in the outer darkness.

Together men and beasts toiled in the fields until the day was done. Then sitting sideways on the broad back of Prince or Beauty, Old Tom Gleeson would jog his way back to the farmyard, rack up his horses by the light of a hurricane lamp and set off for his home.

TOM was a versatile fellow. He could plough a straight furrow, make a good hurdle or thatch and trim a rick. No rule or plumb line for Tom. He had a good eye and a steady hand. His tastes were simple, too. In the morning, the top of a cottage loaf with a knob of butter inserted; in the evening a bowl of onion gruel. His relaxation, a pint at the pub, or a song at the chapel. More often a snooze by his own fireside. Perhaps Bill Rix would come round for a haircut or there might be children's shoes to mend. Sometimes, on a winter's evening, he would stand in the back yard and watch the frozen snow sparkling in the moonlight, or listen to the pealing of distant church bells. Then he would turn in and mutter to his wife: "I reckon tha's what yer call a master fine night. I fare ter think tha's a rare ole frorst."

Tom's year began on March the first. On this day the men assembled in the stable at six o'clock to receive their orders from the steward. "Tom and George, du yow go, together, and start ploughing the fourteen acres. Bill, du yow go and finish that there draining. Where's that there boy?"

"Here I be Mr Leggett. I reckon I'm a bit late corse I couldn't git my buskins on."

"Well du yow leave 'em on all night if yow can't git here afore this. Take yow that ole mare to the blacksmith's and when yow come back, du yow start rolling in the pightle."

AND so the months rolled on, until one evening in late July the men would congregate at the farm for the harvest hiring. The "master" would come out and state the terms. "Seven pound ten this year it is. Any objections?"

Then Tom would hitch up his trousers, wipe his watery nose with a hairy hand and blurt out, "Du we hetta mow the barley this year, master? Corse if we du, I reckon we owter hev eight pounds. Farmer Barker, he a bowt a new binder, and they tell me he's a goin' to tie up all his barley."

"Well, that's as maybe, Tom. Our barley is laid a good bit and I reckon you'll have to mow it, but seven pound ten's my price same as all the others."

Much argument would follow with a possible compromise at seven pound fifteen. The farmer would give each man a shilling and the men were hired. Three weeks later, the harvest over, Tom would set out for Dereham Fair, buy new boots for himself and the children, lose half-a-crown to the purse trick sharpers, or ten shillings on a useless watch. Then, filled with beer and cockles, he would sing his way merrily through field and by-road until he stumbled into his cottage having had a "rare good day."

JIM Gleeson is the son of Robert, who was the son of Tom. Jim works on the same farm as his grandfather used to do. He drives the tractor, operates the mechanical milker and attends to the diesel engine. But no one has yet invented a thatching machine nor an automatic hedge-trimmer. The calving cows still need attention and the mangolds must be chopped out by hand. The craftsman has not died with the birth of the mechanic and Jim is a better man than his forebears.

The village pub has closed its doors and the chapel is little more than a mausoleum of ghostly memories. On a Saturday afternoon, Jim hops on to his motor-bike, picks up his girl in a neighbouring village and together they go to the city of many attractions, pictures, ice-creams, dances, dog-racing, speedway or football, away from the monotony of fields, gold and green or brown and soggy. Jim lives and laughs, calls his master "George" and tells him he can go to hell.

But still the glory of the countryside is not lost on Jim. In the morning he watches the filmy mist rising above the streamlet which flows along the valley and listens to the song of the birds in the spring. In the evening, the smell of honeysuckles and sweet briar is pleasing to his senses and, as the old bells peal across the meadows, their message rings true to his attentive ears, "Oh Thou Who changest not, abide with me." It is true that men and their works are changing with the years, but to the lover of truth and beauty, the glorious tranquility of the countryside has lost none of its appeal.

'Raise the Song of Harvest Home'

Cedric W. Mays, (c1958)

SUFFOLK, Essex and Cambridgeshire are invaded by the extremities of those fertile fields of Ashdon Place Farm, formerly owned by Major Tansley Luddington, my first employer. 'Ashdon Place' stands in Steventon's End, an Essex hamlet with scattered cottages of rural loveliness and The Bonnet, the hamlet inn. The Bonnet was once the meeting place, the social club of Major Luddington's employees, where they gathered for the material comforts of warmth and drink and communion, and to give thanks for a successful harvest.

My mind takes me back to some of the festivities which once were held in that old tap room - where, beneath their deceptive exterior, some astute, self-reliant individuals gave to that village its now long-lost vitality.

Among the farmhands there existed a recognised hierarchy of status, based upon age, experience and occupational prowess. George Smith was horse keeper and in the farmer's absence he assumed command. He once gashed his foot with a careless scythe-sweep. Lacking first aid equipment, he bound a dock leaf over his all-but-severed toe with the tail of his flannel shirt. Ever afterwards he was known as Toe-Rag.

Ignorant of the existence of Veterinary Colleges, before the first symptoms were manifest to human vision, by his sense of small and equine experience he could diagnose thrush, colic, strangles and pregnancy. He was never found wrong. Upon his lower lip was a wart. A horny unsightliness which he tried to hide by his constant chewings on oat straws. Mention of that wart, or a sly peep in its direction, would cause him profound embarrassment. That was quite evident when Tom Symonds, who it was alleged had inherited psychic powers from Gipsy ancestors, offered his powers - for gain.

'Put a bit o' silver in m'hand, Toe-Rag, an I'll wish yer o'd wart away.' George looked him in the eyes and spat in the stall. 'Thankee, Tom. Can do me own wishin'. Right now, I wish y'd mind yer own bloody business!'

When sheaves were carted, George's tenor rang across the golden stubble in exultation. Ships and sailors figured largely in his songs, possibly because the 60-year-old singer had never seen the sea.

Wuddy Smith was a strong man, in more ways than one. Not addicted to daily ablutions, his presence was evident particularly in summer, apart from visual sensory perception. He had a brother church-christened 'Pudden' and distant relatives at Camp's End who, sometimes, but only when there was an acute dearth of labour, were recruited as casual harvesters. There was justifiable doubt of their surnames, a total ignorance of the Christian names, but their nicknames were household and tap-room words . . .

'Pipper an' Pie, Nickett an' Ninn,
They can allus be found
At the Holly Tree Inn.
When they bain't full o' beer,
They be sodden wi' gin.'

Barny Bland, misshapen by a badly humped back, was not physically handicapped. He could whistle like the thrush and the blackbird and he could perform the whole of the farmhand's toil curricula with meticulous conscientiousness and enviable ease. His edged tools were like razors. Not a speck of rust could be found on his fork, spade and shovel. Nightly, they would be wrapped and oiled, like puny children by anxious parents. If one troubled to examine a hedge or ditch which Barny had trimmed, one found the cleanest of cuts on every severed twig and blade of grass. He should have been a surgeon!

With Frank (Poddy) Coote, one always associated noise. At 4 a.m. he would awaken every occupant of the terraced cottages by boot thumping on his bedroom floor, in his curse-accompanied endeavours to get the unyielding leather over his size 15 feet. He was forever singing hymns. He had rote learned every hymn in Ancient and Modern and every psalm in the Psalter, together with alternative tunes and chants. Given an opening line or a whistled bar, he would sing the whole in a peace-shattering, bastard tenor, for beer or bets.

He was never the same after his holiday, one weeknd. For weeks afterwards he wore a strained, pained look. He ceased to sing. The following spring, dressed in new corduroys, with polished straps and buckles below his knee, he made a blushing valedictory confession . . .

'It were on that 'oliday! I met a young gel on the sands. She axed me an' offered me. I were willin' an' we did! Now I be a-going to her fer good!' Singing 'All Things Bright and Beautiful', Poddy strode manfully to Bartlow Station to be steam propelled to the seaside and romance.

THESE were the men who, with others, feasted in The Bonnet, where the harvesters would gather for the Horkey, a ceremony of thanksgiving for a successful harvest. Major Luddington usually gave £5, the tenant farmer £2, and the remainder came from pay-point collections, for weeks in advance.

Horkey day would see Steventon's End in turmoil. Apple-cheeked women would scurry from their homes with baskets laden with cooked meats, hams, pickles, home-baked bread and cheese. Each would vie with the other to produce the best-looking and most palatable cakes and pastries and jams. That old tap-room became a riot of colour and perfume. Bowls of roses, vases of mixed flowers and especially sprays of sweet peas and asparagus fern would decorate the snowy linen. Upon the walls hung pumpkins, marrows and scrubbed potatoes. The pods of peas and beans were pregnant to bursting point, and cabbages and cauliflowers were as round and solid as Cromwellian cannon balls. There were parsnips and pears, carnations and carrots, radishes and roses, and strings of mighty onions, each half the size of a boy's head. Toe-Rag's handicraft was evident in the skilfully plaited cottage loaves, in straw of wheat and oat.

All would be ready and awaiting the harvesters by 7 p.m.

On my last Horkey I was leading the wagonhorses in the field of Woodshot. Most of the harvesters were bragging, Poddy Coote particularly, of the quarts of ale and the plates of beef they intended to 'put away' that evening. Generally, there was an air of excitement and expectancy which increased in intensity as the shocks of corn dwindled in that last field to be harvested. Climax came when Tom Symonds pitched the last sheaf to the loader. Bronzed and sweating, naked from the waist up, Tom looked like some Harvest God.

'Unhook Captain! Take the Horkey Bough!' Toe-Rag gave the ritual orders. Tom uncoupled the traces from the chestnut gelding and replaced them with a rope, whose free end he looped over a branch of a nearby oak. He made a running bight and nodded to the horse keeper.

'Up, Captain!' The massive Clydesdale dug in his hooves and heaved. There came a mighty cracking and swishing as the limb was slivered from the bole. Our cheers rang out. The Horkey Bough had been 'taken'. It was hoisted to the top of the last load and our mugs were filled with strong ale, to drink two toasts; one to the last sheaf, one to the Horkey Bough.

Slowly and majestically the steel-clad wagonwheels rolled farmwards. With wheat ears and oak leaves in their caps, and pitchforks and jackets over their shoulders, the labourers followed. Harvest was over.

AFTER a washing and dressing in Sunday best, the harvesters gathered in conversational groups outside The Bonnet; waiting to take their appointed places at the feast table. Traditionally, Toe-Rag was last to his place. So soon as he sat he rose again and all rose with him. The old horse keeper looked mighty awkward in blue serge. His weather-stained face and rich, gingery whiskers looked grubby against the white points of his starched wing-collar. But when his golden tenor led his fellows in the singing of that immortal hymn, awkwardness was of little account; for here were humble men, giving thanks for rewarded labour.

'Come, ye thankful people, come.
Raise the song of harvest-home;
All is safely gathered in,
Ere the wintry storms begin;
God, our maker, doth provide,
For our wants to be supplied;
Come to God's own temple, come;
Raise the song of harvest-home . . . '

Each word of every verse was sung by all present without reference to printed words, for there were none. No one would suggest that The Bonnet was God's own temple but there was not a man present who was not deeply conscious of the significance of those words. The annual miracles of sowing and reaping were part and parcel of their hard-working lives.

'You can say Grace, boy' said Toe-Rag, looking at me. But I could not. My emotional reaction to that honest singing had erased the simple words from my recollection. Slowly and clearly, as at each of our meals, my father said the words for me. 'For what we are about to receive, may the Lord make us thankful.'

The gruff, communal Amen was followed by chair-leg scrapings on the bricked floor. Conversation, good-humoured badinage and laughter swelled. Aproned women flitted with meat-laden dishes and foaming, frothing jugs.

The feast was on!

After an hour and a bit of eating and drinking, Toe-Rag started the round of individual singing with a song I had not heard before, nor have I heard it since; but I recall the swinging of his heavy gold chain and Alberts as the singer swayed to the lilt of his song:

'Ring-ting, is how the bell goes;
Ring-ting, you pretty young thing.
If you'll be my wife,
I'll buy the ring;
We'll have servants to wait
On our ring-ting-ting.'

In turn, everyone rose and made some contribution - until it came to Wuddy Smith who, beer-wobbly and salivating, was silent. 'Come on, Wuddy, boy!' bellowed Poddy Coote, 'Sing, you old varmint, sing!'

Wuddy was no nightingale but, with his hiccup-punctuated rendering, he brought that house near to hysteria;

'Eggs 'n . . . hic . . . bacon,
Eggs 'n . . . hic . . . bacon;
If y'think I'm gonna . . . hic . . . sing a song,
Ye're bloody . . . hic . . . well mistaken.'

The clock hands stood at well past midnight when the landlord shouted: 'The copper's about folks. He's had a coupla quarts but he's gettin' sarky. Best be gettin' to our beds!'

Toe-Rag banged his pewter ploughing-match prize on the oak table. 'Afore we goes, m'lads, we'll sing the evening hymn. Softly, now!'

And softly and reverently it was:

'The day Thou gavest, Lord, is ended.
The darkness falls, at Thy behest.
To Thee, our morning hymns ascended.
Thy praise shall sanctify our rest.'

I walked through the open door with wet eyes. Listening to that hymn stealing softly through the night, over the fertile fields of my village, I recalled the words of a Persian . . . . 'One glimpse of it within the tavern caught . . . . ' and I was certain that The Bonnet could lay some claim to being God's own temple, after all.

Memories of an Old Farm Kitchen

Gladys V. Nunn (c1954)

ALTHOUGH always spoken of as 'the kitchen' it was really two large rooms connected by a long brick passage running the length of the dairy.

The old grandfather clock stood in the front kitchen and there, also, was the high dresser with its piles of plated dishes and cups and mugs hanging on hooks. We often had meals in this room and in winter passed many a happy evening with our pets on the rag rug in front of the stove.

But it was in the back kitchen that all the exciting things happened. It was a wonderful place. It contained three coppers, a brick oven, a large sink with a pump over it; while a shelf on the wall was the home of the lamps.

The pump supplied all our water. It must have been fed from a good well, for in spite of dairy work, brewing and washing, it never to my knowledge ran dry.

The floor of the kitchen was of brick. The ceiling covered only two-thirds of the room. Then came an empty space reaching up to the roof. Its purpose was to carry off steam from the coppers.

I can remember seeing fleeces of wool from father's flock lying on the brick floor ready to be sown into sacks and sent to Scotland to return later in the form of lovely warm blankets, cloth for suits and serge for our frocks. Our children at school had new clothes. Ours never wore out but were handed down from one to another. Those blankets woven in the 1890s are still in use (1954), with many more years of wear in them.

One copper was always kept going. In it the dairy things were boiled each day. Another copper was reserved for boiling the washing. Alternate Mondays two women came from the cottages and did the whole wash. They started about eight and had a break for tea and cake at ten. They had a good dinner at noon, finished work about three - and for their work received one shilling cach.

The ironing was done by the maids, helped by mother. In turn as we grew old enough we also helped. I can still recall the awful moment when the white-hot 'heater' was lifted from the fire and popped into the box-iron. A second heater was put in the fire to get hot while the first was being used.

FRIDAY was baking day. A batch of bread to last us the week was baked in the brick oven. The dough was made with skim milk and brewer's yeast.

Two faggots of wood were thrown on the floor in front of the oven and while the bread was rising the oven was heated. It took all the wood from two faggots to bring the walls of the oven to the desired glow. It was a big oven and usually twelve or more loaves were stood round the walls. The centre was filled up with pies and cakes and the front of the oven covered with buns made up from the dough. Of course we also made Suffolk rusks, which were taken out, split open and put back to dry.

Butter was made every week and the dairy man also did the brewing of the beer. I can still recall the smell of the malt and hops. The warm beer waiting to be carried in pails to the cellar had a very heady fragrance.

Mother made several kinds of wine and stored it in stone jars. She also preserved fruit, putting it in earthenware jars and then pouring boiling mutton-fat on the top to seal it up. Brown paper was then tied over it.

'Putting a pig away' involved about two days of really hard work. Hams and sides of bacon were rubbed with salt, later put in pickle and finally sent to the bakery to be dried or cured.

All the fat was cut into cubes and boiled down for lard. It was not unusual for two or three earthenware jars each containing about two gallons of fluid lard to be left to cool and then turned upside down on the dairy shelf till needed for use.

Pork pies were made with new lard that had never cooled. The larder would be filled to overflowing with strings of sausages and basins of brawn, which we called pork cheese.

Some of the pork went into the pork tub, to lie in salt till required for use.

ON Friday evening all the men employed on the farm came into the kitchen to receive their wages. Father always brought home £5 from the bank for this purpose. There were usually about eight men, their pay ranging from 10 to 16 shillings per week.

Straw was put on the brick floor to collect the mud from their boots.

Things have changed a lot since those days, many for the better. But from a child's point of view the old kitchen was a grand place to grow up in.

Naturally things did not always run smoothly. There were days when in spite of the most vigorous churning the butter would not 'come.' My grandmother's remedy was to put a hot poker in the bung hole, to drive 'somebody' out. Mother used hot water. I fancy it was a matter of temperament on the part of the cream.

There were times, too, when the bread rose before the oven was ready and had to be kneaded all over again.

As I remember it all, there was never a dull moment. Something was always happening in 'the kitchen.'

The Horse and the Plough

Hugh Barrett (c1955)

WHEN I was a lad - during the early 1930s - I was a pupil on a 1,000 acre estate in East Suffolk. There were three farms of poorish light land not far from the sea, worked as one unit. There was a herd of cows, a flock of Suffolk sheep, pigs, poultry, ducks and, above all, horses. Horses were the beginning and end of all cultivations, the fetchers and carriers as well. It was horse-ploughing, horse-harrowing, drilling, rolling, mowing, harvesting and carting. True, there was a tractor. But no-one really believed for a minute that it could do any work as well as the horse.

Nowadays when harvest is over and the mornings get darker, the machine which generates electricity for the house and buildings starts, and the cow-sheds and barns and workshops are bright. The tractors start, one after the other, spluttering and banging and then moving off to the fields, some with lights so they can start early and work long after dark has fallen again. The predominating sound is that of engines, and the smell of exhaust gases and oils penetrates even to the cowshed, overlaying the sweetness of hay, milk and cows' breath.

How different from the days only 20 odd years ago. I remember on that farm in East Suffolk being called each morning at half-past five, wet or fine, drinking hot tea in the candle-lit kitchen, throwing off the heaviness of sleep and then out and across the dark yard to the stables where the head and second horsemen had been at work for half an hour or more, feeding and grooming the fourteen Suffolk Punches. A hurricane lamp hanging by the door gave just enough yellow light to see the harness with a glint of gold from the brasses. The hindquarters of the horses shone softly, round and enormous. And what wonderful smells. Warm horses, oats, straw, meadow hay and shag tobacco - the last quite forbidden but equally inevitable.

Each man had his own pair. George Walker, the head horseman, had Boxer and Bowler. The second horseman, George's brother Willy, had Matchett and Diamond. Prince and Duke, Captain and Little Boxer, Major and Ruby were all

'Horses were the beginning and end of all cultivations' Photo: John Tarlton AIBP. ARPS.

worked by us as plain horsemen. The rest of the names I do not remember. But there was probably yet another Boxer and Ruby, for these were the most popular names at that time on almost every Suffolk farm. We did have a Ginger, but this name was rather contemptuously given to a rough old horse bought at market and not bred on the farm like the other horses.

WE each harnessed our own pair. For plough-ing, the collar with wooden hames first, leather top lash, then the bridle, or dutfin as it was called, and finally the back strap and plough-chains. The long plough-lines were coiled and hung, along with dinner bag and top-coats, on the hames and as six o'clock struck the head horseman would lead his team out of the stable and across the strawed yard into the lane leading to the fields. The rule that the head horseman was first out of the stable and first into the field was as rigid as any Queen's Regulation and there was sure to be some hard swearing and ill-feeling if any understrapping allowed his pair to jostle past. Six o'clock . . . cold, dark and windy. We walk close to the shoulder of the nearside horse, sheltering behind his bulk; no need to hold the rein. Fifty-six iron-shod hooves and fourteen nailed boots ring on the road and sometimes little sparks, vivid in the darkness, are kicked up from the metal.

There is a tremendous feeling of companion-ship with horses and men. No one speaks much until the field is reached and the line is broken, each man going to his own plough waiting cold-handled for him. Then there are calls of 'back Major, back man', 'weurdy Boxer - hoed up and git over'. All horse talk is pleasant - 'jistep Ruby', meaning she is required to move one step only. I can hear the 'cupiwi' which is 'come to me', the 'weurdy' and the 'steady-man' just as clearly now as on those dark mornings years ago.

The chains on the hames on the collars would be hooked through the eyes on the whipple-trees, the whipple-trees hooked to the pummeltry and the pummeltry to the hake or catshead of the plough. Perhaps it would be so dark that plough-ing could not start at once and, leaving the horses on the headland, we would sit smoking under the hedge, listening to the peewits until the first glimmers of light allowed us no further excuse for sitting.

THE sounds of horse-ploughing are lovely . . . earth shearing from the plough-breast, the squeak of unoiled wheel, creak of leather and the taut jangle of chains. The horses grunt as they take the weight and pull and the ploughmen whistle and talk to them as they walk up and down, up and down. We would go from six to 10 o'clock and then break for bait. The horses would stand facing into the field while the men sat under the hedge eating bread and cheese or a bit of cold meat and drinking cold sweet tea from a bottle. We would talk and gossip about local affairs, the older men of gardens and fields and the young men of girls - often using the Chaucerian word, mawthers. Silly mawthers they seemed to be mostly. By modern standards the talk would seem very limited. Football would rarely be mentioned, films never. We spoke of what we had seen and knew about - crops and stock, beer and horses and the occasional iniquities of the master.

In about half an hour the head horseman would pull out his 'tunnup', solemnly consult it, knock out his pipe and we would follow him back to the plough. On that light land each man's stint for the day would be one acre and this would be finished by about half past two or three o'clock in the afternoon without further breaks, except for breathers at the end of the field. Then we would unhook the chains from the whippletrees and loop them on the hame-hooks, coil the plough-lines and hang them with coats and bags on the hames and set off - riding now - for the stables, leaving the ploughs in the last furrows.

It was good to see the fresh-turned earth, and the ploughs, like sea-birds at rest - not inanimate iron but just at rest. It was good, all of it - the smells, the sounds, the wearying walking up and down the furrows day after day, week after week, it was good. And although I am now farming without a single horse and growing more than would be economically possible using only horses, the work does not seem so rich and satisfying as it was. We lost some of the flavour, some kindness, when the last horse went away.

A Miller Remembers

C. E. Woodrow (c1951)

Billingford Mill - still standing today.

IN days like these when the windmills of Norfolk are few in numbers and those that remain are in peril of decay, it may not be considered out of place for me to record a few reminiscences. I am now eighty years old but have an ineffaceable memory of windmill life, having worked in no fewer than five mills, at different times. I have known tower mills, post mills and water mills - as well as those of later construction.

My father was a life-long miller of the old school. He could prepare the stones used for wheat grinding, a real craftsman's job. And he could produce a sack of flour that the housekeeper of those days welcomed, flour that made appetising bread and built healthy bodies.

The millers who worked those old mills were personalities. They were men of many parts, speaking a language of their own. Fifty years ago in Norwich Corn Exchange I used to hear them speak of their experiences, of slow winds, gales, stocks and sails, of French burr and peak stones, of bolting machines, of steel bills for putting fine cracks in wheat stones. They were mechanically minded, those old millers, capable, industrious, independent men who loved their craft and successfully met the demands of their age.

When my father began business on his own account, he took over the windmill at Billingford, near Diss. Though not large, it was one of the prettiest mills ever built. Cleverly designed, constructed by craftsmen, it was a joy to behold. Into this mill I was carried when I was one year old. Later, when near the age of twelve, I had to work in this same mill. Sometimes I would sit in the cap and listen to the sails going round. There is music and poetry in the wind. It speaks a language of its own, sometimes friendly, sometimes fierce and disturbing.

Few things can be more inspiring than to mount the highest stairs to look out at midnight upon the sweeping sails, to hear the music of the wind in their movements.

And few experiences are more fearful than to be in a windmill on a wild night with only a candle to lighten the darkness and imagination calls grotesque figures to stand out in all shapes and forms upon the walls. Such memories are unforgettable.

FOLLOWING these early experiences at Billingford Mill I worked in similar mills at Scole, Felthorpe, Costessey, Horsford and, later in life, in Peafield Mill, Lakenham.

Horsford Mill was small and needed many repairs, most of which were done by my father and myself. On one occasion we had to take the sails down and I was deputed to remove the last bolt which released the structure from the main timbers. Cat-like I had to cling and was then lowered to the ground with the sail itself.

Night work was a necessary part of the miller's life. Once when I was working the mill all alone, suddenly, without apparent reason, the mill began to stop. It was past midnight and there was a good breeze blowing outside. Fearful that something dreadful had happened, I opened the outside door. There was my father. He had wanted to relieve me and send me to a warm bed. His only way to reach me behind the twirling sails had been to use outside means to stop the mill.

Water power had greater regularity and reliability than wind, as my experience at Costessy Mill showed. That mill developed some 40 to 60 horse power and until the roller process superseded the stone mills, they made hundreds of sacks of flour every week. At one time at Costessey there stood upon the hills above the village a postmill, but this has long since been forgotten.

My love of these mills led me 40 years ago to buy Peafield Mill, a tower mill, at Lakenham. Owners of all such mills were faced with the problem of repairs, for the craftsmen who could do them grew fewer every year.

For the mill at Lakenham I had to call upon the only millwright I knew, Tom Brown, a most capable craftsman.

It was no easy task for him to climb sailor-like, the lofty sails, for he weighed sixteen stone.

And when he asked me to follow him, walking along a plank passed through a window in the tower and across the sail itself, I had a troublesome palpitation within.

The tower of this mill now appears to stand bleak and purposeless, just a relic of an interesting past. To me it is identified with imperishable associations.

Travel

White Roads

M. Janet Becker (c1947)

I FIRST saw Suffolk nearly forty years ago and today it is the ghost of a white road that road that leads my memory back through the happy years.

Roads, white as trickles of milk spilled in grass, were then the natural adjuncts to winding hedges, taller than a man, cascading in season hawthorn, wild roses and brambles, hops and Old Man's beard.

In the fields one often saw groups of women and children and old men, each with a round basket made of withies, known as a bushel skep. As they traversed the bare fields with bent backs, one thought of them as the virtual descendants of gleaners, though theirs was a more meagre harvest, for they were gathering stones.

Every year before ploughing the farmers enlisted their help. It was the necessity for this annual stone-picking that led to the belief hereabouts that "stones grow."

"See my fild," said one farmer. "I plough it in t' spring and there int a stun to be seen. And then after harvest there they are agin - little 'uns and big 'uns, all growed in with the wheat."

The pickers carried their filled skeps to the roadside and deposited the stones in neat mounds on the verge.

By and by would come the road mender, John Jacobs, and he would sit down and break the flints in pieces, casting them by the barrowful on to the crown of the road, there to be ground to brittle dust by the wheels of iron-shod wagons and the hooves of horses.

John wore a black wide-awake, and a Newgate fringe. He was old when I first knew him. He could remember, when he worked as a 10-year-old houseboy at the big farm down the road, that the children of the farmer drank beer because milk was considered unwholesome, and that everything was scrubbed so clean and white you could have "eaten off the floor."

And, sixty five years afterwards, he was sitting outside the house breaking stones and I was on my way through the June mid-day to a music lesson. He called me over to him, and parted the ferns and catstail grass beside him. There lay a little posy of wild roses for me, with all the thorns carefully cut off.

When he was dying at the age of nearly ninety, I went to see him in the cottage where he and his wife lived. Everything in the little room seemed prepared for the gentle angel of death - the walls freshly whitewashed, the counterpane spotless, and his wrinkled hands, so often cut and blood-stained by the stones, now washed and idle.

Out of the window, I saw the tops of the bushes heavy with guelder roses and lilac, while a white road stretched away up the village street, waiting to take him on his last journey to the churchyard.

THE first road I remember in Suffolk led past a cottage garden where gooseberry bushes stood weighed to the ground with ripe fruit. A woman was moving about amongst them, and my mother asked to buy some. The woman filled a paper bag for us, and handed it over the hedge.

"I must go in now," she said; "I'm nursing my five children with scarlet fever."

Another road was fraught with fascination for me because down it every day punctually at six o'clock, blowing an enormous whistle, came the postman to clear the letter box by a distant church.

People ran to their garden gates and held out their letters to him as he passed on, still blowing blasts on the whistle.

I once heard someone say that he did nothing else, meaning that the clearing of that box was his sole duty, but I interpreted it as meaning he did nothing but walk round the world (as I thought) clearing letter boxes, and, punctual as the sunset, he was back again next evening to clear the one by the church. I worried about him never being able to stop, never able sit down and rest. In the late summer, I told myself, he could eat blackberries as he went along, but what did he live on at other seasons of the year?

In time I discovered he was the shoemaker in the next village, and walked a bare two miles! He was a deflated figure, but the road through the water meadows was still beautiful.

ON my earliest walks in Suffolk lanes I was accompanied by Gladys who, by reason of her sweet nature and country birth, was the best nurse-maid for an enquiring London child. In fact, it was upon these walks that she sowed the seeds of my interest in the love of country lore. Every field and path had its strange name, its local ghosts; every flower its nickname or herbal property; every person we met or happpening we encountered added a new fact to my store.

When we saw a funeral procession she gently turned me round to stand facing the way the cortege was going. It would never do to let a coffin pass one by.

If we saw a wedding party we must recall the day of the week to see what thing the bride prized most, for it was:

Monday for health,
Tuesday for wealth,
Wednesday best day of all;
Thursday for losses,
Friday for crosses,
Saturday no luck at all.

One stretch of the road was haunted by an animal called Dyball's Calf. It would come padding along after the late roamer, and then turn into a field near the school. Asked once why a calf should haunt a road, Gladys said one that had been born "wrong" had been buried in the roadway long long ago. Years afterwards in a volume of *Notes and Queries* (or a similar publication) I came across an account of the Saxon custom of burying abortive calves near cattle tracks to ward off evil spirits from the herd.

Then there was Peggy's Path, with a high stile between the road and the field, through which it led. Peggy had hung herself there for love of a sailor.

There was Barnaby Lane, called after St. Bartholomew's Chapel that once stood in a field belonging to the Church of St. Bartholomew the Great, Smithfield - and the Cunifus and Hewlands, two oak-fringed fields, and there was above, above all, The Run.

To extract the most enjoyment out of a visit to this stream across the road, one had to be standing on the footbridge at 4 o'clock. One would hear, faintly at first, then nearer, the clankity-clank and cloppity-clop of a string of farm horses coming down to drink before baiting time. Their harness was loose upon their shiny, sweating bodies.

They moved slackly down the dusty road that dipped to the cool wet sandy margin of the stream.

Shadows of the tall elms came creeping across the meadow. With one accord the horses would wheel, and, refreshed, clop back to the farm.

NOW there are no white roads - they are uniformly tarred; no stream across the road - the County Council has attended to that; no primeval elms - the farmer cut them down last winter; no horses - he uses a tractor.

A Trip by Carrier's Cart

A. W. Osborne (c1957)

WHEN I was a boy the villagers of Denham End travelled on foot for the most part. But on market days they could go to Bury St Edmunds, six miles away, by the 'carrier's cart'. This time-honoured vehicle is worthy of description since it is probably a museum piece by now or long since designated to the junk heap. It was really a high, four-wheeled carriage with a seat on either side running from back to front over the wheels. The passengers climbed in by three steps through a little door at the back, sometimes assisted by a boost from the driver. Once on board they sat on hard, straight-backed seats facing one-another with their knees almost touching. It had no top of any kind and, when it rained, the passengers huddled together under huge carriage umbrellas.

It all seems so primitive now. But in those days a trip on the carrier's cart was something for a small boy to look forward to for days on end. Sometimes there would be a seat for me, but more often I had to stand by my mother's knee, with a neighbour's market basket sticking into my tender ribs. It was a thrilling day when the carrier looked back over his shoulder and said:

'Hullo, me owd boy, you don't fare ter have much room back there with all them mawthers. You better git up here with me.'

Just to sit on the driver's box was thrill enough. But when the good-natured carrier put the reins and the whip into my hands, my happiness knew no bounds.

'There y'are, bor. Don't yew let that hoss run away with us.'

There was no cause for alarm. Neither the uncertain tugs at the reins nor the gentle strokes of the whip could turn old Prince to left or right or shake him out of his jog-trot gait. He was a creature of character as well as of custom. He knew exactly where to lay into the collar and when to settle back into the breechings. He would slow down when he saw a woman in her 'Sunday best' standing by the cottage gate with a market basket on her arm. I fancy he shook his head at the next passenger if the collective weight seemed excessive. He could thread his way through the traffic on Risbygate Street and turn in under the narrow archway leading to the Bell Inn with but little help from the driver.

TO give the women ample time for their shopping, the carrier's cart left at five o'clock and, like time and tide, waited for no man. My mother would collect her parcels and her market basket from the waiting-room and her son from the stables where he had gone to see the ostler harness the horse. Then she would climb into the carriage, make for the seat behind the driver, stow away her parcels and settle herself comfortably to await the appointed hour. And so with the other women, passing the time away by discussing bargains, each one seeking to out-do the other. As the hour drew near the horse was led from the stable, his iron-shod hoofs striking sparks from the cobble stones. The passengers would look up at the clock over the inner archway and say: 'I dew wish he would hurry up.'

On the stroke of five the carrier would come from the bar, wiping a trace of froth from his moustache with the back of his hand, and climb up on to the box. Then he would look back at the passengers and say:

'Now then, are y'all there, together. Time to be drawin' along. Giddup, Prince.'

And so, with a flip on the reins and a flick of the whip, we were homeward bound.

There was little traffic on the roads in those days - sometimes a farm cart or a flock of sheep or a herd of cows or a stray cyclist on a 'boneshaker'.

And once we met a new contraption called a motor-car, greatly to the consternation of our driver who settled his battered bowler more firmly on his head as the car swept towards us at the reckless speed of possibly 20 miles an hour. Prince came the nearest he ever came to shying and our driver expressed the views of all his passengers as he squirted a stream of 'bacca juice after the offending vehicle as it vanished down the narrow road.

It was a delightful drive in summer. The winding road kept to the higher ground wherever possible, affording a pleasant view of the once swampy valley it skirted. Down there a stream glistened like a silver thread. Cows fed knee-deep in lush green grass shot through with the white of daisies and the gold of buttercups. Across the valley, the brown and green and yellow of fallow, root and corn fields swept away to mingle with the deeper hues of distant woods, with one of 'the stately homes of old England' showing through. Through the sleepy village of Little Saxham we went - the ancient, round-towered church crowning the wooded hill - across Fiddler's Green and up Barrow Hill where an ancient windmill beat the air with flailing arms. It will probably have changed beyond recognition by now.

If the day was dull and short, as in the winter, dusk soon fell and the way home was shrouded in darkness made even darker by the flickering light of the candles in the carriage lamps, which cast a fitful light into the shadowy hedges. The horse had no need of the lights. Neither wind nor rain nor darkness could turn him aside. There were times when even the driver seemed superfluous. He was blinded by the darkness and sometimes the swaying of the carriage made him sleepy. He would wrap the reins round the lamp-bracket and give old Prince his head, knowing that he would not pass the sign of the 'Weeping Willow' on Barrow Green.

Here we collected our parcels, paid our fare and crossed the green to reach our home, tired and hungry but well content. To the younger members of the family we were objects of envy. We had made a long and exciting journey in the carrier's cart.

The Carrier's Cart and the First Motor Bus

Mary Durham (c1954)

THERE were two carriers' carts which made the journey from Shotley to Ipswich - a distance of about 9 miles - in those days before the tooting of horns and screeching of brakes on motor vehicles had begun to assault our ears. Except for Tuesdays (market day in Ipswich) when both vans were needed to cope with the demand for their services, they ran on alternate days and I well remember how my mother would sometimes decree of an evening: 'We must put the brick on the drive gate tonight: I want the carrier to bring some fish for supper tomorrow.'

We lived in the rectory, where a long forked drive led from the road to the house, one arm running to the front, the other to the back door. The brick on the drive gate signalled to one carrier that we desired him to call. The sign for his competitor was a bough.

The carriers were truly ubiquitous people. In their quaint hooded boxes on wheels they would convey passengers and parcels of all descriptions and call for shopping orders to be delivered on their homeward journey. With the innumerable stops on the road the journey took several hours and one shudders to think how the modern speed merchant would react to the tedium, to say nothing of the jolts and jerks of the unsprung vehicle.

There was one thing which sharply differentiated our two knights of the road in my childish mind. One owned only one horse. The other was the proud possessor of a pair. I felt very sorry for the lone horse and hoped if we had a parcel of substantial weight to be collected that the mission would fall on the day the two-horse van made the trip. Indeed I pitied all the horses and liked to think that the frequent waits on the road and the long rest in Ipswich, where they were well fed and comfortably stabled, prevented them from becoming too exhausted.

But perhaps the passengers were no less stoical than the horses, as they huddled together on their unyielding wooden seats, chilled to the bone in winter and almost suffocated in summer. And unlike the horses they had to make good use of their time in Ipswich, visiting relatives in hospital, shopping for the household or transacting whatever business had taken them to the market town. However, they were patient folk, these villagers, and looked on the waiting and discomfort as the inevitable accompaniments of a day's outing. I wonder what they would have said if some prophet had told them that within half a century machines would be tearing through the sky, covering the distance from Shotley to Ipswich in as many seconds as the carrier's cart took hours. I think they would merely have dismissed the notion with an incredulous and slightly contemptuous shake of the head.

ALTHOUGH it was sometimes my task to hoist the brick on the gatepost or to stick the bough into the adjacent fence so that it seemed to point a beckoning finger towards the road, I never made the journey to Ipswich myself in the carrier's van. This was because when we were children my father possessed an ancient four-wheeled pony-chaise in which we drove to the town from time

to time. There is something eminently safe-sounding about the term four-wheeled chaise. One is apt to think of it as a symbol of security in contrast with the dashing, dangerous dog-cart so popular at the time with the local farmers. Surely, one says, a vehicle with four wheels cannot over-turn, nor if the pony pulls up suddenly can you be thrown over its head. True as this is, there are other hazards as experience was to prove. On one occasion our elderly gardener was driving my parents and my sister to Ipswich. In descending one of the Freston hills the coach-work gave way in the middle and the chaise was divided into two parts. With a sharp kick the frightened pony broke his traces and careered off down the hill. The old gardener, with true Suffolk tenacity, clung stoutly to the reins and was carried away with the pony, ending up on a heap of stones by the road-side, on which he cut his head severely. When I was told of this act of heroism my eyes filled with tears and I forgave him the surliness with which he was wont to refuse many of our childish requests for favours.

The two-horse carrier's cart pauses at the 'Ostrich' before completing the journey to Shotley.

'I ain't a-gonner do it.' he would say and, in modern parlance, that was that. One might as well have tried to shift the rock of Gibralter as to persuade him to change his mind.

On an earlier occasion, before his marriage, my father was driving one of the pony's predecessors when the animal lay down in the road. Absently he jerked the reins and called: 'get up, pony.' An old labourer plying his sickle by the wayside came up and surveyed the scene morosely. 'Ain't no use a-saying that, sir.' he declared. 'That there pony 'ont never git up, that 'ont.'

And he was right. The poor pony had died in harness.

Another less melancholy story also concerns my father. He was driving the chaise along the Ipswich road, intending to turn left when he came to the turning to Harkstead and Holbrook. However, so engrossed was he in his thoughts that he omitted to pull the rein and the pony jogged steadily along the more familiar route until he reached the outskirts of Ipswich when the mistake was discovered and the ground retraced.

OUR four-wheeled vehicle had, moreover, certain disadvantages as compared to the dog-cart. The roads in summer were white with a thick layer of dust and, being so near the ground, the occupants had to cover themselves with light carriage rugs to act as dust-sheets in order to protect their clothes from ruin. In bad weather splashing through puddles would have been equally unpleasant but for the protection of a waterproof rug.

This conveyance was also useful for driving my father about his scattered parish. The church, that big, gaunt, towerless building which gave rise to the old legend:

Shotley church without a steeple,
Drunken parson, wicked people.

was a mile away from the rectory, while Shotley Gate, at the river end of the village (or rather the rivers' end, for this is where Orwell and Stour meet on their journey to the sea) was over two miles from our house. And talking of Shotley Gate, I can just remember picking blackberries on the hill where the Royal Naval Barracks now stand (1954). But even in early childhood the truth that 'the old order changeth' was brought home to me. Far away in Whitehall an idea was born in someone's brain which altered the course of our local history. Soon the wasteland was cleared and building operations began as the result of the decision to train Britain's future bluejackets ashore instead

'Much excitement was caused among the people of Shotley by the inauguration of a motor-bus service between Shotley Gate and Ipswich station'.

of afloat.

Some years before the First World War much excitement was caused among the people of Shotley by the inauguration of a motor-bus service between Shotley Gate and Ipswich station. I recall how my sister and I got up early one morning in order to ride on the bus on its first trip. It was an open-topped double-decker bus and it ran three times a day to connect with the chief London trains.

However, the old carrier's cart was by no means superseded. It was still essential for supplementary shopping, for a bus conductor will not buy your fish and other sundries and deliver them at your door. And it still carried its quota of passengers, for many villagers preferred to stick to the old familiar mode of transport. The van might be slow but it was sure. It never broke down as the bus was often known to do in those early days, once to the alarm of the passengers half-way up the very same Freston hill which had proved the Waterloo of our pony chaise. There were several accidents, too, though fortunately none with serious consequences. One is particularly vivid in my memory, for I was on my way to Ipswich for a singing lesson and was sitting by the driver - a permissive and much coveted position at that time - when the wheel struck one of the boulders which marked the unraised footpath, jerking the steering-wheel out of the driver's hands. The bus lurched and then plunged through a brick wall into a cottage garden. I descended from my perch to find my father, who was inside the bus, supervising the evacuation of the passengers in an orderly manner - women and children first. Such incidents did not encourage confidence in the minds of those accustomed to the steady jog-trot of the carriers' horses. They served to foster and prolong the belief that the old ways were best and that nothing newfangled was without peril.

During the 1914-18 war, the buses were super-seded on account of the need for petrol economy, and then the horse-drawn carriers' carts, once more the only means of transport for the village population, came into their own again.

Travel when I was Young

D. A. Chillingworth (c1958)

'MO-TOR, pip-pip!!!' - this was the cry, usually starting as a solo and developing into a chorus, that sent everyone in the village hurrying for a safe point of vantage at the dusty roadside to see, and hear, and smell, the only automobile in the district hurtle to the station, four miles away. It was a red monster, gleaming with brass, breathing black smoke and occasional red sparks. The sight of it with its be-goggled occupants was deliciously fearsome to us but just plain fearsome to the many horses it met or passed. This was when we were very young - over 50 years ago. Now the sound of horses' hooves might tempt us to look over the garden gate but as regards mechanical transport only the 50 ft long loads, preceded by a police car, bound for the Nuclear Station cause us any wonderment.

When we were children, journeys, except by train of course, were short by modern standards and were taken by horse and cart (and this covers a variety of vehicles), by bicycle (fixed wheel at first and very tricky), or, less frequently, by boat.

There were two regular carriers in our village, who went to the station each morning, taking passengers and packages for the train and bringing back consignments of grocery and drapery for the village shops. One of them actually drove to Chelmsford (23 miles) every Friday and he also had for hire a dog-cart, a large and small wagon-ette and a brougham. This brougham was in de-mand for weddings, funerals, and on one or two rare never-to-be-forgotten occasions, to convey us to the more distant Christmas party. We adored riding in any of them - the journey was never too long and I never remember feeling cold or get-ting wet, though it must have rained sometimes.

I suppose the big cart umbrella solved this prob-lem. I know it did on one occasion when we were invited to go for a day at The Stone, our favourite beach three or four miles away. Transport this time was by cattle-float, drawn by a sturdy horse. Never was there a wetter day, but our hostess, bless her, rather than disappoint us, tied the huge um-brella firmly over the float and we snuggled into the straw and loved every minute of what must have been a fuggy journey both ways. We spent the entire day in a shed instead of on the beach and I cannot remember at all what we did beyond eating but we returned full of enthusiasm for the trip.

An annual red-letter day was that spent on the sandy beach now occupied by the Nuclear site. Again the journey to and fro was the great attraction as we went, upwards of a score of us, grown-ups and children, in one of the farm wagons from the Hall. Trusses of hay or straw, I forget which, were neatly arranged as seats along each side, with one back to the driver on which the squire's wife sat with great dignity. We had a marvellous view into gardens, and even bedroom windows as we went along.

Another of the thrills of our childhood was having 'people to stay', not necessarily because we enjoyed their company, though of course some were special favourites, but chiefly because, if our behaviour warranted it, we were allowed to go to the station in the hired wagonette, dog-cart, or if necessary, even the precious brougham, to meet the visitors and in due course to take them away. Plenty of time was allowed for the journey, which suited us nicely, and there was, in addition, the excitement of seeing the signal go down at our single-line station and watching for the first puff of smoke which heralded the arrival of the train, which had stopped at five stations in less than twenty miles.

Our rather rare journeys by train, to Southend once or twice a year and to London even less often, were pure bliss. Everything was wonderful - the penny in the slot machines, (where else could you get Indian Pearls in a tin with a sliding lid?) the dusty plush seats in the carriages, with views of holiday resorts on the G.E.R. above, the rattle of milk cans so skilfully manipulated by the porters, the bridges we went over and under, the upping and downing of the telegraph wires, the roar of a passing train, the penny Books for the Bairns which we bought but seldom read until we got home again - everything.

Bicycles were not common but our parents were enthusiastic and encouraged us to learn to ride, realising, no doubt, that this would be the easiest and least expensive way of travelling. Once we had bicycles of our own our horizons widened appreciably. Maldon, Stow St Mary (for the Easter Monday Point-to-Point) and, much later, even Chelmsford were possible objectives. We became much more familiar with neighbouring villages than hitherto and, as 'errand-boys', much more useful members of society. The wonder now is how our tyres stood up as they did to the pre-tarmac roads, for punctures weren't too much of a menace. We even risked cycling to the station to catch a train, which made a day trip to London a cheap outing. At that time you could go there and back for 4/4d on any day by using the return half of a tourist ticket borrowed from an obliging neighbour, getting a return ticket home, and duly restoring the business half to its owner. I'm afraid it can't be done in these enlightened days, so if I haven't made the process clear it doesn't matter! We weren't exactly cheating the G.E.R. but the Comany never intended the tourist system to work that way.

In those far-off days people walked, for pleasure and to get to their work. Children tramped sturdily to school, some of them four miles and more. Footpaths were used regularly by farm workers as well as by holiday-walkers and it was quite usual for people to walk from the station, taking short cuts across fields. I can just remember a very long walk we took on a certain occasion, to a field on the brow of the only hill worth calling one in our flat district, to see one of the first flying machines. It seemed to be made of Venetian blinds and wire but we were not there at the supreme moment when it actually left the ground, cleared the hedge and came down in the next field - its first and last flight.

As regards travelling facilities we have indeed come far along the road called Progress in the first half of the century. Our remote villages are linked up in buses, supplies of all kinds are brought swiftly to our small shops, whence they are delivered at our door in smart vans. I am taken by friends to Chelmsford in just over half an hour in comfortable cars, heated if necessary, and probably fitted with wireless to relieve the tedium of the journey. The Queen Mother was in London yesterday at breakfast-time and in Vancouver this morning. Maybe it is just as well that Nature takes a hand from time to time, as was the case last winter when we awoke to two feet of snow and had, literally, to dig ourselves out. I then found that the only possible method of transport of essential supplies was a pair of sturdy gum-boots, with a pair of equally sturdy 61 year-old legs inside and a large strong basket on my arm. Perhaps things have not changed so much after all.

Memories of 'The Puffing Slug'

H. W. Turney (c1949), Illustrated by Slader Hoare

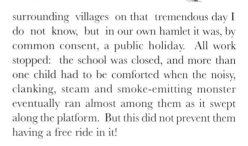

WHEN I am dressing I can see it from my bedroom window if I care to look. I get a glimpse of it between the trees as it crawls along. Its oval, brown, black-topped body and its small black head are quite a familiar sight as it curves along its way.

Little does it realise the way it regulates our village life - and has done for many years. For instance, since his Ingersoll stopped going some years ago, the dear old man who attends to my garden comes to work by it, goes home to dinner by it, and knocks off in the evening to its timing.

For nearly fifty years now it, or its prototype, with its black engine and two brown carriages, has puffed along the single-line track that runs through our village and unites us with the big outside world. And in that period it has exerted a telling influence over the life of the community it has served. So much so that it has become a daily part of our common existence. We always refer to it as "our" train and, in playful mood, have even been known to call it "our EXPRESS." But, on the whole, we prefer our own affectionate appellation of *The Puffing Slug*.

WHAT a stirring day it must have been when the first engine pulled the first coach along that new and glistening track, to the laying of which local labour from the various hamlets had contributed so much. It linked together for the first time little communities which hitherto had led a remote and isolated existence. What happened in the surrounding villages on that tremendous day I do not know, but in our own hamlet it was, by common consent, a public holiday. All work stopped: the school was closed, and more than one child had to be comforted when the noisy, clanking, steam and smoke-emitting monster eventually ran almost among them as it swept along the platform. But this did not prevent them having a free ride in it!

I LIKE the friendly, intimate atmosphere of our Puffing Slug. At the smaller stations and halts, including our own, there are no booking offices, and tickets are issued on the train by the guard who comes along the carriages for that purpose after each stop. Should he fail to appear, well, his guard's-van-cum-booking-office is always open, and we just stroll along and sit on some of the packages while he prepares our tickets, discussing meanwhile how Farmer Green's barley is looking this year and whether these "artificials," as the fertilizers are locally called, are really any good at all.

Since the line was opened we have had but few changes in guards, which speaks well for the friendship between us; for the guards soon come to realise that the train belongs to Us, and we it is who decide quite a lot of things: whether, for example, Mrs Smith's wheel-chair can be left in the corridor; or whether it is fair to charge Mrs Bain for a package which she only put in the guard's van because it was leaking.

There are, of course, some things which we cannot decide, and, indeed, some which even the guard himself apparently cannot dictate - the use of the engine, for instance. A few winters ago, coming home from Norwich, I boarded our train at the little market junction on a bitterly cold, blustering and snowy day, and sat for some time in my unheated carriage waiting for the train to start. Eventually, becoming nearly frozen, I opened the window and called along the platform to the guard, asking why we didn't start.

"We can't," he exclaimed wrathfully. "They've pinched me engine!"

It was only too true. The engine of a heavy sugar-beet train had, literally, failed to make the grade, and had stopped on the single-line track between us and the next station, and our engine had been sent down the line to help her.

YEARS ago the first and third class passengers travelled in the one compartment and were separated only by a curtain drawn across the carriage. One farmer of my acquaintance made a habit of getting in at the third-class end, buying a third-class ticket and then drawing back the curtain and seating himself in the first-class. Now-a-days there are properly separated compart-ments, but, shall I whisper it, even now when the train is full, on market days for example, the classes get very confused and even the guard, bless him, appears to consider separation impossible. But that, of course, we all understand, and on such occasions we ignore him as he ignores us.

Among the many itinerants who used the train in the bad old days was a quack dentist, always on the look-out for victims. It so happened on one journey that the guard, having a violent tooth-ache and not wishing to miss the return journey, was inveigled by this huckster into having his tooth drawn on the open station platform. It was raining and blowing, but this did not deter the dentist who sat the poor guard on a seat, himself kneeled on the guard, put up his forceps - and

pulled. There was a terrific shriek from the guard: "That's my tongue you've got!" To which he immediately received the rejoinder: "Then keep yer d--- tongue out of the way!" - and the tooth was drawn.

In the very hard winter of early 1947, after days of valiantly striving against the snow and ice, the train one dark night ran into a deep drift in the cutting about half-a-mile from our station. The train was thoroughly embedded and unable to extricate itself. The passengers disembarked and, with the help of hurricane lamps, were led, waist-deep in drifts, to the station, where they either got home a-horse or were put up for the night in the village. It was not until three days later, when most of the able-bodied men from the district had succeeded in digging a way for the assisting engine to get through, that the dear old Slug was able once again to crawl along its accustomed route.

Well, those days are past, and the old engine now bears in large, yellow letters the words BRITISH RAILWAYS. But that no more deceives us than do the names on the coaches, one of which has M. & G.N. all over it and the other G.E.R. They can put on whatever labels they like. It makes no difference. It is, and always will be, OUR train - the Puffing Slug.

The Wisbech Tram

Miriam Sykes (c1959)

THE Wisbech Steam Tram (there were actually two or more of them) ran a shuttle service between Wisbech and the villages of Upwell and Outwell, the track following the course of the canal and, for the most part, on the side of the road.

As a small child I loved the tram and it was a great but rare treat to be taken for a ride in it. The square, squat engine with cowcatcher, tiny chimney and clanging bell, the shining woodwork and polished seats running the entire length of the carriages, the jolly passengers and the merry crowds of footballers on Saturday afternoons - all had a great fascination for children, who used to gather in groups to watch the tram pass by.

When I was older and at school, it was my delight to run along during the lunch hour to see the tram come over the New Common Bridge, down the road and into the yard of the Great Eastern Railway Station, where it would come to rest by its own little platform.

Although children loved the tram, horses were often terrified of it and accidents were by no means uncommon. This was not really surprising. It looked a fearsome object as it came puffing noisily along with black smoke and flames pouring from its diminutive funnel. The driver would often stop and shut off steam if he saw anyone having difficulty in getting a horse past.

There were several terrible tragedies, including one where three ladies, leaving the town in their pony trap, met the train as it was crossing the road to enter the station. The driver rang his bell, as was his custom when about to cross over. This sent the pony into a panic and, spinning round, it overturned the trap, flinging the occupants to the ground. The youngest, an ex-school fellow of mine, was killed instantly, her mother was not much hurt, but the third lady was thrown in front of the tram, which passed over her.

The gallant lady, numbed at first and unaware of her injuries, joked with her rescuers as she was dragged from beneath the engine. She spent many weeks in Wisbech Hospital, where her courage and cheerfulness amazed the staff and patients alike.

The whole district was profoundly shocked. The town went into mourning, blinds were drawn and shop windows were shuttered and draped in crepe. There were meetings and discussions about abolishing the tram altogether.

But events of world wide import were taking place abroad and soon all else was to be forgotten in the onslaught of the First World War. Columns of khaki clad men tramped in hobnailed boots towards the coast, marching to a new song those boots inspired:

'You ought to be, you ought to be
In Kitchener's Army,
Seven bob a week
And all you like to eat
Great big boots make blisters on your feet.'

And the tram went quietly about its business, carrying many a service man home on leave. I left the district during the war and many years were to pass before I saw the tram again. Then, in 1935, I learnt that it was now being used for the transport of coal. Remembering its former glory I felt saddened when I came across it standing dirty and neglected in the coal yard, its windows boarded up and coal spilling from its open doors.

For more than another twenty years the tram continued its journeyings, laden with coal. Now it has gone, the track overgrown with weeds, the rails rusted. Only memories remain.

'The track followed the course of the canal and, for the most part, on the side of the road.'

Small Town Childhood

The Bonnet Maker, the Jam Jar Man, & the Bakehouse

Florence E. Burroughes (c1953)

NEARLY ninety years ago my parents with three small children came to live in Lavenham and I am the tenth child of that family.

I can remember going, when quite a small girl, to the British School and sitting on the lower seat of the gallery. There was no free education then and on Monday mornings each child took a penny or tuppence according to what the parents could afford. Near the school was a 'tuck shop' where we spent our farthings and ha'pennies on home-made toffee and rock.

When boys were 12 or 13 years old they often went to work half-days - one week in the mornings and the next in the afternoons. They worked with the men at the mat factory and thus earned a little to add to their parent's income, for wages were small and families often large.

Some of the girls when they left school went to learn horse-hair weaving on a loom worked by two. The girl 'fed' the hook with a single hair and she was known as a server. Mothers with small children unable to go to the factories had looms in their homes. These looms were noisy and took up a lot of space.

Another vivid memory is of a friend of the family who was a milliner. She used to make bonnets and had strangely-shaped wooden blocks on which she modelled them. Ladies from neighbouring villages used to drive up to her door in horse-drawn carriages. Later, when hats became fashionable, she would clean and trim them and I often delivered them to the homes of her clients. The trimmed hat would be tied in a red or blue wrapper secured at the four corners and I was briefed in meticulous detail as to how it should - and should not - be carried.

Next door to the milliner's house lived a young

Horse-hair looms in Roper's factory, Lavenham, just before the turn of the century.   Photograph: Miss Ranson

woman who earned a little money by 'picking' hair. The hair was long and in a bunch and the black hairs had to be picked out from the white, or visa versa. Sometimes I was allowed to pick out a few. After the hair had been sorted in this way it was sent to the women who wove it into cloth. Many of these weavers worked from 6 a.m. until 6 p.m. and their means of lighting was a hanging oil lamp.

The school teacher of my early days told me that her father was a 'wool comber.' Lavenham was once noted for its woollen industry. The old wool combing place still remains and opposite to it is a house known as 'Woolstaplers.' There is another house known as the Wool hall. It was once a communal bake-house. To me as a child it was a very dull place but as we had no means of baking in our houses we were glad to make use of it. There was an old lady there who wore a Victorian or kind of 'coal scuttle' bonnet and we children were always half afraid of her. We must have taken hundreds of cakes there over the course of many years. Most housewives 50 years ago (1900) made their own bread and would take the dough to the bake-house and knead it and put it in the bins there. I've heard they often enjoyed a little gossip while doing it.

There was no 'patent' yeast on sale. The yeast we used was brought by the local carrier from the brewery at Bury St Edmunds, ten miles away.

AS a schoolgirl I was taught to play the piano on an 'old grand.' During the winter the only light we had was from a tallow candle and my music master had to 'snuff' it frequently. He gave music instruction at the Grange, Shilling Street, where Jane and Ann Taylor had lived at the time of writing the poem 'Twinkle, twinkle little star.'

There were few facilities during my childhood for the weekly wash. There were no sinks or even zinc baths - only wooden tubs. These were heavy to lift and often in disrepair. I can remember helping to take a small one to the cooper's to have a new stave or band fitted.

Lavenham was noted for its annual horse fair. It was held on Shrove Tuesday. It was mostly cold and often snowy and slushy underfoot. The excitement began for the children on Shrove Sunday when the 'fun fair' arrived on the old market place. The men soon got to work unpacking and building up the round-about, the swings and the other stalls and booths ready for the opening on Monday.

Also on Monday many well-known horse dealers would arrive with their horses. Soon the High Street was lined with horses on both sides and at one particular spot there would always be donkeys. The paths soon became thronged with people and it was difficult to cross the road, as horses were trotted up and down to attract buyers.

It was a day's outing for people of the neighbouring villages and it was the custom for farmers and others to pay their annual bills to the tradesmen. Often they would be asked to stay to lunch and a huge joint of beef would be provided and followed by plum pudding and bread and cheese. What great wedges of cheese there were!

I remember how eagerly the weekly newspaper was looked for. It was delivered on Saturday evenings by a man who had walked from a town seven miles away. But news of shipwreck or train disaster or mine explosion was supplemented and embellished by men who came and sang in the streets and sold leaflets. These men often brought news to country people who would not otherwise have known of happenings in the outside world.

Another memory is of the old gentlemen who were war veterans, one with an artificial leg, another with only one arm. They wore high hats and long coats and on special occasions they wore their medals. One such gentleman with one arm sat in our pew at church and we children used to find the hymns for him. I remember he sometimes showed his appreciation by giving us a packet of sweets!

The roads in those days were very rough and were repaired with stones which had to be broken by men with hammers. At certain times of the year the surface of the road would be scraped by the roadmen and little heaps of mud would be left in the gutter to be taken away another day. The streets were not well lighted and on moonlit nights not at all and it was not uncommon to step accidently into one of these mud pies.

All vehicles had iron-tyred wheels which made a great noise as they went along the stony roads. One woman with a large family had a wicker pram with wooden wheels, iron tyres and no springs. I am sure there could have been no comfort in it.

I often wonder what present-day children would think of the toys we had. As the jam making season approached we would come out of school to see a man with a handcart displaying paper windmills and sunshades which could be had in exchange for jam jars and a ha'penny. My mother had no rest until the jam jars were forthcoming.

In the spring, boys, were very keen on playing marbles, especially with what were known as 'cockbirds.' These were of lead, made in moulds, and they would be of various shapes representing foxes, horses or cockerels. My brother was kept busy making them for he had every chance to use odd bits of lead from the workshop and there was much boy-bargaining to secure them.

There wasn't much entertainment outside the home. The occasional school concert would be appreciated so much and attended in such force that there would be a repeat performance the next night. From time to time, too, a travelling theatre would visit the town for two or three nights. I can vividly remember attending one performance with my mother and father. The play was 'Uncle Tom's Cabin' and when little Eva was shown dying, with Uncle Tom at her bedside, the scene was to me so very real and so very poignant that I cried and cried.

Then, sometimes, we had a circus. There would be a procession during the lunch-hour headed by a wonderful Britannia seated high up in her carriage. Following her would be performing horses and elephants and, perhaps, most popular of all - the clown. What excitement there was (and a certain amount of fear) as a huge brown bear on a chain was led down the street. As its master made certain sounds the bear would begin to dance and then it would give him a hug. But I think we were just a little relieved when it finally departed.

During the harvest holidays children and women went gleaning and they were glad of the corn to provide them with their winter store of flour. Sometimes they gathered enough corn to feed their fowls for the greater part of the winter. You would see the gleanings spread out to dry on sacks in the sun, often on the path outside their front doors.

Farm workers were poorly paid and after harvest, especially if it had been prolonged by bad weather and their average weekly earnings had been small, they would call on the tradesmen and ask for 'largess.'

Eggs were cheap and at the peak season could be bought 24 for a shilling. At Whitsun it was the usual thing to make an egg custard and it was not thought extravagant to use six eggs for a family dish.

And what would be thought today if tumbril loads of sprats were fetched from the station - as they were - to be spread on the land as fertiliser?

At Christmas time some grocers would give customers a glass of wine and a piece of cake and at any time of the year they would be willing to let their lady customers have cheese 'tasters' and biscuits, a 'taster' being almost as much as one person's weekly ration today (1953).

Children nowadays look forward to their annual outing to the seaside but we had ours at home. Each carrying our own labelled mug or cup we assembled in the schoolroom. Banners were distributed and then we paraded in procession through the streets towards the meadow. Swings were awaiting the first arrivals and games were organised, to be followed by a picnic tea.

Afterwards, parents and friends arrived. There was usually someone with a 7-lb. box of sweets and we scrambled for them as handfuls were thrown on to the ground. Hygiene was little thought of then, I am afraid.

Beccles in the 1880s

G. A. Dunn (c1950)

I AM a full-blooded East Anglian and proud to be that. My father was born in Alburgh, Norfolk. My mother was born at Witham, Essex. I was born at Beccles in Suffolk. I left Beccles forty-seven years ago (1903), and am indebted to that old town for nearly everything that has made life worth living. For go where you will it is the memories and experiences of the early years that stand by you and see you through. And who shall say which is the more important. The large things or the small.

When I was six years, two months and nine days

old I remember hearing for the first time, with comprehension, the greeting "A Happy New Year." and was told that it was the year 1880. Ten years later I was past sixteen and had absorbed (from my own angle) all that is hereinafter set forth. Please consider my bracketed qualification. If you want ancient lore, history, dates and architecture, well, there are the guide books. I bring to you my native town with an atmosphere that has vanished.

We will approach Beccles by way of Gillingham dam, which takes us as far as the bridge. But before crossing into Suffolk we will take a glance at Darby's timber yard and sawmill, an essential local industry. Here are piles of tree trunks, and nearby the clumsy, heavily built, horse-drawn "drugs" which brought them in to the pitside. There are three or four pairs of pit sawyers at work converting the trunks of oak, ash, elm and beech into slabs and boards. You will observe that oak bark is piled in stacks ready for delivery to the nearby tannery, and that a pile of oak sawdust is awaiting collection by the local herring curers. You will hear the screeching circular saws, large ones and small ones. And to atone for their comparative modernity they are driven by a comparatively ancient beam engine, early nineteenth century at least. Its massive over-head beam swings up and down like a see-saw; it might perhaps, at length, have rested in a museum but met its end in a fire. As you leave the yard, Mr Bob Martin, the millwright, will tell you that the slabs of beech he is loading must have two or three years of seasoning before they are converted into windmill fittings. Yes, we had three windmills in Beccles then. It should be realised that everything here recorded excepting only the circular saws (and they are moribund) has gone for ever. Does the atmosphere of old Beccles begin to creep in?

MOVE ahead with me a few yards to the ancient stone bridge with its three arches and low parapets. Beneath it flows the Waveney and no prettier river name can be found in all Britain. What memories the view from the bridge calls up. On the dark evenings of autumn I have seen half a dozen boats moored just below the bridge, each with a flaming torch at the bow and an oilskin-clad occupant cast-netting for smelt.

A few wherries could always be seen. At the corporation quay further down is moored a *billy-boy*, a heavy, clumsy, blunt-nosed craft discharging granite graded to the size of small Brazil nuts for street surface renewals. At the opposite quay lies the *Kelvinside*, one of the four small coasting steamers plying between Beccles, Lowestoft and London. The others are the *Jeannie Hope*, the *Elsy* and the *Aranci*. There is a small craft pushing off from the Norfolk bank, probably the last of the lateen-rigged yachts, the *Woolomoloo*. And messing about at the entrance to The Cut is a weird craft, a sort of box on two floats containing two youths pedalling hard to work two small screw propellers. These are not geared, however, and progress is erratic and negligible. This contraption was named "Takuponskedia."

Further down, the mud didlers are at work scooping up mud from the river bottom with primitive apparatus and using it to "hayn" (heighten) the river wall. Occasionally they would scoope up an object of interest. I have seen a cannon ball with a dent in it which they landed near the town. And further down still is a lonely figure in a small boat tying up to the bank. The evening is coming on and soon he will be babbing for eels. He's so intent on his preparations he doesn't even look up as two outrigger fours swing by manned by members of the local rowing club.

Along the banks down river may be seen water rats (they are not rats but voles) which live in holes in the banks and swim and dive beautifully. And over a rough piece of marsh near the town the snipe in season drum persistently all day long.

But now the smelt comes up the river unheeded. The wherries are all gone. The coasting steamers no longer ply back and forth. The billy-boy and the lateener have vanished. The didlers do not didle now. The outriggers may be laid up somewhere, and eel babbing is probably a lost art. The water voles have disappeared and the snipe no longer drum in the sunshine. All gone and nothing to replace them. But together they constitute another whiff of the Beccles that was.

BUT in Fen Lane close by there are two survivals. The stones of Toll's grist mill are still revolving. They were steam driven in the eighties but not by the old beam engine which stood disused in a forsaken, cobwebby engine room at the rear of the old timber-built mill. (It was never a windmill). This beam engine is evidence that the mill was working long before the eighties. The cooper's business too which flourished before the brewery closed down is still doing good coopering of an ornamental kind.

Beccles has a long frontage to the river. Along the south bank are ranged red-tiled cottages, their yards, gardens and boathouses, with an overhead fringe of green treetops, and above all the massive tower of St Michael's, which is detached from the church and at the wrong end of it. Climb to the belfry and in a wall niche you will see a large gotch - holding, perhaps, a gallon, and inscribed:

> *When I am filled with liquor strong,*
> *Each man drink once and then ding-dong.*
> *Don't drink too much to cloud your nobs.*
> *Lest you forget to make the bobs.*

The bells chime musically. In the eighties they didn't. It was a sort of rat-tat, rat-tat, rat-tat - all on one note. It was a Beccles clockmaker who cut that out and gave us the Westminster chimes. The bells not only tolled for the dead, and pealed joyously at times, but they were "jangled" as a fire alarm. Then our two small manual fire engines would turn out. The pumps were worked by an overhead wooden framework projecting, so that four men a side with an up and down see-saw motion could throw a fairly good jet.

NOW peer over the church wall at Pudding Moor, a picturesque old road leading to nowhere in particular. There used to be three lime kilns on the other side from the church steps, and a little further down, at a corner, was a very large stone which may have served as a mounting block. One day, chancing to examine it closely, I was astonished to find that it was not stone but bone, and certainly a prehistoric relic.

Northgate is a narrow, quaint old street, and is little changed. At its lower end there are the re-constructed buildings of the old tannery: and the brewery, where on certain days of the week an assemblage of women, girls and boys each with a jug or a milk tin would receive, for a penny, liquid yeast (a brewery by-product) to be used in the making of the weekly batch of home-made bread.

From the upper end of Northgate you enter the Old market where centuries ago herring were landed and where, in a more recent period, there were mardling tanks in which flax was steeped. Women were employed to do something to the flax and, of course, they talked all the time. And thus originated the East Anglian verb "to mardle" (gossip). At least that was the opinion of a well-known doctor, one of whose sidelines was our dialect.

Beccles was known in former years as a centre of the clay pipe industry, and one day I saw what must have been the last of it. An old man named Clare came down the lane from the Aldous pot-kiln with a pailful of newly fired clay pipes which he had made. The pot-kiln is worthy of notice too. A variety of very good pots were made there.

And wherein lay the distinctive atmosphere of old Beccles? The old streets: Northgate, Smallgate, Newgate, Hungate, Blyburgate, Ingate, Ballygate, Sheepgate and Saltgate are little changed. The atmosphere was, I think, produced by the people, how they lived and talked and what they did. I could name several local "characters" who were different, original, grotesque even - unlike their fellow townsmen who, however, did not so much conform to a pattern as do the townsmen of today.

In conclusion I will introduce to you a few of my old Beccles friends. Their surnames were: Bird, Sparrow, Crowe, Larke, Eagle, Finch, Martin, Peacock, Starling, Drake, Crane, Cock, Raven, Buck, Doe, Boar, Salmon and Spratt. I knew them well and, in one way or another, they were all good fellows.

Harwich Memories

D. Murrell Simmons (c1959)

MY earliest memories of Harwich - that of a child rising four - is of setting out for a morning walk before the First World War and being startled by a bull-like bellow which caused my mother some alarm till she was told it emanated from a lightship. These vessels, coming in at intervals for a refit, would spend hours testing their sirens. Later I used to wander round the Admiralty pier examining the barnacle-encrusted, many shaped and coloured buoys. The most persistent sound I remember was the mournful tolling of the bell buoy that marked the harbour channel.

How I loved an excursion on one of the old paddle steamers, *Norfolk* and *Suffolk*, with their foaming wake and machinery visible below open skylights! How I enjoyed watching the amusements of the Regatta; the greasy pole - or boys with their hands behind them, biting at treacle-covered buns hanging from a string!

Walks through the narrow alleys were romantic, particularly when the lamps were lit. Sometimes at dusk I would see a porter at the railway station, striding along the carriage roofs with a torch in his hand which he dipped through an opening above each compartment to light the gas lamps.

Before there were cinemas, the great event of the year was the Lord Mayor's procession, when men carried models of ships, illuminated within, shoulder high.

Then there was the Town Crier. How one strained one's ears as the sound of his bell came nearer, trying to catch his announcement; perhaps a notice of firing practice from the Redoubt. (We had to partly open our windows on account of vibration, and a sentry would be posted by a red flag beyond which it was forbidden to pass along the Esplanade.) The announcement always ended with a deflated 'God-save-the-King'.

And I have never forgotten the glimpse through the door of a store with long rows of Dutch cheeses.

For what seem, in retrospect, endless fine days, I played alone in ample spaces, though I thought it would be more fun to live in the tall lighthouse standing within the town.

One afternoon not so long ago I made the mistake of returning. Alas, how distances and buildings were diminished! Only the urchins and the dogs seem to have retained their character.

Market Day and Events on Wilderness Meadow

Alick Reeve (c1952)

I HAVE been much intrigued by the writings of a certain gentleman who ended his remarks by saying: 'I cannot possibly leave East Anglia without a special mention of the little Waveney Valley town of Harleston where all work for the good of the community, and good fellow-ship exudes in such measure as I never before experienced. It is the friendliest little town in the country.'

Now there is a fine testimonial for you. I was born and bred in Harleston and so I agree with it and endorse it. I recall the happy days of my youth there, the things I did and saw and the tales I heard.

My father loved to tell the story of Grand-father 'Truth' Prime who kept the Crown in the Old Market Place where the young bloods always had an enormous bonfire on Guy Fawkes' night. Determined this must cease in the centre of town, the police drafted in extra men. As the evening drew on and everything appeared to be quiet, Grandfather prime easily enticed the police into his back bar for rum punch. The young bloods then quickly got to work and with much material and tar previously prepared soon had the fire going. When the police rushed out, all hope of extinguishing it had gone - to the old man's great amusement.

But he was not so amused next morning when he found that all his gates and stable doors had been used for fire fodder.

Grandfather Prime was one of Harleston's characters. In addition to keeping the Crown and running a large farm at Brockdish he had about 40 horses and did most of the town's carting. A considerable amount of coal, grocery and other heavy traffic came up the river by wherry from Yarmouth to Bungay Staithe and had to be carted from there. He sent broad-wheeled wagons to London and also twice weekly ran a stage coach to Norwich. When the Waveney Valley railway line was opened a proposal was made to him for the taking over of his coach, he to run it for a year until passengers became used to train travel.

With many abjectival expletives he scorned the offer. He had been his own master all his life and wasn't going to work for anyone. Furthermore, he would 'run the railway off the road.' And so he carried on for some time. But on many occasions he returned, himself full of gin and beer but his coach almost empty of passengers, careering round Swan corner at full gallop on the two nearside wheels; and the end of his coach service was not long in coming.

I wonder what he would say today (1952), when nationalisation has accomplished what he failed to do, for it has recently been announced that all passenger traffic on the Waveney Valley line has been discontinued and handed over to the bus company.

HOW clearly I recall the Wednesday sale days when I helped to drive on their own legs hundreds of juicy beef steaks and mutton chops to and from the sale ground.

I recall, too, the scene in the market place with cheap-jacks selling their wares each in his own particular manner. Old 'Blame Ye' West used to arrive in his two-donkey-power cart. He had a stall laden with home-made toffee. To watch him making it was to us a special attraction. A huge mass of toffee hung from a hook and 'Blame Ye' pulled it into a longish rope, spitting on his hands to secure a clean release and repeatedly throwing it back on the hook. In this way he secured toffee of varying shades of brown. Every sale, if only for a penny, was acknowledged with: 'Thank ye kindly and God bless ye.'

Then there was Delhi the fire king, bending white-hot iron with naked hands or feet; the aristocratic dentist operating from an open wagonette (with small band in attendance to drown the groans of his victims); the pill merchant with his 'I don't come here with a velvet tongue to carry you away to oblivion but to cure you of all your ills at one shilling a box.' But I think the most sensational act of all was that of the crockery merchant. 'Here I have a lovely toilet set fit for your future wife. And the price? Thirty shillings - no, 25; no, 15; no, I'll make it ten shillings. No! You shan't have it at any price . . .' And he would dash the whole lot to the ground and thus quickly secure the audience he wanted.

I well remember Harleston's first electric light. It was installed on the end of the Magpie hotel signboard by the local engineering firm, Knights and Stacey. It was a source of wonderment to all, necessitating as it did a fairly heavy oil engine to provide the power. Knights and Stacey were the largest employers of labour in the district. They were agricultural engineers and millwrights and serviced scores of wind and water mills for miles around. They also, in conjunction with the late Capt. Moore of Weybread House, started a bell foundry. The peal of bells in Weybread church, among others, was their work.

Harleston was fortunate to have its cornhall, built in 1849. Its lofty, spacious interior was continually in demand for balls, concerts, theatrical meetings - and the Salvation Army held their Sunday services there. The building was filled to capacity on many occasions for concerts by the Harleston Orchestral Society. For a town of 2,000 inhabitants to provide 50 to 60 instrumentalists (my own family contributed five) and a corresponding number of vocalists capable of rendering such works as the Messiah, Judas Maccabaeus and Sterndale Bennett's 'May Queen' speaks volumes for the conductor, our curate, the Rev Galpin. He himself possessed over 100 instruments the majority of which he could play. He had a lovable personality and was an inspiration to everyone. Harleston will long remember the streams of carriages waiting far down Broad Street to convey the many county families home after the concerts.

ANOTHER local celebrity was Tom Stanton the coal merchant. He was the sole organiser of the Bank Holiday fete and gala. The day's proceedings started with the de-training at the station of the Band of Hope and a troop of mounted Lancers. A procession then formed up to march to the Wilderness Meadow (now the public recreation ground). At the head were the Lancers. Then came the balloonist, then the various friendly societies in their regalia. Bringing up the rear was the one and only Tom. He would be seated precariously in an armchair mounted on a kind of bier carried on the shoulders of eight men. Tom, looking anything but comfortable, would bow regally from right to left.

On Wilderness Meadow there was running for all ages, throwing the cricket ball, bicycle races. The first geared safety bicycle ever seen in Harleston ran away with most of the prizes and left the 'penny-farthings' far behind.

And then the balloon went up. It was filled with hot air from an underground fire which had a flue leading up into the balloon's interior. As the fabric slowly filled it was held down by pegs and scores of volunteers. Then the intrepid Capt. Spencer, seated on a trapeze-bar, gave the signal to 'let go' and the balloon slowly and gracefully ascended into the air, a parachute hanging by its side, the gallant captain waving adieu to the spell-bound crowd.

At least, that is how it transpired on the first occasion. The second attempt was more sensational. As soon as the balloon was released it was caught by a sudden gust of wind and carried on to some tall trees. A huge hole was torn in its fabric and from it poured dense black smoke. The captain could be seen desperately striving to disentangle himself from his harness. Still out of control the balloon went up further, giving the crowd - and the occupant - some anxious moments before it eventually descended safely.

In the evening there would be dancing and a grand display of fireworks.

I cannot leave the subject of Harleston without mentioning the many happy hours spent in our home-made canoes on the river Waveney. They were constructed on a framework of willow branches bent to shape and covered with cheap brown hessian. Then the hessian was covered with painter's waste which we wheedled out of our friendly-disposed local painter. Those were indeed happy days. But then we catered for our own amusement and were not dependent upon film stars and cinemas.

The Railway, the Reading Room, and Halfway Pond

D. E. Hurr (c1955)

I SHALL never forget my holidays at Southwold when I was young. So many treasures were locked away there, including my rather battered model yacht. How I looked forward to taking it to the Halfway Pond at California and watching it sail proudly across the rectangular stretch of water. The agony, too, when she became becalmed in the middle, far from any helping hand.

Southwold has changed little in the years but, in my memory, the Market Place and High Street were dowdier then than now. An old shop in the Market Place, however, sold those wonderful postcards of the Southwold Railway. I spent hours reading and laughing at them but, being at an age when money was minted only to buy sweetmeats, I bought none. I have regretted that ever since. In a fair collection of old postcards I can boast none of the old railway.

Of course the railway must occur in any memories of Southwold. I enjoyed one ride on it to Halesworth. How small the carriages were, little larger than cattle trucks, most certainly not as comfortable as the red omnibuses that now serve the town. Yet I cannot suppress a twinge of regret every time I pass the old station that the railway no longer functions.

Stories of the railway were legend. I remember one I heard of concerning some local lads on leave during the First World War. They agreed to meet at the station on the morning of their departure. But, when the time came, one of their number was late. He got to the station just in time to see the train puffing gallantly away across the common. Yet, when the train arrived at Halesworth, what should his comrades see but the latecomer sitting on the platform waiting for him. He had borrowed a bicycle and pedalled all the way, arriving in sufficient time for him to get his breath back before the train steamed in.

A PLACE of unending interest to me was the Reading Room. My grandfather was a member and I was often able to cross the threshold, whether as an honoured guest or an interloper I cannot recall. What a place of enchantment it was, a rough room with wooden benches and peopled with slow-moving, blue-jerseyed men. I well remember the fireplace (or was it a stove?) on the right of the room and two old fishermen playing chess there. To walk into that room brought the sea and adventure right into a young boy's life.

There was a model of the old *Bittern* there, too. What a grand yawl she must have been and how fine the craftsmen who made her. My grandfather had a framed picture of her hanging in the front room of his house and I knew the lines of the old vessel by heart long before I heard her full story.

the small bridges over the ditches. All had a handrail on one side only, but, as if to ensnare the unwary, the handrail of one of them was on the opposite side to that of the others. I heard tell of one man who had imbibed too liberally at the Blackshore Inn making his way back home across the common. He successfully negotiated three of the crossings by clinging to the handrail. When he came to the last he clutched for the rail on the same side as he had done for the others and fell headlong into the ditch, emerging wet through and covered in green slime. How he explained that to his wife I never did hear.

BEYOND the common was the ferry, a fearsome thing in those days, clanking and grinding as it

The Southwold train in Halesworth station.   Photo: J. Limmer

One of my delights was to watch my grandfather come home from a fishing trip. He would land on the beach beyond the pier and I would run down to the water's edge to help pull the boat out of reach of the breakers. It was a task in which the labour was very strictly divided - my grandfather pulled while I mainly puffed.

But Southwold was full of delights. There was the common where, from the water tower, Walberswick common and church could be seen, a lovely view on a clear, sunny day. There were cows, too, placidly grazing away. And there were

made its laborious way to the far side of the Blyth. Yet it was worth the risk to board such a doubtful monster for on the other side lay Walberswick, a little fairy world of its own, its small green, Bell Hotel, and cluster of cottages almost hidden away from the rest of the country.

On the common I flew my first kite. It was a gay one with miles and miles of string that must surely have reached the farthest star had it all been unwound. My first attempt ended in tragedy. Running backwards, wild with delight at seeing the kite airborne for the first time, I slipped and fell into some cow dung. My suit was ruined and

The ferry across the Blyth which connected Southwold with Walberswick. Photo: F. Jenkins

I was in disgrace. In bad odour in every possible way, I was marched off home. I was never very interested in kites after that.

But my happiest memories of all remain the halfway Pond and my small yacht, her sails filled with the breeze off the sea, crossing that tiny make-believe ocean. Long after I had grown up, I often pictured her, with the sun shining on the unruffled waters, sailing into any harbour that the youthful mind could conjure up.

May Their Tribe Increase

Alice Sterry (c1955), Illustrated by Paul Hogarth

A BACKWARD glance over 35 years to the 1920s may perchance lend enchantment to the view and yet in sober judgement it seems to me that our East Anglian landscape was richer then than now in eccentric characters. In one sense it is doubtful, of course, whether we are not one and all eccentric, in so far as it is impossible to choose any 'normal' man to use as a yard-stick. I do not believe in that oft-mentioned creature 'the common man' but hold that we all come 'trailing clouds of glory' from our Maker. Yet the race of eccentrics who enlivened and alarmed our childhood with their extravagances were no mere deviation from the norm. They stood out as a Giles cartoon might do in a picture gallery full of Mabel Lucy Attwell drawings.

Apart from the colour they gave to life, they served at least one useful purpose - they held the community together. Howsoever far as under the wash-tub might divide Judy O'Grady from the colonel's lady, they held the acquaintance of the 'characters' in common. Their children ran from them with equal terror or hung about their beats with equal delight. I say 'beats' deliberately, for some of them were as regular in their irregularities as the lamplighter or the muffin man.

There was, for instance, 'the man'. (As far as I know he had no other name and in those easy days he seemed to need none - there was much less form-filling then for the likes of him!) Every afternoon of the year, hail, rain, blow or snow, he would march through the town from its southern-most extremity to its northern-most and back again, hatless in those days when a hat was de rigeur even for the poorest of the poor; his jacket unbuttoned, his shirt likewise, revealing a vast expanse of brown, hirsute chest. Overcoat he had none!

He carried a heavy cudgel, never using it as a walking stick, but swinging it so vigorously as to endanger the head of any infant daring enough to come within five yards of him, only none did so dare. During the whole of his six-mile march he talked loudly, but in some such unknown

111

'The Man'

jocular salutation. As the last jangling note was turned out he banged down the lid, picked up the shafts and stumped a few hundred yards further on, there to repeat the performance. And woe betide any child found guilty of following him to the new pitch. He would not tolerate the same audience twice, unless they paid twice!

'THE man' and 'Old Thingummy' belonged to the out-of-door world and therefore, though an element of fear was mixed with our fascination, they gave us no nightmare feelings. The 'wart woman' on the other hand, never came out at all and had to be sought when required in her dark and dirty 'old clothes' shop. She was almost a cretin, with a huge head of silvery-white curling hair, sloe-dark eyes of a piercing brightness and a whispering voice. And she charmed warts! I can vouch for it, for in my ninth year I developed a crop of them in that inexplicable way in which one does develop the abominable things. And 'physicians were in vain,' each and every one of them. As fast as they burned off my affliction from my small hands, so fast did others grow. In desperation an appointment was made for me with the 'wart-woman.' One had to go alone and I thought I was losing my stomach in place of my affliction so sick with funk was I. What she did to them I refuse to reveal! It was very unsavoury! She bade me in that harsh whisper to go home and forget all about it and them! Ten days later I rose in the morning, wartless, and so have remained to this blessed day!

Our best and richest character, was both an indoor and an outdoor one. A chimney-sweep of the old and dirty school, he kept a second iron in his fire by maintaining a 'soft drinks store' in his front parlour. An old 'salt' who had been his next-door neighbour told me in my maturity that those same drinks 'wasn't nothin but coloured water, so they took his licence off him.' Whether this was so I know not. I do know that while I was not over-fussy what sweet stuff I ate or drank, I should have had to be drier than the Sahara before I had accepted the invitation printed on the grubby card in the window: 'If you be dry, step in and try, Happy's lovely drinks'. So ran the

tongue, as that in which one sometimes dreams. His laughter was gargantuan, and punctuated his strange sentences unfailingly. Ageless, homeless, mysterious as the legendary Dutchman he seemed to us. All through childhood he was. And then suddenly he was not. That is all I know of him and 'all I seek to know'.

'The man' was with us every day, even on Christmas Day, but Old Thingummy, the organ grinder, was a weekly treat. Wednesday was his day for our end of the town and our return from afternoon school usually coincided with his arrival opposite our doorway. To rush indoors demanding a half-penny to put into his tin was one thing; to dare to put it in was quite another. He was a fierce little man with a 'wall' eye, a wooden leg, a nose to vie with Bardolph's and a beard almost as long as himself, out of which his red eyes and beacon of a nose peered and jutted disconcertingly. He would stump to his appointed place and without a second's pause would begin to turn the handle of his organ. The repertoire ran non-stop and at a rate of knots from *Annie Laurie* to *Ave Maria*, through *Alexander's Ragtime Band* and *The Last Rose of Summer* to a concluding canter of *Abide With Me*. During the performance 'Old Thingummy' stamped his peg-leg savagely and muttered fearsome imprecations at every passer-by who failed to put a penny into his tin. He acknowledged contributions with the self-same mutterings but with his leg stuck out in would-be tempting slogan - Happy's one and only eruption into poetry, as far as I know. For his chimney-sweeping activities he employed a donkey-cart and beneath the cart trotted his black mongrel, reputed, and I believe ultimately proved, to sleep o' nights upon the family couch with the ancient Happy and his dame. With his 'strawberry' nose, his 'bandy' legs (short children could observe the prospect through them, as could Dickens' Pip through the legs of Mr Hubble!), his choice vocabulary and his unpredictable temper, his charms never palled!

These were only the highlights among a score or more lesser but still shining luminaries who leavened the lump of adult humanity for us. Is the race dying out under the levelling influence of the Welfare State? I wonder. Seeking matches in the general shop in one of our more off-the-map hamlets, I found a bearded lady, worth pounds a week to any showman, picking out winners from the racing lists spread over her counter. She breathed a curse upon me for not being her expected placer of bets and sold me damp matches for my pains. Every stitch of her dress, every particle of her person proclaimed her one of the true eccentrics. May their tribe increase!

'Old Thingummy'

Cupboards, Spice and a Bath by the Kitchen Fire

George J.M. Baker (c1953), Illustrations Nancy Blyth

I WAS born at Halstead in 1892 of a Quaker family. I was youngest of a family of six and I was five years younger than the sister who was nearest to me in age. So it happened that my childhood was associated with two worlds - the old, closely-knit family life of my early years, but which was already disintergrating by the end of the century as one after another of my elders left home, and the new mechanised life that was coming into being with the advent of moving pictures and the internal combustion engine.

We were very much a self-contained unit and the outside world troubled us but little. We did not take a daily paper until the 'Daily News' was reduced to a ha'penny. For late cricket news, my two elder brothers went down to the 'Mechanics Institute' to see an evening paper, and I well remember their bringing home to me as I was sitting in the bath by the kitchen fire the tragic news of Australia's victory in a famous test match, when we none of us doubted England's ability to score the 120 or so runs required for victory!

A very early memory is of the Diamond Jubilee, when a huge bonfire was built on the Market Hill. I can still see the great pile standing not far from the fountain, and still clearer is the later picture of the lurid glow of flame-lit smoke over the heads of the crowd. Sad to relate, I howled with terror and had to be taken home.

Some years later, mother came to tell me one morning in bed the news of the death of Queen Victoria. I expect I tried to appear much more impressed than I really was.

A few other memories from very early days have lingered. Someone must have lent us copies of the 'Graphic' or the 'Illustrated London News,' because somehow I saw pictures of the Spanish-American war and of Nansen's attempt on the North Pole. And there must have been at home a memorial card commemorating the death of Mr Gladstone, with a portrait of the G.O.M. in the middle surrounded by a considerable amount of allegorical trimmings.

These memories are still distinct. Less clear is

the pattern of family life in my very early boyhood while the majority of us were still at home.

I remember the gorgeous blazes father would have in the huge fireplace on his Wednesday half-day, and at Sunday morning breakfast he would read to us the weekly letter (there was a Sunday post in those days) from my eldest sister who was living with an aunt in Dorking. At the conclusion of the meal there was a Bible-reading - or did we read a verse each round the table?   Then there was Saturday tea-time, when there always seems to have been a round pot of dripping from the Saturday joint and woe betide anyone who tried to get too much of the luscious brown gravy beneath. It was a tradition of Saturday tea-time to play 'My father kept a shop like . . .'

But I was so much at the tail of the family that I was too young to share in most of the games. It is chiefly as a spectator that I remember the games of 'buttons' in the 'passage' - we never called it a hall - and the coconut-matting slide across the kitchen and down to the front door. I believe I was given free rides on my eldest brother's 'kangaroo' bicycle, though from others a fee was exacted of one pin.

OUR house at the top of Head Street was a very old one and must, I imagine, have been a horror to run. But in many ways it was a paradise for children. There were big useless passages, ideal for playgrounds, and cupboards. . . cupboards -all

big enough to hide in. On each side of the dining-room fireplace were deep cupboards. That on the left was big enough to serve as pantry and china closet, big enough as well to hold all the family, so that we could play a joke on visitors who came down to breakfast to find the house apparently empty; we then we emerged in a body in high glee, often with Mother at the head, for she enjoyed a joke more than any of us. On the inside of the door were pencil-marks recording our heights with the date written against them. The other cupboard held, as far as memory serves, the family games, mother's workbasket, the coal-scuttle and our slippers. Then there was a dark and mysterious two-storeyed recess under the stairs where reposed great stores of jam. Upstairs there was a big cupboard leading from the front bedroom. I can't remember that it had any particular use and while I was still young it was combined with the interior of a huge chimney to form an extra bedroom.

In an old, condemned cottage close by the back door, apples and pears were stored upstairs, and garden tools and firewood, downstairs.

Best of all for us children was the garden. And chief among its joys were the great fruit trees big enough to climb and have swings in. Each apple tree 'belonged' to a member of the family, though I arrived too late to have more than a small greengage tree to my name.

What memories flood in of apple dumplings the size of cannon balls, of apple pies and apple turnovers, with rich brown sugar oozing out, and most delectable of all, pears stewed all night in an earthenware jar and flavoured with cloves.

As far as money went we were, I suppose, poor enough. Yet how rich we seemed to be in many ways. I have no doubt that the hardest times were over when I was little, for by that time several of my elders were earning. True, I had to wear hand-down undergarments - even, I fancy, my sister's - but no memory of my early childhood is marred by any sense of poverty. I realised nothing of the struggle and self-denial of my elders. What remains is the abiding sense of their goodness and affection.

Aldeburgh in the Thirties

Michael Cornell (c1951)

WHEN he wrote his *Ode To The North-East Wind*, Charles Kingston must have had in mind some such place as Aldeburgh, for I can never think of his 'lonely curlew pile' without recalling the bleak, bleak marshes and dykes which to me set the whole tone of the place. It is perhaps unfair to call Aldeburgh a bleak place, as if it were bleak all the year round. For in summer I have known it almost warm. But it is wintry Aldeburgh which most impresses itself on the memory.

I was a schoolboy there in the nineteen-thirties, and what follows is a picture of Aldeburgh as seen through schoolboy eyes. It is a vivid enough picture, formed during impressionable years.

Perhaps the first sight that met my eyes was the row of old bathing machines, tipped at a bashful angle on their huge wheels. They were a relic of a preceeding age and are, alas, no longer to be seen. They are the only bathing machines I had ever, or *have* ever seen in my life. When *we* went bathing we used no such things. An enormous wooden framework was erected on the beach opposite the school and round this was stretched a long strip of canvas. Thus sheltered from view, we boys changed with the master in charge into our skimpy swim-suits and dashed merrily down the pebbles to await our turn to bathe.

If I remember aright we were always split up into two groups and matron would blow her whistle when it was time for the first group to come out of the water and the next group to plunge in.

And all the while a hired boatman would hover (not too far out) with a wooden step hanging out of the stern of his boat for the more adventurous of us to practise diving from.

A few yards away stood the look-out post, with steps up to the top - a great temptation! Aldeburgh, of course, has a famous lifeboat and much good service has it done. Naturally the beautiful new lifeboat which had, a little before my time, been launched by H.R.H. the Prince of Wales, was a joy to behold. I was particularly impressed by its *two* propellers. But to my boyish disappointment I never saw it in action.

HOW the sea rolled and tossed and roared! All night long I could hear it. And in the early morning, when the sky was still a dark grey, I would awake - the only conscious body in a dormitory full of heavily-breathing beds - and hear a distant cock crow. It was the most miserable sound in creation. It was the final call of the most desolate loneliness imaginable. It summed up the despair I invariably felt at the beginning of a term when in the grip, still, of home-sickness. Oh the joy, every third Sunday, when parents were allowed to visit us and we sat, thrilled with expectancy, looking out of the window of the big schoolroom down the drive, waiting, waiting, waiting, for that joyous yellow car that for me spelt

Bathing machines on Aldeburgh beach in the 1930s

an afternoon of bliss, paddling lazily on the mere at Thorpeness, or picnicking out on the heath.

Once a year, in the middle of the summer term, the whole school was given a holiday and in a body we walked along that straight narrow road, past the mysterious 'halfway house' * (is it really half-way?) and on to Thorpeness itself. Bottles of ginger pop were then bought and boats on the mere requisitioned, the adventurous choosing canoes (for a purpose I shall reveal) while the more sedate, myself for instance, manned the small rowing boats and the masters and the more intellectual boys punted or even sailed. Then it was a case of the survival of the fittest, for the adventurous fellows in the canoes would throw aside all moral obligation and raid, yes *raid* us slower ones and 'bag' our ginger pop and sweets! It was high piracy indeed. I remember resenting it hugely.

Afterwards we all came 'ashore' and gathered ourselves on a bank to have an enormous 'binge.' Snapshots were taken on box-brownies and as the sun slid down behind the dykes and marshes we began the homeward trek. Masters in their amusing battered motors would ply to and from the school carrying loads of tired, dusty but happy schoolboys home from their big outing.

On Sunday mornings we always went to church wearing, if fine, straw 'boaters' - I can't imagine why! We always sat in the north side and I can to this day recall the smell of creosote which was at times almost overpowering. I think the woodwork must have been treated with it and I used to imagine it was the cause of boys feeling faint or sick, for nearly every Sunday at least one boy would be led out, looking very 'frail,' to have his head energetically ducked by the headmaster in the porch. Peering round the pillars we could see the bust of George Crabbe standing in the shadows. But he didn't mean much to us.

OUR walks took us frequently along the heathland and the golf course, and our favourite sport when crossing the railway line was to put pennies on the rails and wait for the train to come along and squash them out of all recognition. The

The houseboat 'Iona'.

local locomotive was nicknamed the 'Aldeburgh Snail' and was the source of much irreverent amusement. When it was bringing us *to* school at the beginning of a term it seemed to go too fast. When the happy day came for the start of the holidays it seemed to go too slow. Actually, I imagine its pace was pretty constant both ways - about five miles per hour, I should think.

Another walk took us in the direction of Orford, and we had much fun scrambling about by the martello tower which lies to the south of Aldeburgh. A feature of curiosity here was the 'Shoe-House,' (the old *Iona* houseboat) which was, we always believed, inhabited by a Mrs Hubbard who had fifteen children!

I wasn't particularly fond of walking but once a week we had 'drill,' which meant parading in platoons, carrying dummy wooden rifles. Sometimes we went for route marches, with me playing the drum in front; and two or three bugles immediately behind me kicking up an awful row! We were particularly smart on Armistice Day, when we used to parade by the cenotaph and moot hall at eleven and observe two minutes' silence.

Poor Aldeburgh has now been 'put on the map' and endlessly publicised. When I last went there it had lost its child-like innocence and had become, to my sour old eyes, 'arty' and 'clever' and 'intellectual.'

Oh Aldeburgh! - when I was with you, the only 'season' you had was the sprat season, and I would be very happy if that were the only season you were to have again . . .

(* The 'half-way house' is the mill house, once attached to a black tower mill which was used to pump water from the marshes.)

116

Urban Life

The Rough and the Smooth

Sylvia Haymon (c1958), Illustrated by Paul Hogarth

IT was a sad day for the boys of our East Anglian town when farmers began to bring their cattle to market by lorry and van instead of on the hoof. Innocent victims of the march of progress, the boys laid aside their shovels and found some other use for the little home-made carts and wheelbarrows with which they had been wont to ply their Saturday trade.

There was a time when every road into the city was jammed on Saturday mornings with slow-moving bullocks and cows, each herd attended by its baggage-train of little boys, trundling wooden boxes on wheels. Local nurserymen had been known to go as high as a shilling for a sugar-boxful of fresh manure.

Round about 3.30 in the afternoon, the chaffering in the Market Place completed, business re-commenced in reverse. The boys attended the bullocks as they plodded stolidly towards their several destinies - to the slaughterhouse or out again to the countryside and a new master.

Generally speaking, the camp-following persisted until the last collector had taken on as much stock as his barrow could accommodate but not if this entailed an appreciable trek out of town.

Once past the tram terminus, the cavalcade began to waiver and dissolve. Like sea-gulls which will scavenge in the wake of a ship a certain distance out to sea but no farther, the boys became uneasy between hedgerows. Far into the unknown land they would not venture, even for profit.

Thankfully would they turn their backs on the swishing tails and swaying rumps they had followed with such single-minded devotion the long day through, to seek once more the familiar safety of city streets.

Only rough boys pursued this calling - 'rough,' in this strictly local context, connoting children who did not wear school uniforms. Upon the basis of this one simple test, our unenlightened little society had no difficulty whatsoever in classifying the children of the town to its own satisfaction into the 'nice' who wore uniforms and the 'rough' who did not.

My brothers being technically nice, it was technically unthinkable that they should stoop to shovelling up cattle droppings in the street as a means of augmenting their pocket-money. But times were hard and Christmas with its attendant expenses loomed close ahead. They decided to try their luck.

FOR a percentage of the estimated profits of the enterprise I agreed to loan my doll's pram and my seaside spade. On the appointed Market Day, before the sun was well up, they slipped out of the house with the intention of intercepting the cattle outside the city limits, where they deemed the competition would be less fierce.

They had made previous provision to account for their day-long absence and my mother, busy with guests that Saturday afternoon, pouring out tea in the decorous gentility of a provincial drawing-room, could have had no foreboding of impending catastrophe.

Into that atmosphere of cloistered calm and

paste sandwiches, my brothers burst, battered but triumphant, rank with the smells of stable and byre. Out on the Caister Road, not far from the very sport where, in an earlier age, Queen Boadicea, facing odds no more desperate, had fled bleeding from the Roman rods, they had stood their ground in a pitched battle with a whole task force of regular barrow boys. While it appears that certain uncomplimentary observations levelled at the doll's pram had set off the spark, the root cause of the conflict was - as almost invariably in deciding peace or war - economic; the regulars' objection to any encroachment upon their monopoly.

It was war to the death or thereabouts, while the bullocks lumbered past all unheeding, strewing their largesse indiscriminately with no appreciation at all of the principle of the closed shop. It was a wasteful business too, as war is always wasteful of wealth and capital resources. The very ammunition - (in the restricted area of the drawing-room it was only too strongly apparent) - had consisted of the actual merchandise in dispute.

'Just the same', my younger brother crowned his gleeful recital with a crow of victory, 'we got ninepennyworth - and please may I have a mincepie?'

As it turned out, they had *most* of the tea. Windows were flung wide and the boys sent to wash and change, but the guests soon excused themselves upon one pretext or other and departed.

They were plainly shaken. They had lost more than their appetites. Gone, too, was their faith in school caps and ties as guarantees of social acceptability - nay, more, as philosophical absolutes in a chancy world.

My share of the transaction was threepence, which may seem a poor return in view of the fact that my doll's pram was never the same again. But there were other gains.

For the first time in my life some glimmer of understanding dawned that the two categories of humankind I had been taught to recognise were neither all-embracing nor mutually exclusive; that there was more to the business of living than being 'nice' or being 'rough'.

The pram was of no consequence. I was certainly getting too old for dolls.

Memories of my Happy Days at Yarmouth

E. L. Barrett (c1957)

I HAD the good fortune to be born at Great Yarmouth at the beginning of the century, in a road nearly opposite the Britannia Pier, and I can look back upon my childhood with a happiness that is not given to many, certainly not in these days when children have so much done for them and are unable or unqualified to make their own fun and games.

Yarmouth in those far off days was not the very popular seaside resort that it is today. Not, I hasten to say, that it was not one of the favourite holiday spots even then - how could it be otherwise when it had miles and miles of golden sands and, it seems to me as I look back, hot and sunny days nearly all the summer. We had rain, certainly, but a short, sharp storm on a hot day, that laid the dust and made everything smell fresh and sweet and was nothing to complain of, although I expect we grumbled a little about it, even then.

It was the beach, however, that was a never-failing source of magic to my small friends and myself. There was so much of it, so many things to do and so much to see that was new to us. After all, the town had 'died' for about eight months, to be re-born at Whitsun with the first few visitors arriving. And then, in July and August, when it was crowded, to our young minds it was at its best.

During the school holidays we used to make for the beach on most of the afternoons in the summer, starting from the Britannia Pier. The people of Yarmouth have been a little unlucky with their Britannia Piers. I forget whether the last disastrous fire was the third or fourth that had burnt it out. But I do remember that the pavilion of my earliest recollections was an elaborate building with a dome at each corner and a larger one in the middle, looking not unlike an oriental mosque. And, of course, the sea had not receded to the degree it has today, so that it was possible to walk out and over the water on what we called the 'irons', in other words the foundations supporting the pier. This was exciting and called for a certain amount of strength of purpose

The ill-fated Britannia Pier of the early 1900s, looked not unlike an oriental mosque.

and flexibility and, considering there were probably about 10 or 15 feet of water below us, a little courage. However, that was only one item in the afternoon's programme. Item No. 2 was 'Madam Cooke'.

'Madam Cooke' was a 'phrenologist' who had a little platform with seats all round near the sea wall. She was a native of Nottingham, I believe, and a very astute and clever woman. She was tall and statuesque, always dressed in black, and invariably wore a short sable cape and a black bonnet in the style affected by Queen Victoria. And before she 'read the bumps', as we called it, of any of her clients she opened a large umbrella so that her audience would not miss a word. She had a very clear and penetrating voice, which was a little embarrassing when she said anything uncomplimentary about her subject - and this she never hesitated to do if it was warranted! After the poor, unfortunate victim had been placed in a little wooden armchair, she would take out a tape measure, find the circumference of his head, put up her umbrella and begin. She would also look at his hands and ears and I must say that her 'readings' were usually very accurate - in the case

of young children she gave the mothers some useful help in the way they should be brought up and what to do to encourage their talents. All this information was given for 1s. - or 2s. if one wanted a typed copy!

MY friends and I had usually had enough of this after sitting down for about 10 minutes, so off we would go again, this time to see if we could get a free show at 'Chappell's'. This was what we should now call a concert party but, unlike most seaside entertainments, as well as a fairly large stage there was a wooden floor and about 200 seats, the whole surrounded by a wood and canvas enclosure. If we had not the money to pay to go in - and we very rarely had - we used to walk all around and try to find a spot where the canvas was loose or where there was a little hole in the wood; even this was not entirely satisfactory as there was usually a man with a stick, ready to chase us off if by any chance we were lucky enough to find a space large enough to look through. Still, we had generally seen one 'turn' before we were sent off, so we considered it worth the risk.

In the days I am writing about, the visitors liked to go out for sea trips in sailing boats, and as these obviously had to be kept in fairly deep water the passengers had to walk up steep wooden gangways to get on board. But if the weather was too rough for the yachts to go out, these gangways were pulled up on to the beach. I am sure the owners of the boats could never have realised how much pleasure they were unconsciously providing for the small children. All one had to do was to climb up to the top, clasp one's knees and slide down, and apart from getting splinters and abrasions on our 'derrieres', and torn knickers, which meant a scolding when we got home, it was great fun!

Then, when the tide was going out, there would be the 'dykes'. These would be caused by the sand being higher in one place than another so that when the sea receded it would leave behind a small river about two or three feet deep. And after the sun had been on it for some time it would become deliciously warm and just the spot to spend a little time paddling and finding star fish and jelly fish. The jelly fish were not the large stinging type but the tiny transparent sort that looked like clear glass marbles. I like to remember that we usually flung the star fish back into the sea, so that thanks to our ministrations they were able to go home to their families!

AFTER all this we would have arrived at the jetty. All we could do about this was to hug the large 'sewer' pipes that ran underneath it and inch ourselves along for a short way. But, apart from getting us dirty, this was not very exciting, so we would go on to the jetty and jump from there on to the sand, daring each other to jump from a greater height until we came to a point where it was too steep to jump and then we would decide that we had had enough of that particular form of entertainment.

By this time, what with all the fresh air and exercise, we would be getting hungry. So we would decide to return by the 'front' after fortifying ourselves with an ice wafer or a cornet which cost a half-penny. The Marine Parade was, in its own way, as exciting as the beach, for there was the Hippodrome with the pictures outside of the 'artistes' to look at and, if we went round to the back, the chance of seeing some ponies or an elephant being taken from one entrance to another.

Another great attraction was the 'Sailors' Home' where ship-wrecked sailors were taken and given food and clothing and a bed. Here there was a room full of curiosities, extraordinary stuffed fish and native work and, what stands out in my mind most clearly, a large glass case with a squirrels' dinner party - about 20 stuffed squirrels together with a waiter serving soup and a long table with a delightful collection of miniature glasses, knives and forks. We were never tired of looking at this.

There was also on the 'front' and near to the 'Sailors' Home', the lifeboat house, a big shed-like building housing the lifeboat, and we were able to climb up the ladders at the side of the boat and look inside. But I think the place we really adored was 'Barron's Exhibition'. We used to think the gipsy fortune teller was a being from another world, with her dark hair and large ear-rings, and we were very envious of the people who could buy a lovely brooch made of gold wire which spelt out their name or, from another stall, a tie, either a lady's or gentleman's, with a beautiful bunch of flowers on it, painted before our very eyes.

At the time of which I write the only form of transport was a horse-drawn carriage of some sort and on our way home we would pass the two or four horse brakes returning from Somerleyton or Fritton Lake or some nearby beauty spot or - and these were much more elegant - the landaus, the graceful open carriages which could be hired for short drives along the front. And the children were not forgotten - they could have a ride on a donkey, or for the tiny children there were little carts drawn by goats. I had special interest in these latter, as in the mornings I was allowed to take them pea pods and all sorts of green stuff, which they seemed to appreciate.

I love Yarmouth, I love my memories of it. But - did the sun really shine all the time as I remember?

My Childhood Summer Holidays at Yarmouth

Marguerita S. S. Bird (c1957)

WHEN I was a child in the early 1900s, when Christmas was over, only Yarmouth was ahead - the whole month of August.

We thought and talked of little else - packed and re-packed our possessions while our mother and father dealt with a large dome-roofed trunk, two hampers (theatrical hampers), a large food hamper, a child's bath full of boots and shoes, a large square hat box, a long bundle of umbrellas, spades and mackintoshes, and Mother's brown bag. Everything except the brown bag went into the van and of course Mother carried her own Dorothy Bag.

The Dorothy Bag was made of string and had two stout handles. At the bottom with chipped blue handle pushing through the mesh was the baby's jerry - then a paper bag of Thomas Ridley and Son's with a pound of Nice biscuits, some harvest apples, a box of Brown's Bronchial Troches, the latest copy of St John's Magazine and some nappies.

Vauxhall Station at last - the wooden platform, lovely fishy smell and air like wine. Some of us went in a Victoria with Mother and the luggage, the rest walked or trammed down until we arrived at East Anglia House, nearly opposite Wellington Pier. It had no front door - you went in through the window - the front garden was just cobbled and there was a long narrow garden at the back which still makes you think of cats. There was Mrs Thomas, the landlady, in a silk apron, who didn't allow ball on Sunday, and an umbrella stand of odd china.

Installed and unpacked the month began. There was the beach all the morning. Mother prided herself that we were all down on the sands by nine! There was P.C. Herring, the beach policeman with whom we all made friends straight away, the man who sold 'Answers' and 'Titbits' and gave away a present with each copy, the horse-drawn bathing machine smelling of salt, stuffiness and people - gorgeous.

We all bathed - Father being a nimble swimmer and diver. I remember being furious one summer when, as I evidently didn't fit into any of the family costumes, I had to wear combs - sewn up where necessary but, oh, so obviously combs.

After our dinner we always went on the Wellington Pier for which we had monthly tickets. I don't know why we never went on the beach in the afternoons but we just didn't. There was always a lovely military band playing in the Wellington Gardens. As we played on the pier, we gazed rather enviously at the lucky children who went on the beach in the afternoon.

After tea came a walk to the harbour - glorious smells again - fish, tar, and that lovely salty tang. We inspected boats. We generally had an early bedtime to dream of another glorious day tomorrow.

We never went alone north of the jetty, as our Mother thought it wasn't nice! But we did go into St Peter's Road (sometimes known as Jetty Road). There was a post office-cum-library where we found our dear little grey-haired Mr Carver and his tall lady-wife. There I got all Mrs Henry Wood's three-volume novels and how I loved them.

Opposite the post office we would find more old friends, Mr and Mrs Scarfe - both rosy-cheeked Norfolk folk, who had a wonderful shop where pails, spades, bananas and oranges and sweets of every kind were to be had, and we had a wonderful welcome each year.

There were so many attractions that it is difficult to know where to begin.

The Hippodrome - we went once during that month and it was a source of great anxiety if the fine weather continued too long as we were supposed to keep that treat for a wet day. It was a grand performance - those clowns, the acrobats, the performing animals, and finally the water scene when the amphitheatre filled with water and the funny policeman swelled up and with other performers swam around.

AT a small side show just outside the Hippodrome, for 3d you could gaze your fill on various eccentricities, one year being the double-bodied man? The man and his other little body were in evening dress, the little body was attached to his 'master' by his middle and was quite perfect but had no head. Our mother and we children loved it;

Father, being a doctor, preferred not to look - perhaps he'd seen his fill of horror in his time and without paying his 3d.

There was a sand artist who nearly always had a marvellous battle scene of a dying soldier with his arms through the bridle of his dead horse. You simply had to throw him a penny.

Who remembers the shrimp ladies with their baskets of pink and brown shrimps? I remember being very sick from eating them and muttering fiercely with my head still in a bowl: 'I'll still eat shrimps, I *will* eat shrimps.'

There was the Old Toll House with its cells and mummified cat.

There were Palmers and Arnolds. I once bought a hair-stuffed doll with real hair from Palmers for sixpence ha'penny.

There was always a good concert party on the Wellington Pier. Ben Laws was there for several years and we learnt most of the songs pretty pat:

'Woo loo moo lo o
Upon my word tis true
Thats the way to spell Wooloomooloo
Now I bet a dollar
There isn't a scholar
Can spell that right first go o
Woo Loo Moo Lo o'.

Firework night on the Wellington Pier was much looked forward to. Wonderful rockets and set pieces, and I well remember one outdoor cinema show in the Wellington Gardens.

I sometimes smile when I hear discussions each year 'Where shall we go this year?' With us it was never 'where', simply 'when' do we go to Yarmouth.

Early 20c Memories of Colchester's North Hill

R. Hemstedt (c1957)

T HE character of a street can change almost beyond recognition in a few years and the changes are hardly noticed by those who are always there. The new shop-fronts go up, the pavements are better to walk on and to the middle-aged man who knew it in childhood the differences seem immense.

Gone are the tramlines and the old street lamps. The multiple store has taken over the little shop Mr Thingummy had for years, new buildings are everywhere, old houses are pulled down and prosperity appears to have come to the place.

North Hill in Colchester seems to me still to have character. As its name implies, it is a hill on the north side of town and it begins life at the junction of Head Street and High Street at what is known locally as 'the top of the town'. It then proceeds at a very steep gradient out towards Sudbury for a distance of about 350 yards and loses its identity at the point where Balkerne Hill joins Middleboro near the cattle market. A few yards further on Middleboro meets the river at North Bridge and continues on as North Station Road.

It is the usual country town street. It contains houses, inns, shops, the local registrar's office, a church, the county technical school, a temperance hotel, solicitors' offices, several dentists' surgeries, ladies' hairdressers, florists, a vicarage, apartment houses, antique shops and a mineral water depot. In my time the hill has had a fish-and-chips shop, a dairy, a cricket school, an amusement arcade, the local labour exchange, a ladies' hat shop, the residence of a famous surgeon, the local office of the 'East Anglian Daily Times' and once, during the war, the police raided a house because it was alleged to be a brothel.

Fifty years ago (1907) the corporation trams would go rattling and swaying up and down the hill and a ride in one of them was a sure cure for indigestion, while on Saturdays life would be enlivened by the shouts and bellows of drovers from the cattle market who always seemed to be in pursuit of an escaped bull or cow.

Those were the days before the carriage of livestock through the streets became the rule rather than the exception. Every Saturday some animal was bound to break away from a herd being driven towards the market, and the afternoon - it was always the afternoon - would be rent with the calls of drovers disturbed at their refreshment in the 'Marquis of Granby' and the shrill cries of dozens of small boys armed with sticks who would rush round in all directions trying to head some large beast back into the fold.

There was always colour and incident on North Hill - and accidents. In those days cycles were big and heavy, with back-pedal brakes, and riders would come hurtling down the slope only to finish up among their wheels and spokes at the bottom, right outside the 'Coach and Horses'. This happened time and time again though I can't recall anyone being seriously hurt.

And what was more remarkable - to me anyway - right opposite to this point was a cobbler's shop and in the window always sat an old gentleman - Mr Chapman I think it was - imperturbably surveying the passing scene whether it was cows, sheep, people or acrobatic cyclists. He never seemed to move but just sat there like a Chinese mandarin, wise and all-knowing, his clay pipe forever in his mouth.

Once I remember one of the early motor cars somehow got out of control at the top of the hill - it was probably a Model T Ford - and began to run backwards down towards the market, its driver frantically turning the steering wheel from left to right in an endeavour to run straight. I can see him now, perched up in his seat, all the time jerking his head round and zig-zagging from one side to the other, mounting the pavement, steering clear of carts and children.

At first I watched fascinated and then joined the rest of the kids running behind him. Here was skill indeed. Down he went, first one side, then the other, only to finish up by colliding with a huge tram standing opposite Northgate Street. A pity really - another 20 yards and he would have been on the level and then on a slight incline towards North Bridge.

The hill has known the tramp of marching feet. Thousands of troops from all over the world have marched from North Station to the tunes of a hundred bands. Standing at 'the top of the town' one day during the 1914 war I saw a sight that thrilled. A Scottish regiment were marching towards me with fixed bayonets. As far as the eye could see were four long ribbons of steel, not one bayonet out of line . . . and the wonderful rhythm of pipes and drums going full blast. And out in front was the biggest man in the world, throwing his staff in the air and performing miracles with a golden rod. Here was Scotland in all its glory - or so it seemed to a very small boy.

IN my childhood, Colchester boasted a good theatre, and a rollicking music hall, alas, now gone for good. If ever a section of the community gave glamour and bohemianism to the town it was the artistes who appeared at these theatres. I used to see them and meet them quite a lot and in the most unusual way. Two houses in particular were given over to 'theatricals' and these establishments hardly ever catered for anyone else. They were situated one on either side of a courtyard with the garden of each running alongside the yard and parallel with it. The house we occupied was in between these two gardens and had been many years before a shoe factory - it is not in existence now. It was possible for me to get up in the attic of the third floor front and lie down behind the curtains and, while having a good view of the garden, be myself invisible to those on either side of me.

The artistes in those days were perhaps more conscientious than those of today because which ever theatre they were currently at and what-ever they might be doing there, whether it was farce, comedy,

drama or music-hall knockabout, they would always rehearse every morning. I would lie up there for hours watching the antics of the various comics, jugglers, acrobats and even a stray contortionist or two who were appearing at the Hippodrome or the old Theatre Royal. There was no need for me to go to the theatre - I couldn't afford it anyway - because there it was all in front of me, those delightful people doing this for me.

I remember in particular, the Bellini Brothers, the famous tumblers who, when they did their act on the stage, punctured it with cries of 'hup!' Then one of them would come forward to the proscenium and explain the next very difficult trick in spite of very broken English. In actual fact the brothers were originally from somewhere near the Aldgate Pump and addressed each other as Bert and Elf.

Bert was the brains of the act while Elf was the strong man. In the theatre they wore an outfit that reminded you of the men's long underwear advertisements and with their waxed moustaches and slicked hair looked the real McCoy. Like all 'theatricals' they didn't get up till nearly 11 and in the garden with their moustaches drooping and windswept hair they hardly looked like acrobats. But they went to it. They would practice one item over and over again. Bert would hold Elf up, then Elf would hold Bert. I wonder what became of them. I suppose the war swallowed them up.

It was in the gardens that I first encountered the eternal triangle. Mr and Mrs X were at the Theatre Royal. A quite elderly couple, they were in a play which I know now to be the conventional thing of that period. As in real life, they were also playing a theatrical husband and wife, and the wife was enamoured of a handsome young penniless type who wanted to get on. As they rehearsed this it was fairly easy for my very young mind to get the idea of what it was all about. One scene in particular: hubby was out of the room and wife and boy friend would embrace very passionately, only to be discovered. In the garden this scene was played against the summer house which apparently represented a room. Hubby would come out of the side of the summer house and a terrific row would ensue and the youthful admirer sent packing. That was in the mornings. Later in the day and before the

evening performance the same scene was often enacted though much more passionately and without the presence of hubby. It was all very puzzling to a small boy hardly yet of school age and later on in life when I got to know de Maupassant I suppose it would have been much more clear.

But even then I remember thinking to myself that things are not always what they seem.

Norwich - The Wagonette, and Bread for the Troops

Gladys O. Howard (c1954)

I WAS born in Barrack Road, Norwich, and until I was eight years old attended a small private school, afterwards going with my sister to the Octagon School (now non-existent) in Calvert Street.

My father owned a large bakery business, and held the contract for supplying bread to the troops at Cavalry Barracks, and also at Britannia Barracks after it was built in 1886. We had two bake-offices, one of which had what was then the largest oven in Norwich. It held 500 loaves at one baking.

The bakers worked very long hours for an average wage of £1 a week. Work usually started between four and five o'clock in the morning on every day except Sunday. On Friday it started at 12 midnight in order to bake enough bread for the week-end.

Every year in May the militia - the 3rd and 4th Battalions of the Norfolk Regiment - would encamp on Mousehold Heath. This of course meant a great deal of extra work for us as all the canteens had to be supplied. Extra labour was engaged and the miller would lend us one of his huge flour wagons and a driver. Every morning a soldier on horseback would bring the requisition for the day's bread, which had to be delivered by twelve noon ready for inspection by a board of officers.

On one or two occasions something happened

Old Norwich from the quayside

to the ovens at the barracks for I can remember that we had to cook the troops' dinners too. A fatigue party brought them down and collected them. What happened to our other customers' dinners I don't know but the army had to come first. Until houses began to install their own cookers we used to charge a ha'penny or a penny for cooking a dinner, according to the size of the dish.

As time went on we supplied large quantities of pastries to the canteens, and on Good Friday mornings hot cross buns had to be delivered to the barracks very early, so that the soldiers could buy them before church parade.

A STIRRING sight in the Norwich of those days was the military band, mounted on horseback and complete with kettledrums. As it came through the streets everyone ran to their doors to watch and to listen to the music. I well remember, too, the 'church parade' to the cathedral on Sunday mornings.

Two or three times a day the military postman would clatter by on horseback to collect the mail from the post office.

On Sunday mornings we were allowed to hear the band on the barrack square and each evening it would play while the officers were at dinner.

During the summer, military sports were held on the drill-field which later became Mousehold aerodrome. The events were announced by Childerhouse, the local bellman (who was much in demand for advertising all such functions in Norwich). Military tournaments were held in the Agricultural Hall and were a source of great excitement. I remember that 'Old Snap' used to chase children and snatch off boys' caps with its dragon teeth. A man with a collection box would walk by its side. For the rest of the year 'Snap' was kept in a skittle alley in a nearby public house.

We were proud possessors of a wagonette. On Sundays and holidays, father would take us for a jaunt in the country - on whole-day trips sometimes as far as Great Yarmouth. We took with us large hampers of sausage rolls, sandwiches and cakes. The wagonette hadn't a cover so we carried a large umbrella. One such jaunt in the wagonette was during the jubilee celebrations of 1887, which I remember well.

We were brought up more strictly than girls are today. We had to be home before 9.30 in the evening and even up to my marriage I was never allowed out after 10.

The Dames' School, Town Crier & Tombland Pigeons

Ernest De Caux Tillett (c1953)

MORE than sixty years ago (1890s) I lived in one of the large Georgian houses immediately overlooking Tombland and next-door-but-one to that partly shown in the illustration (see next page). The ground floor was mainly occupied by my father's legal practice, and the first and second floors, residentially.

How many thousands of times must I have passed under that venerable archway, my first school (one of the 'dame' type) having been

125

There was plenty of space and little risk in trundling a hoop . .

located immediately to the left as one emerges into the Cathedral Close in the house now numbered 75.

The school was conducted by two maiden ladies whose name was Freeman and whom we children addressed as 'Miss Freeman' and 'Miss Lucy.' (Locally, almost everyone had heard of 'Freeman's Norwich Hollow Biscuits,' with the makers of which these ladies, I believe, were related).

Although by present-day education standards the school's curriculum would doubtless be regarded with mingled amusement and derision, I shall always feel that the groundwork received there tended to prove helpful in the following years. One of our textbooks was entitled: 'Stepping Stones to General Knowledge' and consisted entirely of question and answer dealing with such diverse topics as the discoverer of the circulation of the blood and the names of the planets! Another publication which we used for our studies was a folding sheet of English history dates comprising, for the most part, the names of the monarchs reigning from 1066 to 1837, the memorising of which was rewarded by a half-day holiday.

Every Monday the older scholars had to be prepared to repeat from memory the collect from the previous day's Church of England service and I am afraid that even at this remote date the exacting duty which resulted during Advent still prejudices my views on many of those beautiful passages.

BUT 'the Close' as we called it was not only the scene of my early schooldays but to a large extent of my recreation. There was plenty of space and little risk in trundling a hoop, and Pull's Ferry, the old water-gate, afforded other

126

attractions. I remember once, though, receiving a big scare when engaged in the pleasing pastime of kicking loose stones (the bigger the better) down a water grating so as to hear the resulting plop. For suddenly I saw standing over me the Close porter, or janitor, resplendent in long embroidered coat and top hat laced with gold. His name was Hubbard. I cannot recollect whether he was the sole guardian of the Close's amenities nor whether he was succeeded on retirement by any other official. But that the post has fallen into abeyance these many years there seems no doubt. We credited 'Mr Hubbard' with living in quarters at the Ethelburt Gate, from which he was expected to emerge, after the gate was closed, to admit those 'Close' residents returning home after the hours laid down by the dean and chapter, a practice similarly prevailing with the other entrances so far as bolting and barring was concerned.

To digress for the moment while on the subject of a Norwich character, and to write of another - who can recall the inimitable town crier, Childerhouse, the little man with the stentorian voice? His official garb also consisted of a long coat and tall hat, the former bearing the city arms. And who can still remember his announcements of the Chapel Field garden fetes 'to be 'eld next Monday evening' invariably concluding with the words: 'Admission twooooooopence!'

I believe Childerhouse (who, by the way, sported prominent side whiskers) lived in the Cow Hill (St Giles' Street) district. Anyhow, we boys thought so and also believed that he partook of special diet (of which treacle was a constituent) the better to maintain his vocal chords at concert pitch! I can still see his quite impressive little figure striding down the street, bell tucked under one arm and grasping a batch of papers. His reputation extended beyond the city and one of the tasteful series of 'Wrench' picture postcards, showing him in full regalia, must have carried his likeness far afield.

Childerhouse had a successor, but although a finer type of man physically, he did not possess the same personality. Later the office fell into disuse and lapsed - unfortunately so, perhaps, as a city of such historic associations as Norwich might well have retained so long-standing and interesting a position on its official establishment.

BUT to return to Tombland: How well I recollect the frequent Sunday church parades of troops stationed at the neighbouring barracks and, following the service at the cathedral, the drill for which we certainly had balcony, if not dress-circle seats. I vividly remember how the scene, after the word 'Dismiss!', became a mass of flowing scarlet.

Tombland would not now permit so brave a show; the car park and the public conveniences would present too great an obstruction. In the days of which I write there was a cab rank, accommodating four or five growlers, with a shelter for the jarveys, on one side of the street, while opposite, were three portable shell-fish stalls to which surely even the Norwich Society, ever jealous of the amenities of the site, would have taken no exception. The small fountain still survives, although on the market day on which I recently (1953) visited the spot aqua pura was so

The inimitable town crier, Childerhouse,
the little man with the stentorian voice.

hemmed in by motor vehicles that I fancied the car park attendant viewed me with some suspicion as I thrust myself betwixt and between them on my mission of rediscovery.

Like Trafalgar Square, Tombland had its pigeons. They were fed by the cabbies, I believe, but as is so often the case under similar circumstances, the flock had the habit of getting out of hand and a periodical thinning-down became advisable.

In Tombland Alley (quite one of the quaintest and most interesting thoroughfares hereabouts) lived a worthy named Dewing. He was the parish clerk and his better-half earned the undying emnity of my brother and me by recommending mother to 'rub in' goose fat on our chests as a preventative of colds.

It was one September night in the early 1890s that in my top-floor bedroom I was awakened by unusual sounds outside and looking through the window I saw a sea of upturned faces lit by the glare of what afterwards became known as 'Cooper's fire.' Cooper's confectionery manufactory was situated at the corner of Queen Street and Upper King Street (since rebuilt and forming a suite of offices) and was separated by the width of the latter thoroughfare and one house, occupied by a family called Forester, from our house. No untoward happening took place as far as we were concerned but the collapse of a chimney resulted in the death of Police-Constable Hook, a tragedy which at the time made a big impression on my youthful mind.

A final childish reminiscence is connected with the Lower Close. In that part where the road narrows in the direction of Thoroughfare Gardens, there stood behind a wall a tin hut, since removed, where I attended meetings of a local Band of Mercy (the name given to junior branches of the R.S.P.C.A.) organised by two young ladies named Lucas and whereat I made my initial public stage appearance in a falteringly delivered recitation entitled 'The Fakenham Ghost' (the 'ghost' proving to be a harmless donkey which effectually scares an old lady returning from market after dark).

Childhood Memories of Old Norwich

Guy P. J. L'Estrange (c1950)

SPRAWLING in an armchair by the fireside during a recent indisposition, I allowed my mind to ramble at will amid time-mellowed recollections of my boyhood days. Some of them dated back between forty and fifty years to the turn of the century, and the vividness of quite unimportant details often astonished me.

One of my earliest memories is of bunting strung across the street near Thorpe station in my native city of Norwich. Echoing down the years, I hear my nurse's voice explaining, "The new king (Edward VII) is going to be crowned tomorrow." Strange to say, I cannot remember the decorations in other parts of the city.

Much about the same time, I saw a man jump into a pony trap outside the station, and pull off his beard as he was being driven away. When I told my mother, she said it was probably something to do with the police. I was puzzled, for to me a policeman was simply a big man in blue uniform and helmet, but I asked no questions.

I first attended school at the age of seven. It was kept by two maiden ladies, sisters, one of whom wore starched neckwear, like a clergyman's. Anxious to be helpful, I told her politely that she had put on her collar back to front. I received no reply, and was about to repeat my remark in a louder tone, assuming that she was a little hard of hearing, when I caught her eye and decided to remain silent.

There were two classrooms, one for the older pupils (grown-ups of nine and ten), the other at the back for beginners. We sat on forms at a long table, I being next to a lovely little girl (to this day, I have no doubt of her loveliness) named Ida, who mothered me in all sorts of endearing ways. Every girl wore a white pinafore, but the boys were attired in a variety of styles, and I thought I had never seen anything so splendid as a cap with a glazed peak belonging to one lad. It fascinated me, that cap, the result being that the wearer and I became close friends.

For a blissful fifteen minutes each morning and afternoon the school played such games as "Poor

Mary is A-Weeping" in the playground. How embarrassed I was every time pretty little Ida summoned me, as her "sweetheart," into the ring! I know I should have been bitterly disappointed had she ever chosen anyone else, yet I felt acutely uncomfortable as I submitted to her kisses, wondering, as I always did, why girls had such moist lips.

BEFORE I left this school, I became acquainted with ha'penny comics, *Chips* being my favourite. I delighted in the exploits of the front page heroes, Weary Willie and Tired Tim, but the ingenious Casey Court Kids appealed to me still more. At nine, much to my parents' astonishment and disapproval, I took to buying the *Eastern Evening News* (then the same price as a comic or two ounces of sweets) and could not explain its enchantment. It used to contain a feature headed "News in a Nutshell," which I loved.

The *Magnet*, with its stories of Billy Bunter, first appeared about this time. It originally cost, I think, a halfpenny. Then there were the *Diamond Library*, 64 pages for a penny, with its thrilling stories of such heroes as Dixon Brett - detective, and the *Nugget Library*, containing 56 pages for the same sum, relating the adventures of those frolicsome schoolboys, Tufty and Co. I revelled in them all, for I spent most of my spare time reading.

The first pierrots seen at Norwich (at any rate, the first I remember) established themselves in a meadow at Thorpe Dene, opposite Harvey Lane. You paid twopence or threepence for a seat, but could stand outside a barrier of iron hurdles for a penny. One of the songs was all about the strange things which might be expected to happen in 1910, still some years distant, and a particular verse ran:

In the year nineteen-hundred-and-ten,
There will be a great difference then,
Girls will leave off their skirts,
And wear trousers and shirts,
In the year nineteen-hundred-and-ten;
  Pom-pom!

This picture of the future seemed to me ludicrous in the extreme, and I laughed until my sides ached. But some of the older people were unamused. It was "not quite nice" to suggest that women would ever step out of their voluminous skirts to don male habiliments. Later, the entertainers moved to Thorpe Gardens, not far from Whitlingham station, where they appeared in naval uniform and called themselves Pierrot Cadets.

IN time, Nelson became my great hero, and it was a treat to be taken to see his statue in the Close, especially after it had been decorated for Trafalgar Day. One of my mother's maids gave me a book about him, and I have it still. I begged to be sent to the Grammar School where he was educated, and there I duly went at the age of eleven. People told me he had carved his name on a brick as a schoolboy, but I searched for it high and low without success.

The headmaster at that time was the Rev. Eustace Fyffe Gilbard, a tall, scholarly man, much loved by the seniors and feared by the juniors. An older boy, Dudley Narborough (now Bishop of Colchester) took me to school for my first day there, and left me with some other newcomers in the pedagogue's study. One nervous youngster whispered to me: "I believe we're expected to call him 'Sir'," and I stamped heavily on his toe just in time for his scream of anguish to make the headmaster jump as he entered the room.

Soon afterwards, an old servant, coming into my bedroom early one morning to pull up the blinds, had tears in her eyes. "Master Guy," she exclaimed, "the poor old king is dead!" With my mind still fogged by sleep, I thought she referred to an unknown Mr King, but was soon made to understand. Then I remembered standing at a window on the gaily decorated Prince of Wales' Road, about a year previously, and seeing a stout, bearded figure pass in an open carriage, attended by a long procession.

A day or two later, my form-master, Mr Liddell, told his class that the school would be closed on the day of the king's funeral. To his horror, the boys, meaning no disrespect to the deceased monarch, cheered lustily as they invariably did when an extra holiday was announced.

Nearly everybody wore something black, if it were only a tie or a jet brooch, during the next week or two. Some tradesmen draped their shop windows, less spacious then than now, in mourning.

A feature of drapers' establishments in those

days was the shop-walker, immaculate in morning coat and glossy collar, who asked your requirements at the door, and then bawled them forth in sterntorian tones. "Miss So-and-so, forward! Black-edged handkerchiefs for this customer, if you please." Finally, having made your purchase, you were bowed into the street with all the courtesy imaginable.

IN June 1911, Norwich was en fete again, this time for the crowning of George V. The decorations were kept up after the coronation, others being added until the city was rendered unrecognisable by its triumphal arches and canopies of artificial flowers, and I learned that the new king would soon be seen in his Norfolk capital. He intended to visit the Royal Show, held that year at Crown Point, on the second day.

I saw him at the show, and was disappointed beyond words. Most of his published pictures depicted him in a resplendent uniform of an admiral of the fleet, with the broad blue ribbon of the garter aslant across his chest, and here he was, a short figure with a bald patch on his head, dressed like any other man. "Fair as a Saxon!" commented my mother, admiringly. I looked again, tried in vain to identify him with the highly coloured presentation plate I had fastened to my bedroom wall, and gave up with a sigh.

That night there were fireworks and an enormous bonfire on Mousehold. My parents took me as far as Foundry Bridge, whence I had a not very good view, and we soon went home again. The streets were crowded. Trams, decorated with bunting and coloured balloons, would take you all round the city to see the illuminations for, I think, sixpence.

THE floods of 1912 are another vivid memory. I remember going with my sister through torrential rain to keep an appointment with a dentist. Her umbrella blew inside out, and she had to relinquish it. Somewhere in Norwich a pretty, fair-haired girl, who was to become my wife one day, rushed upstairs with her family as the water invaded the ground floor of their house. Streets were transformed into rivers. Many people, rendered homeless, were given temporary shelter in schools. Others marooned in bedrooms had provisions carried to them in boats. Even on Prince of Wales Road there was a good-sized lake, near a new picture theatre known as the Prince of Wales Palace.

I do not remember when Norwich had its first cinema, but I recall the place, a shabby old building called the Victoria Hall, in St Stephen's Street. It was approached by a narrow flight of stairs. I never went there, but soon became acquainted with the Theatre de Lux, in St Andrew's, which appeared next. Stalls were 3d. and the balcony 6d., children being admitted for twopence and threepence, and the entertainment lasted two-and-a-half hours. Soon other picture theatres, the Haymarket (not the imposing building which exists now) and the Electric Theatre on Prince of Wales Road, sprang into being, and the films were given added realism by sound effects. A special piece of apparatus, worked by an attendant, imitated the noises made by horses trotting, water-falls, pistol shots, thunderstorms and so on.

The first "talkies" to be seen at Norwich were shown at the Agricultural Hall in 1912 or thereabouts. They did not amount to much, these "talking pictures," as they were called, and attracted very little notice. You saw a figure on the screen singing a popular song such as "Who Were You With Last Night?" the voice and accompaniment being provided by two large gramophones set on either side of the screen.

I liked the "pictures," but what I liked better were the regular musical evenings at home. Friends arrived with sheet music, and, though I had discovered Dickens at the age of twelve, I did not want to read when I could listen to the piano reproducing the masterpieces of Chopin, Beethoven, Liszt, Mozart and Mendelssohn.

One evening, feeling utterly reckless for some reason which I have forgotten, I put a stink bomb in my pocket (these things were new and could be bought at most toy shops, three in a box for twopence, then) before I entered the drawing-room. What my mother would have said if she had known, I cannot think, but she never did know, for I was powerless to crush the pernicious thing after listening to a Chopin nocturne. So I saved it until the geography lesson next day, when it caused quite a stir, in more than one sense of the word.

TALKING of entertainment reminds me of the Christmas and Easter fairs. People who declare that fairs are not what they used to be speak nothing but the truth. Forty years ago (1910), a series of temporary theatres, with glittering facades and blaring steam organs, faced the Shire Hall for the duration of the fair, providing a cinematograph and variety entertainment at a cost of two or three coppers. On the platform outside the entrance to the auditorium, clowns, dancing girls and strong men gave free exhibitions of their skill to draw a crowd.

These were in addition, of course, to the shooting ranges, freak shows, coconut shies, roundabouts, and "aunt sallies." In time there came the mat toboggan ("A penny on the mat"), now known simply as "the toboggan"; the cake-walk, subsequently called the rag-time glide and other topical names; the joy wheel, a circular platform which revolved at varying speeds, whirling off all who sat on it; and, at last, the hoop-la. The last-named novelty soon outdid all other games of chance in popularity, and it was the aim of everybody who threw a hoop to encircle an alarm-clock, though there were other attractive prizes.

As a child, I looked forward to the fair for weeks. With Christmas or Easter drawing near, I was thrilled to the core if I caught sight of a wagon laden with wooden horses on its way to the fair ground. It was not that I hungered for a ride on the roundabouts or was consumed with an overpowering desire to hurl wooden balls at a row of pipes in the gaping mouth of an "aunt sally." I was quite satisfied with a single trip on the gilded "Venetian gondolas" (the prancing horses never appealed to me) each day, and that was all I usually had. Merely to wander about the fair-ground, with the shouts of the showmen and the strains of the steam-organs in my ears, was bliss enough for me.

BEFORE I conclude, let me return to school for a more sombre memory. I cannot recall the date, but it was probably the summer of 1911, and all the boys were assembled in the big hall for end-of-term examinations. The headmaster was very ill. As brows puckered over papers, the door opened and the science-master, one of Mr Gilbard's oldest friends, entered quietly, murmured a few words to his colleagues on the rostrum, and then turned a white face to meet the gaze of the assembled school.

"Boys, the headmaster is dead."

Like most of the boys, I attended "Gillie's" funeral at the cathedral. The seniors predicted that the old school would never be the same again, and indeed many changes were effected when the new "head" the Rev. W. F. Brown, took charge. He it was who divded the school into "houses," and the handsome sports shield for which they were to compete each year was his gift.

I have many pleasant recollections of Mr Brown, who took a great interest in the religious life of his boys. He prepared many of them, myself included, for confirmation, and I took my first communion from his hands. I remember well my confirmation, with three or four schoolfellows, in the Bishop's private chapel. We and our parents attended tea at the palace first, and after the service Dr Pollock chatted with each of us alone.

I still possess the little altar manual given me some days later by the headmaster. The inscription on the fly-leaf reads: "G. P. J. L'Estrage, from W.F.B., in memory of Advent Sunday, 1913."

'The Man in the Moon came tumbling down . . .'

Sylvia Haymon (c1958), Illustrated by Marjorie Budd

SOME people may have wondered why, with the whole world to choose from, the Man in the Moon, when he came tumbling down, asked the way to Norwich. Not I. I happen to come from there and it does not surprise me in the least.

In a sense, Norwich is for me a haunted city; haunted by the ghost of the child I was. I look back at my old - or rather, my young - self as I might look into one of those glass paperweights that have a tiny figure inside: shake them and a miniature snowstorm swirls about the little figure, then settles again.

Even so I peer in it myself, inviolable in that magical world of youth. I shake the glass globe. The memories swirl like snowflakes, and gently subside.

It is a small town I see - yes, small, even though its population is well over 100,000. Small because one could compass it as a whole - not an indeterminate agglomeration of suburbs, world without end, middle or beginning. The town has a unity imposed by history. Cathedral, castle, market - these lay at its heart and all roads, like veins and arteries, led to them.

Ah, the Market! Saturday was the day. A jostle of people in the narrow streets, townsfolk, countryfolk, competing good-humouredly for elbow room with cars, trams, bicycles, cattle and horses.

Do you know what 'lokusses' are - or locust beans, to give them their proper name (which nobody ever did)? I used to buy them twelve for a penny in Norwich Market. They looked like small pieces of wood that had been dipped in varnish and were still tacky. My recollection was that they tasted better than the best kind of toffee - until, quite recently, I came upon some in a London store. Then, alas, I discovered that not only did they look like varnished wood, they tasted like it too. But perhaps it was I who had changed and not the 'lokusses'.

I used to invest another penny in half a pint of

tiger nuts - not nuts at all but some kind of seed, I imagine, brown and shrivelled, about the size of a small pea and tasting vaguely of vanilla. In summer I bought ice-cream off a painted cart like the gondola of a merry-go-round, manned by Mr Marcantonio, a wistful little monkey of a man with the longest waxed moustachios in captivity.

His ice-cream was none of your hygienic wrapped stuff but a thick yellow custard tailored to your individual requirements with a paddle and a little metal contraption that held the wafer. It tasted heavenly - and as for those moustachios, oh they were a sight to see!

There were sweet stalls piled with Everests of candy where my elder sister, who was not yet allowed to use face powder, used to buy little sausage-shaped bon-bons which she would rub on her nose and cheeks before popping into her mouth. They were coated with some powdery stuff which, to her great self-satisfaction, overlaid her natual rosiness with a corpse-like pallor.

There were stalls where you could buy square white cheeses smooth as jelly, on little rafts of straw; flower and fruit vendors galore and stalls where they sold tortoises and Norwich canaries - and behind them all, the delicate, pierced tower of St Peter Mancroft and the ageless flint of the old Guildhall, climbing away from the Market Place up the steep gradient of St Giles.

ANYONE who dismisses Norfolk as flat is hereby challenged to take a cycle ride round Norwich. To a child, it was a matter of honour not to get off and push. Standing up on the pedals, weaving dangerously about the narrow streets, heart and lungs pumping fit to burst, one held on and on. Another yard, yet one more, and then - what bliss! The sweet triumph of breasting the rise, victor alike over the force of gravity and the frailty of the flesh! Conversely, there was the perilous joy of swooping downhill like an arrow, in a small hurricane of one's own making.

There is a tract of gorse and heather called Mousehold Heath at the edge of the town. There were barracks there when I was a child and a fine, knife-edged hill to fly a kite from or feel the wind in your teeth. There was a prison there, and down the road from the prison a copse where a woman once was found with her head hammered in.

All these things are Mousehold Heath to me - soldiers, kites, men caged in and violent death, or the acrid smell of gorse and heather that murmured with bees; all these and more.

There, on the Heath, George Borrow had seen his first gipsy encampment. There, Robert Kett, the great rebel, had gathered to his standard the poor and the oppressed and led them, in the end, down to defeat and death in the valley below. Among the gorse and heather the child that was I relived their lives in its own person: *I* was Borrow, *I* was Kett.

That ancient oak - had it posed for Old Crome?

I was Crome. Below me lay the city, still much as he had painted it - green water-meadows, the winding ribbon of the river and the cathedral steeple pointing to Heaven.

'Lokusses' and Robert Ketts, Mr Marcantonio's moustachios and the wind on the heath - random scraps from the incongruous patchwork of childhood. You may not recognise Norwich from my description because the Norwich I have been describing is part of me, just as, for better or worse, I am part of Norwich.

'The Man in the Moon came tumbling down
And asked the way to Norwich . . .
I hope somebody directed him . . .

The Street Characters of Old Cambridge

Alice Mary Bond (c1952)

AN article on our beloved Parker's Piece in Cambridge brought back many memories of childhood days spent there.

It also made me think of people of those days of the past, the characters that we loved and the fun they brought into our lives. Time or custom or fashion did not alter them. Year in, year out, they were the same. There was the cinder-dust man. Old Singie Tarbrush, he was called. He did not collect house refuge - only cinder ash. He came round once a week with his pony cart. He was smothered with ashes and his flat-topped hat had a thick layer of dust upon it. There was dust, too, on his pony. He wore clothes that were too big for him and dreadful old shoes. His face was always dirty and his whiskers were covered with

ash like the rest of him. I have never seen so
dirty a man.

We children used to make him angry. 'Does
your mother use Sunlight?' or 'Did your mother
forget to bath you last night?' we would ask him.
He would put his nose in the air and brush the
dust from his hands in Charlie Chaplin style and
ride away.

It was all great fun.

Then there was our little oil man. He came
every week. He was so small he might have been
one of Snow White's dwarfs. He pushed a little
cart with two large cans inside and some small
ones hanging outside. He had a very big voice
for such a small man and he called: 'Oil, lamp
oil, today.' He sold a lot and made a good living.

The vegetable man was known as 'Old Goo-
on,' for he was forever saying that to his sleepy
horse. He would call out: 'Taters or cabbage or
turnips or onions. Goo-on, there!' But whatever
he shouted at it, his horse went only one pace.

We had a shrimp and mussel man who wore
ear-rings. He had a voice that could be heard a
long way off and people were always out to buy
before he arrived in the street. The wood man
called 'billet or block-o' and also sold peat at
several pieces for a penny. The trotter man came
round in the evenings. He sold sheep's feet at
a ha'penny each. We liked to hear his call:
'Trot-o, trot-o!' in the dark evenings.

And what fun we had watching the scissors
grinder, who pedalled his machine with such thin
legs in such tight trousers. He had a nice singing
voice and as the sparks flew he would sing . . .

'Large knives or small knives,
Carving knives or table knives,
Any knives I grind . . . umperellers I mend.'

He was not the only singer in the street. One I
remember was known as 'New Penny.' She wore
many skirts, some long, some short, which she
held up with one hand as they were always
slipping down. Her great hat was a mass of
feathers that wanted curling and her toes were
poking out of her shoes. She sang the same verse
of the same hymn all the time and the strange
notes that came out of that poor creature had to
be heard to be believed. Her hymn was: 'All the
storms will soon be over.' She always stood in the
gutter with her hand held out to any passerby.

Then there was a little old
man who stood on the
market selling almanacks.
I never saw anyone buy
from him but there he stood
in all weathers calling: 'Old
Moore's Almanacks. Old
Moore's perdicaments of
the weather. Penny each.'

The hurdy-gurdy man
was our special favourite.
He came every week to
play the latest tunes to
us. We were always
intrigued by the cradle
that was strapped on
to the organ for it
had a baby inside. We
wondered however the
baby could sleep through
all that noise. But it did.

In the early morning came the bloater man with
fine, fresh bloaters for breakfast. The muffin man
and the tripe man came once a week. The little
old tin man came with his kettles and saucepans
and all kinds of tin-ware in his basket. He made
them himself. He had very bright blue eyes and
wore a moleskin waistcoat. He was proud of his
craftsmanship and would keep saying: 'None
better, my dear, none better.'

I remember Old Bungo, Old Hambone, Old
Ooten Gootens, Old Liza who sold button-holes
outside the New Theatre. I remember, too, the
'Pop-shop Poppies.' They were a race apart from
all the others as they brought unhappiness
wherever they went. They thrived on people who
were out of work, people who, somehow or other,
had to find the rent. The Pop-shop Poppies
always seemed to be fond of drink. They were a
despicable lot.

A character of more recent years was Sluice
Parker. What a fellow he was. What a merry wit
he had. He sold plants at the door. He called
them 'everlasting begonias.' But they always died
within a couple of days. Someone asked him once
if he knew his duty towards his neighbour. 'Yes,'
he said. 'Keep your eye on him.' He had an
answer for everything. The last time I saw him
was just before his accident. He came to my

back door, looking very ill. He had, as usual, a pot plant, one of his 'everlasting begonias.' He said he was ill and going deaf. 'Oh, lady,' he said, 'ain't it hard to be deaf. Just think, lady, a pal asked me to have a pint and I didn't hear him.' I told him I was sorry for him but didn't want his plant. But I helped him on his way. I went to the gate with him. I shall always remember the look on his face as he turned to me and said: 'It is very hard, lady.' I said goodbye. I did not think that day was the last time I should see one of Cambridge's best known characters. He died following an accident soon afterwards.

Just lately another well-known character, called 'Spiv,' has died in rather sad circumstances. But he went to his rest amid the great kindness and affection of the British Legion in our city.

Memories of Bonfires, Bicycles & Butter by the Yard

Cecile Arburn Spring (c1952)

FIFTY years ago I was a child in Cambridge. I was taught the piano and harmony by the borough organist there, and singing by a very famous singing-master living at the time in the town. Above all I was watched and guided with loving interest by the then organist of King's College chapel, Dr. Mann, whose Festival Choir was at its zenith. Choirs from Norwich and King's Lynn came each year to take part in some great choral work conducted by him - very often the first provincial performances of new works (especially Elgar's) took place in the chapel at these festivals.

But it is not of music that I write but of smaller happenings that I remember between my tenth and twenty-fifth years. Bicycles were only just beginning to be popular. Though my father rode a 'penny-farthing', women had not mounted these high steeds. But about the year 1898 I learned to ride on a bicycle hired from a shop. It had one cross-bar about half way up and was easy to

mount or dismount. When I became proficient I had a cycle of my own. I think mine was only the second ladies' bicycle to be seen in the Cambridge streets.

'. . . only the second ladies' bicycle to be seen in the Cambridge streets.'

Cycling for ladies was frowned upon. It was harmful to girls, my mother was assured. I well remember when coming into my house one day I had to stand at the kerb to allow a lady (no less than the wife of a master of a college) to pass. She remarked to me: 'I am surprised that your mother allows you to ride one of those vulgar machines.' However, it was but a year or so later that I saw her youngest daughter riding one, carrying a hockey stick and wearing a very muddy short skirt.

An early memory takes me back to my school days and it concerns the lions on the top of the side steps of the Fitzwilliam Museum. I was told that when they heard one o'clock strike, they came down to drink at the 'Run' (the little stream which flows on each side of Trumpington Street - and used to flow also in St Andrew's Street). Many times I stood and waited for Addenbrooke's Hospital clock to reach one o'clock before I would go home to dinner (and get into trouble for being late). But the lions never seemed to hear the clock strike. It was an awful discovery when one day I realised that they never would hear. Are children still told these tales?

Speaking of this 'Run': a very famous mathematician, I remember, seemed to be fascinated by it. He used to cross it and recross it at each little bridge, remaining on the road till he came to the next, then returning to the pavement - and so on until the little stream disappeared underground at Pembroke College.

Another famous divine used to remain close to the house side of the pavement. When any building jutted out he would skirt it and then return close to the houses again. Perhaps he was nervous of the running water!

Three great events of the year occurred when my grandfather hired a wagonette in which four people sat on either side facing one another, with a black furry rug at our feet on the floor, and we taken as children on three great excursions into the nearby fens. First we went to see what fields were sown and how far the corn was up. The second journey, near mid-summer, was to see the corn ripening, and the third was to see it cut and stacked.

My grandmother and mother wore special clothes for these outings - grey alpaca dust coats which protected their usual black garments from the great clouds of dust that rose around us as our wheels grated along those fenland roads.

Harvest festivals in churches and chapels were in those days great occasions. They were very real and vital to all of us, for hadn't we seen the corn growing, then ripening, then gathered in.

CAMBRIDGE market on Market Hill was chiefly for the sale of country produce. One stall I remember in particular. It stood opposite the end of St Mary's Passage and my father visited it each week almost as a ritual. It had poultry and butter for sale. Chickens were from 1s. 6d. each and butter, if I remember correctly, was a shilling a pound. The butter was sold from long baskets measuring a yard and lined with the snowiest of white cloths. The long rolls of butter were an inch or so thick, a length of one yard weighing a pound, and half a yard half a pound. I do not remember ever seeing it weighed at the time of sale. A knife guided by the eye with a turn of the head from side to side severed the roll in the middle and so your half pound was cut off.

To celebrate the visit of any great personage to the university, or on Guy Fawkes' night, or at any excuse for celebration, the Market Place was the scene of many a raging bonfire fed by anything movable that would burn and which the undergraduates could carry. Lengths of garden fence often required a dozen or so willing carriers. And then came the awful rush when the cry of 'progs!' arose - for I believe it is a fact that only those caught in the act of carrying fuel and throwing it on the blaze could be apprehended by the proctors with their bulldogs or by the police. Exciting but all rather terrifying.

Looking back I am struck by the remembrance that certain journeys seemed then great distances. To take a ride from Christ's College to the railway station on the top of one of the old horse-drawn trams was almost an adventure. The trams had what I believe is termed a knife-board seat on the top. It had no roofing cover of course. It went from one end of the tram to the other so that the passengers faced the houses. In summer time to try and look into the first-floor open windows was considered a good game. That of course was rather rude (though I must confess it was very tempting). At the two termini the horse was taken out and transferred to the other end and back the tram went.

Midsummer Fair on the common was not a gathering at which young ladies were seen - certainly not alone. But I remember being escorted there by my father, just one quick visit and home again.

A very lovely walk lingers in my memory. It was from FitzWilliam Street to Downing Street, through tall gates at both entrances and under an avenue of trees, mostly lime. That walk is something which the inhabitants of today cannot enjoy. Cows used to graze here but were mercifully (to my mind) kept safely behind railings. Cows grazed also on New Square, wandering to and fro across the path.

136

A line of hansom cabs used to stand on a rank outside the Senate House. It was a never-ceasing wonderment to me how those rather large, heavy men in bowler hats managed to heave themselves into the very small, high-up seats on the back of the cab. The horses seemed to wear nose-bags perpetually when on the stand and, as I passed, usually contrived to give a sneeze into them, blowing the oat husks all over me. Inside the cabs the drivers slept and snored as they awaited customers.

I remember another joke told in all seriousness in my youth - that sausages were made from old cab horses and that to prove it one had only to put a line of them on the cab rank and they'd 'move up' as the front one was taken away.

So much for a few recollections when the thought of the Cambridge sausages of *those* days also brings pleasant memories.

College and Social Life in Cambridge c1919

Phyllis Mills (c1955), Illustrated by R. Sell

I SAW Cambridge for the first time in 1919 when I had been married a week. My husband had been an undergraduate from 1910 to 1913. He had then gone to the Sorbonne, meaning to stay there two years and take a degree. But, after his first year, the war intervened. He joined the army and never went back to Paris. Now he was demobilised and he had spent the first six months of his civilian life in Cambridge working on a thesis in the hope of a fellowship. In his spare time he had renewed his acquaintance with the Cam and had coached his colleagues' 'getting-on' boat.

Now his thesis was finished. It had been sent in and we could only await the result. He had a job with a salary on which we could marry - at least we thought it was enough.

So, in spite of the horrid warnings of our elder relations who seemed to think we were heading for poverty and disaster, we planned our wedding. It was not easy to find anywhere to live in

'To take a ride on the top of the old horse-drawn trams was almost an adventure.' Photograph: Ramsey & Mospratt.

Cambridge but an hotel in Petty Cury let us have four tiny rooms in its annexe. They were officially 'furnished' and we filled the many gaps with wedding presents and furniture from our homes. Our week's honeymoon coincided with a big railway strike but we managed to arrive in Cambridge only a day later than we had planned.

Cambridge looked its beautiful best that autumn in day after day of golden sunshine. The Virginian creeper blazed fiery red, Cotoneaster berries glowed on the grey stone, the trees in the Backs were every shade of flame and russet.

Petty Cury was noisy and narrow but from our windows we could see Christ's gateway. I thought that nothing could be more congested than Mincing Lane, where I had worked before my marriage, but it was nothing compared with the traffic that now surged below us. Petty Cury was not then a one-way street and cars and lorries interlocked like superior jigsaws. Bicycles were pushed at less than walking pace, the narrow pavements were always overcrowded and pedestrians plaited themselves in and out of the array.

Our minute rooms were at the top of the house and a married undergraduate and his wife lived on the first floor. A seedsman's shop occupied the ground floor. Strange smells wafted up to us when he opened a new bag of fertiliser. But he was very kind and would take messages from people who called when I was out. He knew almost everyone in Cambridge by sight and would often point out a lady who had left cards upon me. That gave me the chance to return her call before she reached her home, providing that I was given this information during the recognised calling hours. The first call and its return were a purely formal exchange of cards that might or might not lead to friendship.

THE hotel cooked for us in an underground kitchen at the other side of the street, bringing our meals across the road and up two flights of stairs yet, miraculously, serving everything piping hot. We had no tap in our abode but they took it as a matter of course that they should provide hot water for a bath every morning. We had borrowed an ancient hip-bath that dated from my father-in-law's undergraduate days.

Young couples like ourselves lived in nooks and crannies all over the town. Some rented houses in Chesterton Road and de Freville Avenue. It was a short cut as well as an exciting experience to cross the river by the ferry, known as the 'grind,' to reach the outskirts.

Never before had I led so crowded a social life. We were constantly asked to parties, as well as to more formal lunches and dinners. Sherry parties were an innovation given by

'Petty Cury was narrow and noisy'

The 'Grind'

the more modern inhabitants. Tea-parties, always a great feature of Cambridge life, abounded. And every morning at 11, the 'Whim', then in Rose Crescent, and its rival cafes were crowded with coffee drinkers.

I did a good deal of chaperoning for mixed parties in college. The girls at Newnham and Girton were not allowed to go to the men's rooms without a duenna in attendance and I, being about the same age as my charges, filled the bill satisfactorily.

We did a good deal of entertaining in return, as far as our restricted means and space would allow. I didn't realise just how many our tiny rooms would hold until I had them packed every evening by young men who heaped gowns on our narrow staircase and discussed the problems of the universe over a cup of coffee and chocolate biscuits.

Some of the undergraduates had married during their military service. The older dons found their young wives and babies a puzzling problem. They could remember the time when fellows were not allowed to marry and university babies were few and far between.

The women's colleges were not yet officially recognised. The girls had no gowns and only titular degrees. Their clothes were far more formal than those of the girls who have succeeded them. Never were they seen without stockings and rarely without hats. They wore little make-up and the rules and regulations that governed their lives were far more strict than any that prevail today. But they seemed perfectly happy, although their very existence was ignored by most lecturers who addressed their audiences simply as 'gentlemen'.

MY husband actually achieved his fellowship, much to our delight. I had given little consideration to the financial side of this honour and it was a pleasant surprise to discover that, along with it, went £200 a year free of tax and the privilege of dining in hall every night if he chose.

During our first year the senior proctor asked my husband to deputise for him at a congregation, as he would be in Canada on the date for which it was fixed. On his return, he suggested that the arrangement might be permanent for his term of office, as far as special functions were concerned. This senior proctor happened also to be public orator and could not double the two roles on the Senate House platform. So my husband would make his appearance with the bulldogs, looking acutely self-conscious in gown and boards. It was specially lucky for me, even if he didn't enjoy it much, for, as the proctor held office for only a year, their wives were asked to everything and I had a good view of all sorts of ceremonies. Many distinguished men were given honorary degrees, especially in the first year after the war.

The late King and the Duke of Gloucester - then Prince Albert, and Prince Henry, were then undergraduates at Trinity. They went about with a complete lack of ceremony and except on special occasions there was nothing to distinguish them from the other men.

During that winter the 'Fairy Queen' was produced at the New Theatre. There were concerts, plays at the A.D.C. with an all-male cast and dances. We watched rugger matches on winter afternoons and cheered the college Lent boat when it went head of the river.

I found the price of food a worry. Butter was 5s. 6d. a pound but it was still rationed. Eggs were 6d. each. Margarine was reasonably priced but it was very nasty. Cream, on the other hand, was plentiful and one could buy luscious cakes. The undergraduates could be seen every day carrying boxes and bags from the confectioners and bunches of flowers. I loved their cosy tea-parties in college, with plates of delicious food on the hearth rug and crumpets and muffins toasted at the fire. And there were lunches when the young hosts made superb omelettes or cooked the sausages that one bought at a shop off Sidney Street that were better than anything I ever tasted.

There were, too, meals from the college kitchens that taught me to appreciate superb cooking.

WE found a house in the spring - as much too big for us as the rooms at Petty Cury were cramped. It was one of a Regency terrace and I loved it dearly in spite of its unsuitable size. We now had a spare room - in fact we had half-a-dozen, mostly unfurnished. We had friends to stay and paying guests for May Week and spent our profits on dancing the daylight in at the balls.

Cambridge was still practically in the country. The college had not yet built on the other side of the river and the library was in King's Parade. Fields surrounded the town where there are now suburban roads and new houses.

I stayed in a road on the way to Grantchester some years after we left Cambridge. At the bottom of my host's garden was a strip of the river. Punts and canoes, each with its portable gramophone or wireless set, jostled one another; houses clustered all round.

This was once that part of the river called 'Paradise' where we would tie up our punt under the May tree while larks sang above the shining golden fields that were a sheet of buttercups, and waterhens scuttled round us.

Now our Regency terrace has been pulled down and a new telephone exchange has been built on the site. It is an admirable building in its modern factual way but I think of the well-proportioned windows and stately facade of the old houses. I remember our beautiful door with its fanlight and the gently worn steps that led up to it. The staircase had a mahogany handrail and wide shallow steps, and on the first floor was a room with pillars from a four post bed set into the panelling, and roses and a great pear tree grew in the garden where we sat on summer evenings.

The seedsman's shop is now a branch of a multiple grocer, and above it is a cafe called, not inappropriately, the Eros. It would be easy enough to climb the stairs that once led to our eyrie. But the ghosts of our lost youth live in the upper floors. I leave them undisturbed.

The Crumpet Man, Rock Maker & Old Horse Trams
L. J. Tibbenham (c1951)

SIXTY years ago (1890), Carr Street, Ipswich, was not the shopping centre that it is today, but a very narrow thoroughfare mostly made up of private houses with a few shops dotted about in between.

The street twisted like a snake and the roadway was of stones and was always dirty. As a small boy I used to bowl my hoop and spin my top in the road, for there were no back gardens and the road was the only place in which to play. There was little traffic, just an occasional horse and trap. I remember one day I ran with my hoop as far as White Horse Corner and there I was frightened by a high stepping horse. I left my hoop to its own resources and it became entangled in the horses legs. I can still see the driver's fierce look as he tried to strike me with his whip.

The narrowness of the street will be obvious when I say that one of my elder brothers was very expert with a peashooter and he used to blow peas from our attic window across to the windows opposite. We did it - I feel unutterable shame at the memory today - to see a poor blind man run his fingers over the panes to make sure they had not been broken.

There was no water inside our house and, of course, no sanitation. We had a tap in the yard. Also in the yard was a fairly large receptacle which I believe everyone called a 'bumby.' It was a smelly affair in which all the house refuse was dumped as well. Every so often it was cleaned out - always at night, and as far as we boys were concerned it was a secret business. We were all packed off to bed. But we used to lie awake and hear the tramp up and down the side passage of the scavengers. It must have been an awful job. When it was finished my father always gave them a good round of beer. I guess they needed it.

The 'bumby'.

For illumination we had gas. The jets were very tiny and burned with a yellow flame (the incandescent burners came along later). We supplemented the gas jets with oil table reading lamps. At night, in case of emergency, a small jet was always left burning on our landing. Sometimes, as the gas pressure varied, the jet would jump up to a foot in height, with a high-pitched screech that frightened the whole family.

There were six of us in the family, but ten people in all lived in the house. We were happy enough although we were overcrowded. We had three small bedrooms, one of which was an attic, and the larger bedroom was used as a parlour on Sundays. That was a special treat. The living room was very tiny. It measured about nine feet square and in it was a small, five-bar fire grate in front of which my father every Sunday morning used to frizzle the bacon for breakfast. He used a weird contraption that used to hang upon the front bars. I can taste that hot frizzled bacon now.

WE had a number of queer neighbours. For example there was the crumpet man. He would be about the streets quite early crying: 'Hot crumpets.' He had a bell and he carried a board on his head. It was supported on a green baize ring like a cushion. The crumpet man's father used to make rock. He was a big fellow with curly hair and a bald patch in front. He had great brawny arms and he used to throw the rock over a hook attached to the wall of his shop which we could see from our front window. No doubt his work was hard. He would spit on his hands and sweat as he pulled the slowly cooling rock. It was of all colours and various flavours. It cost one penny a quarter and it was good, too. We purchased this rock in small lumps like marbles which he used to produce in a small, hand-operated machine attached to his counter.

Next door was a hairdressers. This was the 'news shop' of the district and I should imagine it was the local bookmakers shop too.

My mother used to send me there every few weeks with a message that he was not to put any of that greasy stuff on my hair. It seemed to her, I think, that it made my hair grow too quickly, as our hair always seemed to need cutting. (I wish I had the secret of that imaginary hair grower today!). The cost of a haircut was twopence, that of a shave a penny. The barber would ask us whether we would like a mechanical hair brush. We always said yes. His boy would turn a large wheel which worked an overhead contraption and through a rubber belt would revolve a circular brush on one's head. It was quite a pleasant feeling.

In the winter months - and indeed during most of the year - there was a baked potato can opposite the Cross Keys public house. It was very popular. One could get a huge potato with a pinch of salt and a nip of butter for one penny or without these extravagant etceteras for a halfpenny.

No street was complete in those days without a coffee shop and in Carr Street the coffee shop had a dull-looking window with a large ginger cat always lying in it. There was little else in the window except a large rice pudding, a stiff concoction that was sold at a penny a slice. I never crossed the threshold of this establishment so cannot say what fare it provided but I could see that it contained a trestle table and two forms.

The most popular shop with me was a sweet

141

shop near White Horse Corner. By standing on my toes I could just see into the window and was always intrigued by the notice: VARIETIES ONE PENNY PER QUARTER. The first word was too difficult for me to pronounce, so my elder brother used to place the order for me. 'Varieties' consisted of animals made from boiled sweet stuff, and I used to tell him to ask for elephants as they were the largest.

and cockles and they could be eaten in the shop with plenty of vinegar.

I REMEMBER very vividly losing a sixpence which my mother had entrusted to me to buy some baking powder at a nearby grocer's shop. I must have been very nervous about being sent on such an important errand and I lost the sixpence. This was indeed a terrible catastrophe. Sixpence,

Carr Street as it was in 1890

Another shop very popular with the small folk was at the top of two steps. It was owned by a dear old lady with side curls and, of course, the conventional cap. We could buy anything here for a farthing upwards . . . marbles, tops, cottons, needles, notepaper, ink, even the penny cane which every parent kept handy to control his large family.

The shop at the corner of Brook Street was what we called an oyster saloon. There was not much of a saloon about it, but it was considered to be very manly to stand in the shop and swallow a dozen oysters. I can remember only the acrid smell that came from the inside when I passed the open door. Next to it was a greengrocers, which I believe belonged to the same man, and I think the oyster shop also sold whelks, mussels

in those days, was a lot of money. One can imagine my mother's anger when I reported the loss. I was clouted and sent back to find it. This seemed impossible. I had no idea where I had lost it. But in those days the floor of a shop was covered with about an inch of sawdust and I scratched about on the floor and I found it. What great relief was mine. I made my purchase. But, in my elation, I asked for borax and I took it to my mother with great glee and, as she had been waiting for it, she dumped it into the pudding without a thought. Dinner that day was not a success. As the pudding was turned out it kept getting smaller and smaller until there was not much to see for six hungry boys and the grown-ups round the table. But there were no ill effects.

I was proud of my mother. She was called the

Duchess of Carr Street and she did look a swell in her bustle and flouncy skirt and a high bonnet and a black parasol. And when she went out to see her friends she always carried a neat little basket containing an 'at home' cap: no married lady was properly dressed indoors without a lace cap.

As boys, we of course had to make our own amusements and our own friends. Children were plentiful in the neighourhood and were nearly all

and we would go nearly wild with delight.

In those days transport was very limited. But there was a single-decker tram, drawn by a horse with a bell dangling on its front harness. The tram operated on a single track and could pass another tram only on a loop, so that one tram would sometimes have to wait for the other. I never had an opportunity of riding in this luxurious vehicle. I suppose my parents had no

The Promenade by the Orwell with Hog Highland in the distance.

boys. I think that in three families there were quite a couple of dozen of us. The older boys had to look after the younger ones. We each had a three-wheel pram and we often made a procession down the street, with three boys abreast in each pram. Then off we would go to the river promenade to catch crabs, and we went even as far afield as Hog Highland where in the summer time we would bathe in the river in the natural state. We never thought of danger. Or we would go to Gainsborough Heath. This was a wonderful outing. It usually took place during the school holidays, when we would be ordered by our mothers to be out all day. We were deliriously happy with a bottle of tea or liquorice water and some bread and butter. The freedom of this open heathland was an exciting change from our tiny back yards

coppers to spare. All I knew was that it used to disappear towards the viaduct in Spring Road.

GRADUALLY, as the years went by, the street took on a new shape. I should think more than half of it was pulled down and rebuilt in its present form. My father was always talking about it but I never realised what was taking place. All I know is that we were lucky and that my father's little house was one of the few places left. I saw the Lyceum Theatre built. I saw the site cleared and a large hole dug out for its pit and after its short life I saw it demolished.

There were at least three public houses in Carr Street, and every night I would sneak out of bed to see the drunks go home. I was really terrified. But they fascinated me as there was nearly always a fight. I have seen many such fights, even with women too. I am glad those things do not happen now.

There was quite a variety of shops in this street of ours; a wood turner who had all kinds of turned pieces of wood in the window; a harness shop, a very essential shop, for this was a 'horsey' period; the newspaper printing works, the beginning of the *East Anglian Daily Times* - If I woke up in the night I could always hear the roar of the printing presses, and, near the harness shop, a newspaper shop. It was a very tiny place. I was always horrified by the sheets displayed outside the window. They always seemed to show murders, fires, earthquakes and all kinds of dreadful things. Inside was the

The beautiful timber-framed house at Cox Lane corner lost to redevelopment.

usual collection of penny dreadfuls which were all the rage at the time and every February the most grotesque Valentines were sold by the yard.

Adjoining the alleyway of the Cross Keys was a very large house, half-timbered and surrounded at the back by a 10-foot wall. I remember it very well because it came up to our back yard and shut out every bit of sunlight. For some time, I recall, the house was occupied by a very fashionable doctor who used to drive out with a pair of high-stepping greys.

Another half-timbered building was the shop at Cox Lane corner where the man made his rock. It had a wonderful corner post. In later years, when alterations were being made to the street, this building was purchased, or at least the woodwork, by my brother. We little thought, my brothers and I, when we used to watch the brawny, perspiring man making his rock, that one of us would one day buy the old place. I believe the old house was reconstructed and re-erected elsewhere, possibly in the United States, as a genuine old English timbered house.

Sunday School Treats and Things a Penny would Buy

L. R. Garrard (c1956), Illustrated by Joan Pickford

WHAT a wonderful thing memory is! It is something we all possess but no man in the world is wise enough to tell us how it works. A sound, a smell, a taste, a sight - and the years have vanished in a flash and we are back again in our childhood days, living over the simple but important pains and pleasures that made up those early and formative years.

For example, the lady who handed me a chocolate some time ago was doing something more than she or I anticipated. No sooner had that chocolate touched my tongue than I saw and tasted once again the chocolates of 40 and more years ago (pre First World War). 'Packer's!' I exclaimed and I was right. No other flavour in the intervening years had roused that particular memory. better chocolates there may be, certainly more expensive ones. But the door of memory could be opened by that key and by that key alone. I was a boy again, clutching in my hand the penny that was so rarely received and so carefully expended, gazing long and anxiously into the sweet-shop window, before going inside to make my all-important purchase. The penny was too precious for careless use and the result of a wrong choice too disastrous to be contemplated.

Penny, did I say? No, those whose memories are being stirred by these words will confirm the fact that a *farthing* was often the extent of one's purchase in the early 1900s. Five toffees could be bought for a farthing. I have counted them far too many times to be mistaken on that. As a scholar at St John's Infants' School, Ipswich, and then at California Boys' School, I found several shops in that part of town where this humble purchase could be made.

But what endless possibilities were opened up to the possessor of a whole penny . . . sherbert suckers which were paper bags filled with the powder of unforgettable flavour and provided with a tube of liquorice through which the powder could be sucked and which had the additional advantage that it could be eaten after it had served its primary purpose. Which leads to liquorice ladders and liquorice bootlaces, long strips of doubtless somewhat indigestible material, shining black without and dull brown within.

And what about cokernut crisps or jap nougats or tiger nuts? Or aniseed balls, 16 a penny (if I remember rightly) for the large size and 40 a penny for the small. Perhaps time has falsified my figures in this particular instance but it has not removed the sight and flavour of those brown balls as hard as marbles which by careful rationing at least one small boy in Ipswich tried to make last out from one Saturday to the next. Then there were those balls that change colour as one sucked them, which necessitated constant withdrawal from the mouth between thumb and finger to see the colours appear and disappear one by one. It was rumoured in our school that one boy, knowing his teacher's favourite colour, used to suck them till that colour appeared before handing over his morning gift.

Removal to another part of the town, and to another school, meant a transfer of custom from the shops in the Spring Road area to one in Woodbridge Road opposite Samuel Road, and another in Tacket Street near to Foundation Street. Four ounces a penny was the usual price and only occasionally was the penny used to buy two ounces - such as Packer's chocolates.

Writing about sweets has set the saliva working and I must dip into the drawer of the same desk in which the aniseed balls were once stored to find something that has cost 12 times as much. Perhaps sweets are better today as well as more expensive but they just cannot arouse that same anxious interest, that same careful economy, that same sense of possession. Sweets today are . . . well, just sweets.

NO one can convince me that the boys and girls of today enjoy their treats and outings so much as we did all those years ago. Probably almost every generation has argued in the same way but I do not mind. The pleasure and excitement of that greatest of all half-days were so intense that it is not within the capacity of human nature to feel more. The Wednesday afternoons in July were set apart by the education authorities for such excursions. Whether we had to go to school on all the afternoons except that of our own Sunday school I do not remember.

The excitement began, of course, very early in the day - an anxious glance towards the bedroom window to see the state of the weather. If it was bright, would it last? If it was dull, would it clear? Morning weekday school was intolerably long and dull. Why we could not be given the *whole* day we just could not imagine. Then the rush home to a scrambled dinner; the putting on of a pair of rubber plimsolls ready for the races; the arrival at the chapel school room at half past one. The wagons were not due till two o'clock and that half hour had to be filled with the calling of names, the dividing into classes and the giving of warnings concerning what we must or must not do when we arrived at the meadow. All this was very boring and completely unnecessary and I must confess that the prayer offered by the superintendent or a teacher was the prayer of all the year I found hardest to endure.

By this time we could hear the wagons and carts arriving. No modern motor-coach could possibly arouse the feelings stirred by the sound of those heavy wheels and heavy horses. Carters, millers and other tradesmen kindly lent their vehicles for the occasion, some of them drawn by one horse and some by two. Would that superintendent *never* give the order to load up? Yes, it came at last but the infants had to go first, the girls next and we boys last. Into the wagons we crowded, jostling each other for the best positions. Sometimes a boy could sit in the coveted position beside the driver and even hold the reins. Next there were the sides where we could sit with a leg dangling over. To my mind the best place was on the tailboard, facing backwards. I can feel now that peculiar sensation as the road slipped away under me.

myself and few sweets came my way. Presently came tea-time. We sat in circles on the grass and were handed paper bags with our ration of food, while the teachers came round with great jugs of tea.

After tea, the races. Parents lined up on either side and the course was set with a teacher forming the turning point or finishing point at the other end. The concourse seemed enormous, the shouting deafening and the race endless. I must have won at least one race, for I recall receiving a fishing rod as a prize, a rod that was used once at the Round Pond in Christchurch Park and then forever abandoned.

After the races, the prizes. Mrs Holden herself came out from the house to present

The journey from the centre of Ipswich to 'Pinetoft', Rushmere, was not one inch too long, for a great proportion of the joy of the occasion was in the ride itself. Occasionally we burst forth into song. I am afraid that the only one that I can recall now was one which began: 'Shut up the public houses . . .' This we bawled each time we came to such a place on the way. Evidently our vocal efforts were in vain, for I notice that those public houses are still there and still open today.

At last 'Pinetoft' (kindly lent by Mrs Luther Holden) was reached and I feel now that soft grass beneath my feet. *Was* the park really big? It seemed to stretch for miles, with woods in which one could get hopelessly lost. There was the minister with boxes of sweets, which he threw out on the long grass. I found myself pushed right and left by boys greedier and stronger than

them. I see her now. She was a great worker for the Society for the Prevention of Cruelty to Animals and her carriage and pair were a familiar sight on the market in Princes Street every Tuesday. What lovely horses they were! Their tails were never cut; or rather, the coachman, Mr Reynolds, just cut off enough hair to prevent them from sweeping the ground. The carriage was beautifully kept; one could see one's face in the shining black panels. Perhaps there is a little personal pride in this, for my father painted and varnished it.

Soon the treat was over and the return journey began. Along the Rushmere Road, past the horses' water trough at the junction with Woodbridge Road, down the two hills to St Margaret's Street - I can see every inch of the way. No, there never will be again such treats as those.

Schooldays, the Horse Bus and the Electric Trams

L. R. Garrard (c1957)

OCCASIONALLY there breaks out in conversation or in writing a rivalry between acquaintances. Each one seeks to outdo the others in going back to the earliest possible memories. 'I can remember something that happened when I was four,' says one. 'I can remember something when I was three,' says another. And so it goes on. Perhaps this problem can never be decided even concerning ourselves, for so often something that we see or hear or read recalls to us an experience of early childhood that for long years has remained unknown.

At the moment my earliest memory is of a horse bus in Ipswich. Why we should remember one thing and forget a thousand other things no one can say but I can see myself on the top of a horse bus in Spring Road at the junction with St John's Road where an extra horse was hooked on to pull the vehicle up the hill. My guess is that I was two years old and I have no desire to discover whether or not this figure is correct. For very many years one of these horse buses stood in a garden at Claydon.

Switching for a moment from buses to trains - how dark Ipswich tunnel was to a boy of five travelling to London with his mother! With his feet on a long metal container filled with hot water, which was put into the carriage by a porter before the days of steam and electric heating, he nestled closer and closer to his mother as the darkness of the tunnel became more intense. That tunnel had two entirely different lengths - the actual one of probably a few hundred yards and the one created by nameless terrors, amounting to endless miles. And the one is as real as the other.

Horse buses were followed, of course, by electric trams and these now obsolescent vehicles made Ipswich one of the most progressive towns in the country.

The purpose of this article is not to give a technically accurate description of them but to place on record simple childhood memories.

There is, for instance, the unforgettable shriek of the tram as it rounded a bend, especially, it seems to me, at Major's Corner. In the course of time the tram lines had a serrated edge, like that of a saw, where the tram wheels cut into them. The driver naturally applied his brake as he neared the bend but I thought he was steering the tram along the lines and I admired him for his cleverness.

If I were an artist I could draw one of those trams, accurate, I make bold to say, in every detail. There were the varnished seats extending the whole length of the tram, for we had to sit and face the passengers on the opposite side. In the seats, at both ends, there were little trap doors and opening one of these I found inside the sand that was used to apply the emergency brakes. One notice painted above the doorway seems rather out of date now: 'Gold coin is not accepted in payment of fare.' Years later I was on the end of Felixstowe pier, keeping myself

Double-decker horse bus at Ipswich in the early 1900s

away from the rain and wind in a shelter that somehow or other seemed strangely familiar. The sight of these words above the door explained to me that a one time Ipswich tram was being used for a new purpose. But it was the upper deck that was naturally more attractive to a small boy and my fingers itch to sketch the details that are so vivid in my memory, the winding staircase, the bell push, the reversable seats, the green trolley standard with its notice: 'No smoking forward of the trolley standard', the trolley arm, ending in a

sense of burning injustice is with me still, but I suppose the Statute of Limitations would, after all this time, prevent me claiming damages from the Ipswich Corporation. Still, an ex gratia payment would be most acceptable!

The upper deck was, of course, open to the sky - very pleasant in summer but not particularly so in winter. I recall one pouring wet night coming from Whitton. The seats were saturated, so I put my feet on them and sat on the backrest. I sat backwards to prevent the rain blowing in my face,

Tramcars at Ipswich station in the early 1900s.

little wheel that ran along the wire. I see now every swing upwards and downwards and sideways of that arm and I hear now the sound of that wheel. Simple things all these memories are, and from one point of view perhaps hardly worth recording. But then life is made up of a multitude of similar recollections, and impressions have a far greater influence upon us than solid facts. I recall the half-pride, half-humiliation that was mine when a conductor would not believe me when I told him I was under 12. It was a source of pride to be thought older than I really was but it was a great humiliation to be turned off the tram in St Helen's Street because I had but a halfpenny and he demanded a penny. The

until a sudden shout from my companion caused me to jump down just in time to prevent the back of my head coming into violent contact with the Norwich Road railway bridge.

No, modern means of transport are commonplace and unromantic. Or will a boy of today write and feel in 40 years time as I do now? I wonder.

I THINK it is Rudyard Kipling who says somewhere that it is a great mercy we adults cannot suffer as we did when we were children. Such a statement is startling and in some connections probably false. But it does help to remind us how real and acute were our mental sufferings in early childhood. Most adults will agree that *places* look much smaller than they did when we were young, that *distances* are much shorter. But the same principle holds good regarding our joys and our sorrows. Yes, Rudyard Kipling was right. If the trials of later years had given us the same proportion of suffering as those of childhood, life by now would be unbearable.

My first day at St John's Infant School, Ipswich, was rendered less happy than it would have been by a great terror. Someone at home had told me that when I got to school the girls from the big school would undress me. Of course, all that was meant was that they would help me, and others, to take off our outer garments. But I had fearful visions of being stripped by these great girls and subjected to all manner of horrors. However, the fears did not materialise and I soon found a place in the school. A faded photograph helps to make real and permanent those early memories. With a crowd of other children there I am in a velvet suit and a lace collar. The musty records of the education committee could doubtless confirm or otherwise the names of the headmistress and teachers, Miss Levett, Miss Thompson, Miss Fletcher are names that I rightly or wrongly recall.

I can see now the sheet of paper with my name perfectly written at the top, and I was told to copy it again and again until the bottom of the page was reached. Yes, and there were the cardboard clocks by means of which we were taught to tell the time, and a hundred other things that cannot now be mentioned.

The day of transfer from the infants' school to the big boys' (then known as California School) was an eventful one. I have clearer visions and deeper impressions of the *playground* than of the classrooms, though I believe the hours of lessons under the headmaster, Mr Cracknell, and such teachers as Mr Thompson and Mr Wardman were not ill spent. What giants those boys seemed to one frightened youngster! They must surely have been men but a little mental arithmetic tells me that the *oldest* of them were not more than fourteen. Thus once again I learn that life is largely a matter of proportion and comparison.

WERE winters colder then? Well, at all events, that playground was sometimes deliberately flooded with hundreds of pailfuls of water before we left school in the evening and next morning it was a sheet of ice. Yes, and there was a game we played there of which I have never even heard in any other place and how to spell the word I do not know, unless it is 'arwoosh.' On cold days the biggest boy would stand in the corner of the playground facing outwards and then the rest of the boys would gather in front of him, facing the same direction. To the chant of 'arwoosh' they swayed backwards and forwards upon each other and the heat engendered had to be felt to be believed. This game, and the ice-covered playground, and the cocoa tins with holes punched through each end and filled with smouldering rag which became very hot as we ran along and let the air blow through them - these and other things convince me that winters really were colder then - or were they?

From California School to Foundation Street Boys' School, which, I believe, has now disappeared. My chief impression of this school is, I think, the rivalry that existed between the boys of that place and of the Central School a little further down. The scholars of the latter paid (if I am not mistaken) 6d. a week to keep the school rather more select and the consequent sense of superiority that these scholars had was something that we bitterly resented.

I recall now the serious thoughts and feelings that were mine as I stood at the gate and looked back into that playground for the last time. Life *is* like that; a few years of close contact with others and then a scattering far and wide. Those boys are men of 50 and 60 now. But the only picture that my memory retains corresponds with the photograph in my album - boys as they were - for the mind, like the camera, can freeze into immobility those whom life is ever moving on.

Half Century of Changing Customs 1900s-1950s

L. R. Garrard (c1957)

IT is surprising how quickly the new becomes the normal. We are shocked by the disappearance of something old, or the appearance of something new, but in a few weeks we accept as commonplace the thing that shocked us. Two world wars have, of course, quickened the speed of change and also caused us to forget the old. We look upon anything pre-war (particularly pre-1914 war) as belonging to another age.

Following my references to change in such spheres as transport and education, I have been thinking of other, mostly unconnected, differences between today (1957) and 40 odd years ago. If I remember Ipswich in particular, it will simply be because I remember that town best. But almost the same changes have doubtless taken place elsewhere.

Of course the horse-drawn passenger vehicles have disappeared. No longer does the cabman's shelter stand on the Cornhill, nor do the closed or opencarriages. We had better not enquire concerning the fate of the horses. Half-asleep they waited for possible passengers, occasionally tossing their heads to get the last few grains of food from the straw nose-bags suspended from their harness. The clop-clop of their hoofs no longer echoes in the slumbering streets, so comparatively devoid of traffic that boys played marbles in the middle of Major's Corner and Barrack Corner, simply picking them up for a moment or two while some carriage or wagon went by and then getting on with their game once more.

And is there any place in the world where the custom is continued of spreading straw or other sound-deadening materials on the roadway in front of a house where someone is ill? I can see it now, spread for a distance of several yards and stretching from kerb to kerb. I can hear again the difference in sound as the striking of the iron shoes and the rattle of iron-tyred wheels gave place to the impressive silence as horse and vehicle went over the stretch of covered roadway. Are people less ill today? Or have their ears become so accustomed to the multiplied noises

of modern towns that the old custom is no longer needed? Or was there (I rather think there was in some cases) a curious kind of pride and desire for sympathy that caused the relatives of sick people to proclaim to the whole street and town that someone in their house was ill.

This leads me to funerals. No, even these are not what they were. Of course, the horses with their nodding black plumes have gone, but so also have the funeral coaches with the coffin in front and room for about six passengers behind. We no longer boast, as our grand-parents did, that at so-and-so's funeral there was the longest procession of funeral carriages ever seen in the town and that hundreds of blinds were drawn as the procession passed. Those were the days of ostentatious mourning. A remark that I remember reading somewhere in one of Oliver Wendell Holmes' books has today almost lost its point. Describing a man who was always miserable, Holmes says something to this effect: 'One day he was rather more cheerful. It was as if he had got out of the carriage immediately next to the hearse and got into another one about six carriages further back.'

I was but a small boy when I lived in Cemetery Road, and time may have distorted my figures, but it seems to me now that on Sunday afternoons literally hundreds of people made their way up the road to visit the graves of their relatives and to put fresh flowers upon them. It was the 'thing to do', and they did it. I see now the keeper at the gate ready to turn back children who were not accompanied by an adult. I was myself turned back because he did not consider that the sister who had charge of me was old enough to be thus described.

THE lesser accompaniments of funerals are too numerous to specify . . . the mutes standing at the house door . . . the funeral cards with a black edge that varied in width according to the nearness or otherwise of the relationship . . . the black hat-bands, again varying in width from several inches to about half-an-inch - it being reported, I remember, that one man used a shoelace at the funeral of his mother-in-law! . . . the pulpit draped in voluminous folds of black cloth . . . the equally voluminous clothes which kept many a seam-

*People turned out
in their hundreds
to watch a funeral
procession go by.*
Photo:
E. S. Singleton Ltd.

stress working all night so that they would be finished in time . . . the memorial service the next Sunday, when special pews were reserved for the black-garmented relatives and friends, when the deceased's favourite hymns were sung and a more or less sincere tribute was paid by the minister, which caused black-edged handkerchiefs to be applied to tear-filled eyes.

This is not an exaggerated picture, and we can surely congratulate ourselves on a more sensible and restrained attitude to such things today.

Occasionally in Cemetery Road we had the morbid excitement of a military funeral, for the Ipswich Barracks were then in full use. I hear again the band playing in double-slow measure the Dead March. I see again the union-jack-covered gun carriage. I hear and see again the livelier music and the quicker pace as the empty gun carriage returned from the cemetery.

Much could be written of the changes that 40 or 50 years have made, changes in shops and houses, in streets and people, changes for the better and changes for the worse.

As an example of the former I will mention a certain butcher's shop. I see now the open slab covered with joints of meat, these in their turn being covered with flies. I see now the butcher (who shall be nameless) flicking off the flies with a dirty cloth. I see them rising in swarms, only to settle down again a moment or two later. More hygienic butchers covered their joints with strips of butter-muslin under which, of course, the flies crept undisturbed. Possibly a great number of funeral processions up Cemetery Road could be traced back to butchers' shops with their flies, to milk jugs on doorsteps with the money inside them ready for the milkman to take, as with a measure suspended from the side of his can he poured into the jugs a bluish-tinted liquid that in a raucous voice he proclaimed to be 'milko'.

After such morbid and depressing information I would finish with a reference to weddings if I could remember anything about them. But for some unaccountable reason, whilst I can see vividly all the details of a funeral character, I cannot recall one single thing about a wedding. Doubtless the dresses were just as elaborate, the flowers just as expensive, the tears just as copious. But some other pen must describe the changes that brides of half a century ago have witnessed. The bridegroom, poor fellow, was probably as insignificant then as he is today; a necessary part of the function - but whoever waited at a church door or rushed across a street to see a bridegroom? In Ipswich or Timbuctoo, in 1900 or 1957, he stands in the background nervously fingering a tie that nearly chokes him. *He*, at all events, will never change.